A History of Liturgical Books

Eric Palazzo

A HISTORY
OF LITURGICAL BOOKS

*from the Beginning
to the Thirteenth Century*

Translated by Madeleine Beaumont

A PUEBLO BOOK

THE LITURGICAL PRESS COLLEGEVILLE, MINNESOTA

This book was initially published in French under the title *Le Moyen Age: Des origines au XIIIème siècle* © 1993 by BEAUCHESNE EDITEUR.

A Pueblo Book published by The Liturgical Press

Design by Frank Kacmarcik, Obl.S.B. Cover illustration: manuscript, Gospel Book dedication page, Hildesheim, ca. 1015, APL.

Library of Congress Cataloging-in-Publication Data

Palazzo, Eric.
   [Moyen Age. English]
   A history of liturgical books from the beginning to the thirteenth
century / Eric Palazzo ; translated by Madeleine Beaumont.
      p.   cm.
   "A Pueblo book."
   Includes bibliographical references (p.) and indexes.
   ISBN 0-8146-6167-X (alk. paper)
   1. Catholic Church—Liturgy—Texts—History and criticism.
  2. Church history—Middle Ages, 600–1500. I. Title.
BX1973.P3513   1998
264'.02'009—dc21   97-52988
                                                        CIP

For Claudia

Contents

List of Bibliographical Abbreviations

Andrieu, *OR* = M. Andrieu. *Les "Ordines romani" du haut Moyen Age.* Spicilegium sacrum lovaniense 11, 23, 24, 28, 29. Louvain, 1931–1961.

Andrieu, *Pontifical* = M. Andrieu, *Le pontifical romain au Moyen Age.* Vol. 1, *Le pontifical romain du XIIe siècle.* Vol. 2, *Le pontifical romain de la Curie romaine au XIIe siècle.* Vol. 3, *Le pontifical de Guillaume Durand.* Vol. 4, *Tables alphabétiques.* Studi e Testi 86–88, 99. Vatican City, 1938–1940, 1941.

Baroffio, "Manoscritti liturgici" = "I manoscritti liturgici." *Guida a una descrizione uniforme dei manoscritti e al loro censimento.* Ed. V. Jemolo and M. Morelli, 145–200. Rome, 1990.

Becker, *Catalogie* = G. Becker. *Catalogi Bibliothecarum Antiqui.* Bonn, 1885.

Bischoff, *Schatzverzeichnisse* = B. Bischoff. *Mittelalterliche Schatzverzeichnisse.* Vol. 1, *Von der Zeit Karls des Grossen bis zur Mitte des 13. Jahrhunderts.* Munich, 1967.

Brommer, *Cap. Ep.* = *Capitula Episcoporum.* Vol 1. MGH. Ed. P Brommer. Hannover, 1984.

CCSL = *Corpus Christianorum: Series latina.* Turnhout.

Chavasse, "Evangéliaire" = A. Chavasse. "Evangéliaire, épistolier, antiphonaire et sacramentaire: Les livres romains de la messe aux VIIe et VIIIe siècles." *Ecclesia Orans* 6 (1989) 177–225.

CNRS = Centre National de Recherches Scientifiques [National Center for Scientific Research].

CP = A.-G. Martimort, ed. *The Church at Prayer,* new ed. Vol. 1, *Principles of the Liturgy.* Vol. 2, *The Eucharist.* Vol. 3, *The Sacraments.* Vol. 4, *The Liturgy and Time.* Trans. M. J. O'Connell. Collegeville,

Minn., 1986–1987 [A.-G. Martimort, ed. *L'Eglise en Prière*. Vol. 1, *Principes de la liturgie*. Vol. 2, *L'Eucharistie*. Vol. 3, *Les sacrements*. Vol. 4, *La liturgie et le temps*. Paris, 1983–1984].

CRME = Centre de Recherche sur le Manuscrit Enluminé [Center for Research on Illuminated Manuscripts].

Deshusses, *Grégorien* = J. Deshusses. *Le sacramentaire grégorien: Ses principales formes d'après les plus anciens manuscrits*. With bibliography and historiography of the research. Vol. 1, *Le sacramentaire, le supplément d'Aniane*. Vol. 2, *Textes complémentaires pour la messe*. Vol. 3,*Textes complémentaires divers*. Spicilegium friburgense 16, 24, 28. Fribourg, 1971, 1979, 1982.

Ebner, *Missale Romanum* = A. Ebner. *Quellen und Forschungen zur Geschichte und Kunstgeschichte des Missale Romanum im Mittelalter: Iter italicum*. Freiburg, 1896.

Ekenberg, *Cur cantatur* = A. Ekenberg. *Cur cantatur? Die Funktionen des liturgischen Gesanges nach den Autoren der karolingerzeit*. Stockholm, 1987.

Fiala and Irtenkauf, *Liturgische Nomenklatur* = V. Fiala and W. Irtenkauf. "Versuch einer Liturgischen Nomenklatur." *Zur Katalogiesierung Mittelalterlicher und Neuerer Handschriften*, Zeitschrift für Bibliothekswesen und Bibliographie, special issue (Frankfurt am Main, 1963) 105–137.

Gamber, *CLLA* = K. Gamber. *Codices liturgici latini antiquiores*. 2 vols. Spicilegii friburgensis Subsidia 1 (Fribourg, 1963, 1964). *Supplementum, Ergänzungs- und Registerband*. Spicilegii friburgensis Subsidia 1A. Fribourg, 1988.

Gy, "Collectaire" = P.-M. Gy. "Collectaire, rituel, processionnal." *Revue des Sciences philosophiques et théologiques* 44 (1960) 441–469. rpt. in *La liturgie dans l'histoire*, 91–126. Paris, 1990.

Hesbert, *AMS* = R.-J. Hesbert. *Antiphonale Missarum Sextuplex*, according to the Gradual of Monza and the Antiphonaries of Rheinau, Mont-Blandin, Compiègne, Corbie, and Senlis. Brussels, 1935.

Hesbert, *CAO* = R.-J. Hesbert, ed. *Corpus Antiphonalium Officii*. 6 vols. Rerum esslesiasticarum documenta, series major. Rome, 1963–1979.

Hughes, *Mass and Office* = A. Hughes. *Medieval Manuscripts for Mass and Office: A Guide to Their Organization and Terminology*. Toronto, 1982.

Huglo, *Livres de chant* = M. Huglo. *Les livres de chant liturgique.* Typologie des sources du Moyen Age occidental, fasc. 52. Turnhout, 1988.

Jungmann, *MS* = J.-A. Jungmann. *Missarum sollemnia: Explication génétique de la messe romaine.* 3 Vols. Théologie 19–21. Paris, 1950–1953 [Jungmann, J. A. *The Mass of the Roman Rite: Its Origins and Development.* Trans. F. A. Brunner. 2 vols. Westminster, Md., 1951–1955].

Klauser, *Capitulare evangeliorum* = Th. Klauser. *Das römische Capitulare evangeliorum.* Vol. 1, *Typen.* Liturgiewissenschaftliche Quellen und Forschungen 28. Münster, 1935.

Leroquais, *Bréviaires* = V. Leroquais. *Les bréviaires manuscrits des bibliothèques publiques de France.* 6 vols. Paris, 1934.

Leroquais, *Livres d'Heures* = V. Leroquais. *Les livres d'Heures manuscrits de la Bibliothèque national.* 3 Vols. Paris, 1927. *Supplément aux livres d'heures manuscrits de la Bibliothèque national, acquisitions récentes et donation Smith-Lesouëf.* Paris 1943.

Leroquais, *Pontificaux* = V. Leroquais. *Les pontificaux manuscrits des bibliothèques publiques de France.* 4 vols. Paris, 1937.

Leroquais, *Psautiers* = V. Leroquais. *Les psautiers manuscrits latins des bibliothèques publiques de France.* 3 vols. Mâcon, 1940–1941.

Leroquais, *Sacramentaires* = V. Leroquais. *Les sacramentaires et les missels manuscrits des bibliothèques publiques de France.* 3 vols. and atlas. Paris, 1924.

Liturgica Vaticana = *Biblioteca Apostolica Vaticana: Liturgie und Andacht im Mittelalter.* Ed. J. M. Plotzek and U. Surmann. Issued by the archepiscopal museum of Cologne. Stuttgart, 1992.

LQF = Liturgiewissenschaftliche Quellen und Forschungen. Münster.

Martimort, *Lectures liturgiques* = A.-G. Martimort. *Les lectures liturgiques et leurs livres.* Typologie des sources du Moyen Age occidental, fasc. 64. Turnhout, 1992.

Martimort, *Martène* = A.-G. Martimort. *La documentation liturgique de Dom Edmond Martène.* Studi e Testi 279 (Vatican City, 1978). Completed in A.-G. Martimort. "Additions et corrections à la documentation liturgique de Dom Edmond Martène." *Ecclesia Orans* 3 (1986) 81–105.

Martimort, *Ordines* = A.-G. Martimort. *Les "Ordines," les ordinaires et les cérémoniaux.* Typologie des sources du Moyen Age occidental, fasc. 56. Turnhout, 1991.

MGH = Monumenta Germaniae Historica: Studien und Texte. Hanover and other places.

MGH, *Ep.* = *Epistolarum tomus.* 8 Vols.

MGH, *Sc.* = *Scriptorum tomus.* 32 Vols.

MGH, *Po.* = *Poetarum Latinorum medii aevi tomus.* 6 Vols.

Pfaff, *Medieval Latin Liturgy* = R. W. Pfaff. *Medieval Latin Liturgy: A Select Bibliography.* Toronto Medieval Bibliographies 9. Toronto, 1982.

PL = J.-P. Migne, ed. *Patrologiae cursus completus.* Series Latina. Paris, 1844–1891.

Rasmussen, *Pontificaux* = N. K. Rasmussen. *Les Pontificaux du haut Moyen Age: Genèse du livre liturgique de l'évêque.* Spiciligium sacrum lovaniense. Louvain, in press.

Salmon, *Office divin* = P. Salmon. *L'office divin au Moyen Age: Histoire de la formation du bréviaire du IXe au XVIe siècle.* Lex orandi 43. Paris, 1967.

SC = Sources chrétiennes. Paris.

Taft, *Liturgie of the Hours* = R. F. Taft. *The Liturgy of the Hours in East and West: The Origins of the Divine Office and Its Meaning for Today.* Collegeville, Minn., 1986.

Thiel, Liturgische Bücher = E. J. Thiel. "Die liturgischen Bücher des Mittelalters." *Börsenblatt für den Deutschen Buchhandel.* Frankfurter Ausgabe, vol. 23 (October 17, 1967) 2379–2395.

Van Dijk, *Origins* = S.J.P. Van Dijk and J. H. Walker. *The Origins of the Modern Roman Liturgy: The Liturgy of the Papal Court and the Franciscan Order in the Thirteenth Century.* London, 1960.

Vogel, *Introduction* = C. Vogel. *Medieval Liturgy: An Introduction to the Sources.* Trans. and rev. W. G. Storey and N. K. Rasmussen. Washington, D.C., 1986.

Vogel and Elze, *PRG* = C. Vogel and R. Elze. *Le Pontifical romano-germanique du Xe siècle.* Studi e Testi 226, 227, 269. Vatican City, 1963–1972.

Preface

Eric Palazzo went from art history to the study of medieval liturgical sources, into which he now initiates liturgist-apprentices and medievalist-apprentices. In addition, he has seen in many medievalists both a strong interest in the liturgy and the place it occupies in medieval life, and the fear of a little-known domain and one apparently difficult to explore. Hence the purpose of the present work.

This book is akin, even after a lapse of thirty years, to *Introduction aux sources du culte chrétien du Moyen Age* by Cyrille Vogel, the last edition of which was translated into English in 1986 by William G. Storey and Niels K. Rasmussen. In his time, Vogel was a pioneer in the collaboration between liturgists and medievalists; since then, this collaboration has grown and obliges us to adopt new perspectives. There is also the fact that Vogel, our colleague in Strasbourg, now deceased, had deliberately limited his study to certain liturgical books and as a consequence left gaps that needed filling. Finally, Vogel was interested principally in the transition between late antiquity and the High Middle Ages; this left the field open for what seems to me to be Palazzo's purpose: a presentation of liturgical sources centered on the Carolingian and Ottonian periods—which are essential as regards liturgical sources—but also complemented by appropriate attention to the subsequent development of medieval liturgy.

Since its topic is medieval liturgical sources, Palazzo's book also takes its place next to the series "Typologie des sources du Moyen Age occidental," some fascicles of which have been published while others are to be published under the auspices of the Institute of Medieval Studies of the Catholic University of Louvain. The purpose of the "Typologie" is clearly defined, and works such as those of M. Huglo and A. G. Martimort have allowed us to appreciate its usefulness. Palazzo's book should be utilized before one has recourse to the specialized studies of the series. I think that it offers students the basic manual they need for their work.

To me, this book seems fundamental in several ways. First, it supplies serious overall information on the liturgical books, both in the categories the author has personally studied (the understanding of which he advances in several cases) and in those published by other researchers.

Second, Palazzo seems to practice naturally the essential give and take with the history of civilization, of which M.-D. Chenu gave a remarkable example and which, J. Le Goff had the kindness to say, characterizes my work on the liturgy in history. Palazzo does this in two ways: by showing an attentive respect for the religious quality proper to the liturgy—a respect I deem essential—and by acknowledging the place of the liturgy within the larger framework of history as well as the interactions in which the liturgical practice is involved. In addition, Palazzo exhibits a quality for which most liturgists (I among them), envy him, that is, his competence in matters of paleography and codicology. As I write this, I remember a remark the master paleographer B. Bischoff made to me one day, "I have the highest esteem for the liturgical science although I myself am not a liturgist. F. Wormald, for his part, has the twofold competence." Such a twofold competence is what we need.

Finally, this book is a very good example of the proper attention to the way liturgical books were used in the celebration and pastoral practice of the Middle Ages, which I had the opportunity of studying in the course of the years in my conversations with M. Huglo and N. K. Rasmussen: one must take into account simultaneously the measure of oral usage in liturgical practice,[1] the complementarity of books in a common celebration (as rediscovered in the liturgy after Vatican II), the modest significance of *libelli* composed for a specific occasion, and the compact books (breviaries, for instance). Palazzo excellently applies himself to all this.

Pierre-Marie Gy, O.P.

Easter 1993

---

1. See the unpublished doctoral thesis of Th. Elich, *Le contexte oral de la liturgie médiévale et le rôle du texte écrit*, 3 vols. (Paris: Paris IV-Sorbonne and Institut catholique de Paris, 1988); summary in J. Pierce, "Using Liturgical Texts in the Middle Ages," *Fountain of Life*, In Memory of Niels K. Rasmussen, O.P., ed. G. Austin (Washington, D.C., 1991) 69–83.

Preface to the English Language Edition

Almost three years have elapsed since this book was published in the original French and The Liturgical Press offered to make an English translation, a proposal which makes me feel honored. First of all, I wish to express my most sincere thanks to this publishing house as well as to the translator, Madeleine Beaumont, for the work that has been done.

This book contains the version of 1993, without any revisions. Indeed, at no time did the opportunity arise to review any part of the initial text, an undertaking which would have required a labor out of proportion with the purpose of the translation. Therefore, I have limited myself to correcting the unfortunate errors which had crept into the text and which I had regrettably overlooked. I have also established a list, by no means exhaustive, of bibliographical additions containing those references which have become available since 1993 and also those which, though already existing at that date, had escaped me.

Since its publication, this book has been the subject of reviews in various international journals and in several languages; among the reviewers were eminent specialists of the liturgy and its books. Some of these writers—to whom I am deeply grateful—have gone even deeper into the matter and given their own personal opinions on some question concerning the history of the liturgy or on a precise point of the history of one or the other of its books. The personal character of these remarks, my firm decision not to rewrite entire passages, as well as a certain form of intellectual honesty, have led me to refer the readers directly to the reviews themselves. Thus, I would like to list those of P. Bernard, *Bibliothèque de l'Ecole des Chartes* 152 (1994) 579–581; M.-N. Colette, *Cahiers de Civilisation Médiévale* 38 (1995) 64–66; P.-M. Gy, *Revue des Sciences Philosophiques et Théologiques* 78 (1994) 276–277; d'A. Häussling, *Archiv für Liturgiewissenschaft*

35/36 (1993/1994) 256–258; A.-G. Martimort, *Bulletin de Littérature Ecclésiastique* (1994) 256–258; H. B. Meyer, *Zeitschrift für katolische Theologie* 116 (1994) 372–373; R. Pfaff, *Ecclesiastical History* 46 (1995) 356; J. Pierce, *Worship* 68/5 (1994) 478–480.

Finally, in a more personal way, I wish to thank all the colleagues, students, and friends who thoughtfully—often on the occasion of informal exchanges—told me that my book had been of help to them at some point in their research.

Eric Palazzo
Orléans, France
May 20, 1996

Acknowledgments

This book was born during my stay in Göttingen at the French Historical Mission in Germany during the academic year 1990–1991. Michel Parisse, then director of the Mission, had suggested that I take advantage of my year in Germany to prepare a manual of introduction to the liturgical books of the Middle Ages in order to answer the historians' growing demand in this domain. The excellent working conditions enjoyed by the members of the French Historical Mission made it possible for me to gather and organize the needed documentation. The sessions of the introductory course to the liturgical sources of the Middle Ages, for which I am responsible at the Superior Institute of Liturgy, gave me the opportunity to test the chapters of the book with the students. My connection with the liturgical section of the Institute of Research and History of Texts (part of CNRS) allowed me to complete the writing of the book under the best possible conditions.

In this enterprise, I received the help of many friends. Among them, I have the pleasure of thanking—for their encouragement as well as their critical reading of my text—Fr. Anselme Davril, Fr. Paul De Clerck, my master, Fr. Pierre-Marie Gy, François Héber-Suffrin, Dominique Iogna-Prat, Guy Lobrichon, and Michel Parisse. I am also grateful to Mlle. Monique Cadic for having agreed to publish this work at Beauchesne Publishing House.

Finally, nothing could have been done without Claudia's attentive reading, unflagging support, and affection day in day out.

The Liturgical Year: History and Definition

The liturgical year as we know it today is the result of a number of successive transformations that for the most part took place in the course of the first centuries of Christianity.[1] Discounting the variations and changes in details that have occurred as time went on, one can affirm that by the year 600, the structure of the liturgical year has been established, at least in its main features. The people of the Middle Ages were living according to a rhythm combining seasonal activities and the christianization of time, in the framework of a liturgical cycle composed of large periods.[2]

The liturgical calendar is divided into:

—the Temporal Cycle, that is, the feasts determined by the events of the life of Christ and the ferias (ordinary days);

—the Sanctoral Cycle, comprising the feasts of saints plus the common of saints (of martyrs, virgins, and so on). For the common of saints, no precise attribution is foreseen.

GENERAL STRUCTURE OF THE LITURGICAL YEAR[3]

Advent

—4 weeks before Christmas, punctuated by the 4 Sundays of Advent

1. See the fundamental work of T. Talley, *The Origins of the Liturgical Year* (New York, 1986); R. Taft, "The Liturgical Year: Studies, Prospects, Reflections," *Worship* (1981) 2–23.

2. On the notions of liturgical year and liturgical cycle, see M. Metzger, "Année, ou bien cycle, liturgique?" *Revue des Sciences religieuses* 67 (1993) 85–96.

3. For more details concerning this structure, which does not take into account variations, often local ones, in the course of the centuries, see *CP*, vol. 4, and *Gottesdienst der Kirche: Handbuch der Liturgie wissenschaft*, vol. 5, *Feiern im Rhytmus der Zeit 1, Herrenfeste in Woche und Jahr* (Regensberg, 1983–). See also the tables in Vogel, *Introduction*, 404–410.

—December 25: Nativity of Christ
—Octave of the Nativity
—January 6: Epiphany

Ordinary Time (1)
—6 weeks punctuated by 6 Sundays after Epiphany (the feast of the Annunciation is on March 25)

Paschal Cycle
—Septuagesima: 70 days before Easter, marked by Septuagesima Sunday
—Sexagesima: 60 days before Easter, marked by Sexagesima Sunday
—Quinquagesima: 50 days before Easter, marked by Quinquagesima Sunday

Lent
—Ash Wednesday, Quadragesima: 40 days before Easter

Paschal Time
—Holy Week:
—Palm Sunday (entrance of Christ into Jerusalem)
—Holy Thursday, Good Friday, Holy Saturday, Easter Sunday (Resurrection)
—Ascension: 40 days after Easter
—Pentecost: 50 days after Easter

Ordinary Time (2)
—25 to 32 weeks after Pentecost, punctuated by the Sundays after Pentecost

Introduction

"In my opinion, this book stresses remarkably the importance for both the historian and the liturgist of a history of the liturgy anchored in history at large, or rather constituting a domain of this history, perhaps one of the most secret, but also one of the most important." So writes Jacques Le Goff in his preface to a collection of articles by P.-M. Gy.[1] However, the relationships between history and liturgy have for a long time been characterized by a profound misunderstanding and even by a reciprocal ignorance on the part of the practitioners of the two disciplines. In our day, this attitude is yielding to an ever growing interdisciplinary closeness. In order to understand this evolution in western Europe and especially France, one must go back to the beginning of this century.

The separation of Church and state in France in 1905 and the dechristianization of western society as a whole have left their unmistakable mark on academic traditions, especially among historians and ecclesiastical circles. In the universities, the teaching of religious history has been completely amputated of one of its essential components, the history of Christian worship. Conversely, this discipline flourished only in the restricted circles of religious and clergy, often woefully ignorant of the important stages of the evolution of historical sciences. The recent history of the Catholic Church, the Council of Vatican II in particular, has given birth to a new generation of liturgists, people who are historians and are also actively engaged in worship.[2] One of the foundations of Vatican II was the rediscovery of the tradition of the Church, and for that reason, it has given rise to innumerable works on the history of the liturgy. Sensitized by the acute

1. P.-M. Gy, *La liturgie dans l'histoire* (Paris, 1990) 5.
2. To appreciate the impact of the council on the theologians and historians of the liturgy, see for example the reflections of Y. Congar, *Le Concile Vatican II: Son Eglise, peuple de Dieu et corps du Christ* (Paris, 1984).

historical sense of the great precursors, such as Fr. Marie-Dominique Chenu,[3] the participants in the Council have made, in a very short period of time, great strides in advancing our knowledge in that field. To make this possible, the investigation of liturgical sources has been singled out. Guided by such masters of the first half of the twentieth century as Bishop Duchesne,[4] the historians of the liturgy have rediscovered the importance of these sources (and especially that of the liturgical books) for the reconstruction of the ancient liturgies which would supply the basis for today's reform. Because this reform has utilized the texts describing liturgical practice, the task has consisted in large measure in researching the origin of the different books used in worship. For every kind of book, people have striven to discover the archetype, the original state of the texts of missal, gradual, lectionary, and so on. Aware of being heirs to the Roman liturgy, the liturgists have endeavored to find the origins of the practices and texts in use in Rome between the fourth and eighth centuries. Endowed with a new historical sensibility, the researchers at the same time have examined more exactly and tempered the role Rome played in the past in the completion and diffusion of a model liturgy, and they have uncovered forgotten liturgical traditions.

Following the example of the scholars at the end the nineteenth century,[5] the Vatican II liturgists and, before them, those working between the World Wars, have widely explored the sources of the history of the liturgy, that is, the liturgical books, these "fresh documents," according to Fr. Chenu's felicitous expression.[6] Their rediscovery has been accompanied by a new fascination with the liturgical manuscripts which have transmitted the sacred texts. The gigantic work on liturgical manuscripts undertaken by several scholars in this century produced a concrete result: the completion of catalogues.[7] In certain cases, these catalogues have fostered the formulation of a general ty-

3. From the monumental corpus of M.-D. Chenu's work, I shall only mention here a book whose history was so turbulent, *Une école de théologie: Le Saulchoir* (Paris, 1937; 2nd ed. 1985). It is a true pleading for the renewal in the study of theology and the history of the Church.

4. See the Part 1 of this manual.

5. See the Part 1 of this manual.

6. Chenu, *La liturgie,* 124.

7. See the nearly complete panorama for the entire world in N. Sacksteder, "A Provisional List of Inventories of Latin Liturgical Manuscripts and Incunabula of the Middle Ages," *Ephemerides liturgicae* 99 (1985) 60–82.

pology of the liturgical books of the Middle Ages on which modern research still relies.[8]

Among historians of the liturgy, some have taken into account the specificity of these documents, especially from the viewpoint of the codicologic and paleographic aspects of the manuscripts. Other scholars have restricted themselves to the study of the text (for instance by establishing its archetype), often facilitated by new discoveries of modern science, such as microfilm.

This period of great fruitfulness for the history of the liturgy, in which we are still living today for the large part, has not yet led into a real opening to historical sciences and to the different movements that have left their imprint on them since World War II. Notions as innovative for the historian as the "long duration,"[9] social history, the history of worldviews and ideas, anthropology have made but small inroads into the restricted circle of the specialists in the liturgy; they have failed to appreciate the richness that their studies on the books and the practices of the Christian cult could bring to the historian of worldviews and the anthropologist.

Nonetheless, it is well known that the in-depth study of liturgical books has transformed our view of certain parts of the history of the Middle Ages. For instance, this new approach has converged with, confirmed, and refined what we know about the Church's institutions and the ecclesiology in the Middle Ages.[10] These books are also precious witnesses, in many ways, of the political and social history of antiquity and the Middle Ages.[11] A proof of this is the interest that historians and liturgists have shown for the works of E. Kantoro-

8. See in particular the work of V. Leroquais, *Les manuscrits liturgiques latins du haut Moyen Age à la Renaissance,* the opening lecture at the Ecole pratique des Hautes Etudes (section of Religious Sciences) on November 30, 1931, 16 pages; Th. Klauser, *"Repertorium liturgicum* und Liturgischer Spezialkatalog, Vorschläge zum Problem der liturgischen Handschriften," *Zentralblatt für Bibliothekswesen* 53 (1936) (text reprinted in *Gesammelte Arbeiten zur Liturgiegeschichte, Kirchengeschichte und christliche Archäologie,* Jahrbuch für Antike und Christentum Ergänzungsband 3 [Münster, 1974] 82–93); K. Gamber, *CLLA.*

9. See the basic article of F. Braudel, "La longue durée," *Annales ESC* (1958) 125–153 (rpt. in *Ecrits sur l'histoire* [Paris, 1969] 43–83).

10. See the basic work of Y. Congar, *L'ecclésiologie du haut Moyen Age* (Paris, 1968).

11. As an example, see the recent attempt, a little too systematic, made by B. Baroffio, on the basis of the liturgical manuscripts kept in Italian libraries, "I codici liturgici, specchio della cultura italiana nel Medioevo: Punti fermi, appunti di lettura, spunti di ricerca," *Ecclesia Orans* 9 (1992) 233–270.

wicz.[12] Sometimes, the historian of the Middle Ages needs to understand liturgical rites in order to shed light on the way a given social category of persons is constituted. For example, the rites of entrance into knighthood, the dubbing in particular, have important links with liturgical rites and their texts (such as the *ordines* of coronation).[13]

For a few years, the history of the liturgy has benefitted from the abundant contributions of anthropology and the opening of new avenues offered by its methods.[14] The principle of the construction of an anthropology of Christian rites and worship—which in any case is not new—gives historians of the liturgy a wider vista on the object of their study.[15]

Lastly, let us recall the connections, close although difficult to pinpoint, that exist between liturgical sources, art history, and archeology. The iconographic interpretation of a painting or of the plan of a church no longer in existence is often enhanced when the history of the liturgy plays its part in it.[16]

12. E. K. Kantorowicz, *Lands* regiae: *A Study in Liturgical Acclamations and Medieval Ruler Worship* (Berkeley-Los Angeles, 1946).

13. See J. Le Goff, "Le rituel symbolique de la vassalité," *Simboli e simbologia nell'alto Medioevo* (Spoleto, 1976) 679–788 (rpt. in *Pour un autre Moyen Age: Temps, travail et culture en Occident, 18 essais* (Paris, 1977) 349–420; J. Flori, "Chevalerie et liturgie: Remise des armes et vocabulaire 'chevaleresque' dans les sources liturgiques du IXᵉ au XIVᵉ siècle," *Le Moyen Age* 84 (1978) 245–278, 400–442.

14. The bibliography on the anthropology of the liturgy is too abundant to be presented here in its entirety; let us simply refer readers to the work of F. Isambert, *Rites et efficacité symbolique* (Paris, 1979), and especially to that of J.-Y. Hameline, "Eléments d'anthropologie, de sociologie historique et de musicologie du culte chrétien," *Recherches de Sciences religieuses* 78 (1990) 297–424. See also *Traité d'anthropologie du sacré*, vol. 1: *Les origines et le problème de l'"homo religiosus,"* ed. J. Ries (Paris, 1992).

15. See for example the study of J.-C. Schmitt, *La raison des gestes dans l' Occident médiéval* (Paris, 1990), in particular chapters 3, 8, and 9.

16. In the domain of architecture, see the pioneering work of C. Hertz, *Recherches sur les rapports entre architecture et liturgie à l'époque carolingienne* (Paris, 1963), and the comprehensive article of S. de Blaauw, "Architecture and Liturgy in the Late Antique and the Middle Ages: Traditions and Trends in Modern Scholarship," *Archiv für Liturgiewissenschaft* 33 (1991) 1–34. In the domain of the decoration of manuscripts and in that of monumental art, let us mention, among numerous others, R. E. Reynolds, "Image and Text: A Carolingian Illustration of Modifications in the Early Eucharistic *Ordines*," *Viator* 14 (1983) 59–75; O. K. Werckmeister, "The Lintel Fragment Representing Eve from Saint-Lazare, Autun," *Journal of the Warburg and Courtauld Institute* 35 (1972) 1–30; E. Palazzo, "Iconographie et liturgie, les mosaïques du baptistère de Kélibia (Tunisie)," *Archiv für Liturgiewis-*

In an increasingly interdisciplinary context, the need for a history and a typology of liturgical books is acutely felt. This book was conceived to answer this need. A preliminary word of caution is necessary: readers will not find here a history *of the liturgy*,[17] but rather a history *of the liturgical books*, though some facts concerning the history of the Mass, of the chant, and of the sacraments are mentioned. This information is not meant of course to replace the classical books on these questions.[18]

Far from being the first manual since the beginning of this century to be devoted to liturgical books,[19] the present work takes its place between the classical book of Cyrille Vogel[20] and the "abstracts" of the series "Typologie des sources du Moyen Age occidental" from Louvain.[21] It differs from these in its perspective and its concerns,

senschaft 34 (1992) 102–120. On the relationship between liturgy and archeology, see the recent studies of J.-Ch. Picard, "Ce que les textes nous apprennent sur les équipements et le mobilier liturgique nécessaire pur le baptême dans le sud de la Gaule et l'Italie du Nord," *Actes du XIᵉ Congrès international d'Archéologie chrétienne, Lyon, Vienne, Grenoble, Genève, et Aosta, 21–28 Septembre 1986* (Rome, 1989) 2:1451–1454; V. Saxer, "L'utilisation pour la liturgie de l'espace urbain et suburbain, l'exemple de Rome dans l'Antiquité et le haut Moyen Age," ibid., 917–1031.

17. See in particular, *CP* and *Gottesdienst der Kirche: Handbuch der Liturgiewissenschaft*, 8 vols. (Regensburg, 1983–). See B. Neunheuser, "Handbücher der Liturgiewissenschaft, in den grossen europäischen Sprachen, 25 Jahre nach SC, der Liturgiekonstitution des 2. Vatikanums," *Ecclesia Orans* 6 (1989) 89–103. See also the book—too little known—of I.-H. Dalmais, *Initiation à la liturgie* (Paris, 1958); [I.-H. Dalmais, *Introduction to the Liturgy*, trans. R. Capel (Baltimore, 1961)]. For an overall review of the manuals of liturgy, see B. Botte, "A propos des manuels de liturgie," *Questions liturgiques et paroissiales* 33 (1952) 117–124. See also the very useful bibliography in Pfaff, *Medieval Latin Liturgy.*

18. I am thinking especially of Jungmann, *MS*, a history of the Roman Mass.

19. We shall mention P. Cabrol, *Les livres de la liturgie latine* (Paris, 1930); [P. Cabrol, *The Books of the Latin Liturgy*, trans. Benedictines of Stanbrook (St. Louis, [1932])]; L. C. Sheppard, *The Liturgical Books* (New York, 1962); A. Hughes, *Medieval Manuscripts for Mass and Office: A Guide to Their Organization and Terminology* (Toronto, 1982) (essentially focused on musicology). For additional references, see Vogel, *Introduction*, 1–29.

20. The title of Vogel's book in the French edition is *Introduction aux sources de l'histoire du culte chrétien au Moyen Age* (Spoleto, 1966), with a reprint prefaced by B. Botte (Spoleto, 1975). Then the book was translated into English and, mainly, revised by W. G. Storey and N. K. Rasmussen, *Medieval Liturgy: An Introduction to the Sources* (Washington, 1986).

21. To date, the following books have been published: M. Huglo, *Les livres de chant liturgique*, fasc. 52 (1988); and two volumes by A.-G. Martimort, *Les "Ordines,"*

especially in the study of the crucial passage from oral practice to the written document; in a special attention to the process that formed each of the liturgical books; by a fresh look at what the knowledge of codices, paleography, and iconography bring to the study of manuscripts; and also in an interest in the medieval terminology used to designate the different books. Finally and above all, the leading characteristic of the book is an awareness, as far-reaching as possible, of the historical dimension of liturgical books, their significance for the history of the Church, the history of worldviews, and social history.

This synthesis of over one millennium of western liturgical sources aims at being at the same time an introductory manual to their study. One section is devoted to each type of book, each type specifically designed for a given form of celebration (Mass, Office, sacraments, and rituals) and destined for a clearly identified liturgical agent (pope, bishop, deacon, monastic, and so on).

This work focuses on the sources of the *Latin liturgy,* and therefore on a fundamental aspect of the religious life of the medieval West, between the fourth and thirteenth centuries. With the Fourth Lateran Council (1215), a new period in the history of liturgical books begins which will last until the Tridentine reform. There are occasional allusions to books of particular rites (Ambrosian, Mozarabic, Celtic), and readers will benefit from consulting the passages which Vogel devotes to these. A historiographic summary of the discipline of research on liturgical books, from the scholars of the sixteenth and seventeenth centuries down to our day, will serve as an introduction.

---

les ordinaires et les cérémoniaux, fasc. 56 (1991), and *Les lectures liturgiques et leurs livres,* fasc. 64 (1992).

Part One

**Historiography of the Research
on Liturgical Books**

I. The Science of the Liturgy

1. PRECURSORS (SEVENTEENTH TO NINETEENTH CENTURIES)

Since paleo-Christian times, liturgists have occupied a central place among the great figures in the history of Christianity. Often they are at the same time officiants whose active part in the celebrations gives life to the liturgists' reflections on the meaning of the celebration in the Church; they are also theologians who live their faith through the liturgy in which they participate. Theologian-liturgists have a connection with mystagogy because they explain the mysteries of the very celebration and lead others to contemplate them.[1] From the Carolingian period to about the fifteenth century, the liturgists of the Middle Ages worked for both a better understanding of liturgical actions and the creation of liturgical books and particular feasts, often by composing entirely new prayers and songs.[2]

In the sixteenth century, when the process of liturgical codification was for the most part completed, the science of the liturgy began to appear, and then progressively developed, particularly in the seventeenth century. The labors of several scholars from that period became the scientific foundations of the modern history of the liturgy. Whereas the medieval liturgists favored the allegorizing interpretation of the rituals,[3] the liturgists of the sixteenth and seventeenth centuries were

---

1. See the reflections of P.-M. Gy, "La tâche du liturgiste (Homélie prononcée pour le vingt-cinquième anniversaire de l'Institut supérieur de Liturgie)," [homily given at the twenty-fifth anniversary of the Institut supérieur de Liturgie], *La liturgie dans l'histoire* (Paris, 1991) 321–324.

2. See the list of medieval liturgists and their works published by Vogel, *Introduction*, 12–17.

3. See R. E. Reynolds, "Liturgical Scholarship at the Time of the Investiture Controversy: Past Research and Future Opportunities," *Harvard Theological Review* 71 (1978) 109–124; "Liturgy, Treatise on," *Dictionary of the Middle Ages*, ed. J. R. Strayer (New York, 1982–) 7:624–633.

above all historians whose work helped their readers discover the importance of tradition in the Church, the meaning of rituals and prayers, the origin of the treasury of prayers, in a word, all that contributes to a living knowledge of the liturgy through history.

The extent of the field covered by these pioneers of liturgical science is impressive. Several among them not only gathered an important documentation but also wrote commentaries, some of which are still indispensable today.[4] We must note that many among the writings of this period deal precisely with the liturgical books, their history, their typology, and above all the standard edition of the texts.

During most of the eighteenth century, this interest in the history of the liturgy, especially the study of its sources, continued to grow. However, the political and cultural turn taken by history at the end of the eighteenth century greatly slowed down this trend. It was not before the middle of the nineteenth century, with the birth of the "Liturgical Movement," that the history of the liturgy and the study of its sources made a fresh start.[5] This Liturgical Movement, which viewed the liturgy as a social fact, granted a special place to archeology in the widest possible sense of this word, in sum, all that more or less concerns historical sources in general. Several of the protagonists and leaders of this movement were great historians of the Church, some even were well acquainted with liturgical sources. As an example, let it suffice to cite the uncommon itinerary of Bishop L. M. Duchesne (1843–1922), who for twenty-seven years was the director of the Ecole Française de Rome, and whose scientific work strongly contributed to the future orientations of the liturgical science.[6]

2. LITURGICAL RENEWAL IN THE TWENTIETH CENTURY

The theological and liturgical renewal of the first half of the twentieth century, whose fulfillment was Vatican II, had its roots in the Liturgical Movement of the nineteenth century. In fact, the former was an extensive prolongation of the latter—whose first concrete result was a better formation of clergy, monastics, and lay people. Here again history played a prominent role, now shedding light on contemporary

4. See the list given by Vogel, *Introduction*, 17–20.

5. On this topic, see the in-depth study of J.-Y. Hameline, "'Les origines du culte chrétien' et le mouvement liturgique," *La Maison-Dieu* 181 (1990) 51–96.

6. Finally, it will be good to consult the series of articles devoted to Duchesne in a special issue of *La Maison-Dieu*, no. 181 (1990).

liturgical practices and fostering new orientations in pastoral ministry, now justifying decisions favorable to a liturgical reform.[7]

The decades of the twentieth century preceding Vatican II were the chronological framework in which some of the inspirers of the council, and some of its actors, were formed. There are many liturgists and theologians—sometimes theologian-liturgists—who distinguished themselves during this period of great intellectual fecundity for the Church.[8] It is enough to mention the names of A. Baumstark (1872–1948), whose method of comparative analysis of the Eastern and Western liturgies in the Church opened vast horizons to liturgists;[9] J. A. Jungmann (1889–1975);[10] and B. Botte (1893–1980)[11] to measure the amplitude and diversity of the progress made in the course of this century.

3. LITURGICAL STUDIES AFTER VATICAN II

By defining in the Constitution *Sacrosanctum Concilium* on the holy liturgy, promulgated December 4, 1963, the general principles, the restoration, and the development of the liturgy, together with its "nature and importance in the life of the Church," the council provoked a renewed enthusiasm for the historical science and the teaching of the liturgy. In Germany especially, the historical science of the liturgy became the object of advanced theoretical reflections aimed at defining in depth its ends, its interaction with other disciplines of the human sciences, its theological postulate, its effect on pastoral ministry.[12]

7. See A. Haquin, "Histoire de la liturgie et Renouveau liturgique," *La Maison-Dieu* 181 (1990) 99–118; see also *CP*, 1:72–84.

8. For research on the bibliography and/or career of such and such a liturgist, one should consult the helpful lists established by Rasmussen, "Some Bibliographies of Liturgists," *Archiv für Liturgiewissenschaft* 11 (1969) 214–218; 15 (1973) 168–171; 20 (1978) 134–139; 25 (1983) 34–44.

9. A. Baumstark, *Liturgie comparée: Principes et méthodes pour l'étude historique des liturgies chrétiennes*, 3rd ed., rev. B. Botte (Chevetogne, 1953); [A. Baumstark, *Comparative Liturgy*, rev. B. Botte, ed. F. L. Cross (Westminster, Md., 1958)]. The bibliography of Baumstark is found in *Ephemerides liturgicae* 63 (1949) 187–207.

10. Known especially for his important work, *Missarum Sollemnia*; see the obituary by P.-M. Gy, "L'oeuvre liturgique de Joseph Andreas Jungmann," *La liturgie dans l'histoire* (Paris, 1990) 308–315.

11. See especially by this author his book of memories, *Le mouvement liturgique: Témoignages et souvenirs* (Paris, 1973). On his life and scientific work, whose importance is considerable, in particular for the history of the first centuries of Christianity, see pp. 301–308 of the same book and *La Maison-Dieu* 141 (1980) 167–171.

12. On this, see the comprehensive article, together with the preceding bibliography, by A. A. Haüssling, "Liturgiewissenschaft zwei Jahrzehnte nach Konzilsbeginn,"

Today the history of the liturgy is generally admitted among historical sciences; nevertheless, it remains confined within restricted ecclesiastical circles, primarily because it is insufficiently taught. Hence the necessity of a real effort on the part of lay people who want to be initiated or even to become specialists in this discipline.

Archiv für Liturgiewissenschaft 24 (1982) 1–18; E. J. Lengeling, "Liturgie/ Liturgiewissenschaft," *Neues Handbuch theologischer Grundbegriffe*, enlarged ed., ed. P. Eicher, vol. 3 (Munich, 1991) 279–305.

II. Studies on Liturgical Books

1. HISTORIC REVIEW OF THE RESEARCH

Several famous names in liturgical science have marked the research on the history of liturgical books. We must again go back to the sixteenth, seventeenth, and eighteenth centuries to meet those who established the foundations, and even sometimes more than the foundations, of the historical investigation of liturgical books.[13]

Who is the historian who has not one day in the course of his or her research encountered one of the Benedictine scholars of the Congregation of Saint-Maur? J. Mabillon (1632–1707) and E. Martène (1654–1739) are in effect, the true forerunners, among other things, of the modern research on liturgical books. On the essential points, their works are still authoritative and remain the requisite basis for this or that particular research. We are indebted to Mabillon for the indispensable *De liturgia gallicana libri tres*,[14] and also, in collaboration with M. Germain, the *Museum italicum seu collectio veterum scriptorum ex bibliothecis italicis eruti*,[15] in which several major manuscripts of the High Middle Ages, such as the famous Missal of Bobbio, are edited and presented. Besides the printed books we owe to Mabillon, we not infrequently find notes written in his own hand on the end page of a manuscript, for he, like Martène, spent a large part of his life consulting the collections of ancient monastic libraries.

---

13. As far as we know, to date there exists no overall historiographic study on this topic; without any doubt, it would deserve to be undertaken.

14. Published in Paris in 1685 and reprinted in *PL* 72, cols. 99–448.

15. Two volumes published in Paris between 1687 and 1689; the second volume, containing among other things collections of *ordines*, was reprinted in *PL* 78, cols. 851–1408.

The major work of Martène,[16] a pupil and disciple of Mabillon in Saint-Germain-des-Prés, is *De antiquis Ecclesiae ritibus.*[17] This work is the result of thorough research on customaries, ordinaries, rituals, and other liturgical books preserved in several ancient holdings. Martène, guided and prompted by Mabillon, elaborates on each of the subjects treated in these documents, explains the rituals, and describes them exactly as he finds them in the sources he uses.

Bent on retrieving the medieval tradition of earlier monasticism for the benefit of their Congregation of Saint-Maur, Mabillon, Martène, and others who followed their example[18] had as their principal purpose the writing of the history of Benedictine monachism, particularly through liturgical rituals and practices. To this end, they regarded the liturgical manuscripts of the prestigious past of the order as privileged sources that must be thoroughly studied. In addition to these investigations—historical in character and justified by reasons external to the study of the sources themselves—there was a new awareness of the criticism of written sources per se. Mabillon's remarks on individual medieval manuscripts already demonstrate a rigorous process of scientific analysis, rare at the time. The same is true of the descriptions of liturgical objects and even of architectural vestiges of the Middle Ages found in *Voyage littéraire de deux religieux bénédictins de la Congrégation de Saint-Maur,* written by Martène and U. Durand.[19]

The motives that prompted the research of Mabillon and Martène caused them to become acquainted with the oldest documents of the

16. On the life, work, and personality of Martène, see J. Daoust, *Dom Martène: Un géant de l'érudition bénédictine,* Figures monastiques (Rouen, 1947).

17. Published for the first time in Rouen in 1700–1702, the four volumes of the second edition (Antwerp, 1736–1738) are more frequently used; there has been a reprint (Hildesheim, 1967–1969). On the genesis of the work and the study of the sources Martène used, see the remarkable work of A.-G. Martimort, *La documentation liturgique de dom Edmond Martène,* Studi e Testi 279 (Vatican City, 1978), completed by his "Additions et corrections à la documentation liturgique de dom Edmond Martène," *Ecclesia Orans* 3 (1986) 81–105. See also B. Darragon, *Répertoire des pièces euchologiques dans le "De antiquis Ecclesiae ritibus" de dom Martène,* Bibliotheca "Ephemerides liturgicae," Subsidia 57 (Rome, 1991).

18. See the thorough article of R. McKitterick, "The Study of Frankish History in France and Germany in the Sixteenth and Seventeenth Centuries," *Francia* 8 (1980) 556–572; for France, see 564–572; P. Gassault, "Motivations, conditions de travail et héritage des bénédictins érudits de la congrégation de Saint-Maur," *Revue d'Histoire de l'Eglise de France* 71 (1985) 13–23.

19. Published in Paris in 1717 and 1724.

medieval past. However, their purpose was not to edit and classify ancient manuscripts, in contrast to several other learned liturgists, their contemporaries, whose work was focused on the search for the original, and secondarily on the elaboration of a typology of medieval liturgical documents.[20] In a certain way, as will be seen in the following section, these objectives were also those of the scholars of the nineteenth and twentieth centuries.

The name of Jacques de Joigny de Pamèle (1536–1587)—Pamelius being the better known form—is intimately linked with the study of lectionaries, antiphonals, and sacramentaries.[21] He was the first to publish the Gregorian Sacramentary, a task which A. Rocca and especially H. Ménard (d. 1644) successfully continued.[22]

A contemporary of Mabillon, J. Tomasi (d. 1713) was one of the pioneers in the publication of western liturgical sources.[23] He researched the earliest manuscripts, but he did not neglect the present because, aware of the imperfections of the liturgical books promulgated by Pius V, he saw himself as a reformer. His *Codices sacramentorum nongentis annis vetustiores* (Rome, 1680) places in the limelight four manuscripts of prime importance for the study of sacramentaries, in particular the Vat. Regin. 316. Among other things, we are also indebted to Tomasi for the publication of documents indispensable to the reconstitution of the earliest forms of the lectionary of the Mass and the antiphonal of the Office; here again, we find that he used manuscripts which were to be the basis of the work of scholars in the twentieth century.[24]

As regards the research on and the publication of the sacramentary, the name of L. A. Muratori (d. 1750) must be taken into consideration. His *Liturgia romana vetus*[25] deals with Roman and Gallican documents.

---

20. See the list in Vogel, *Introduction*, 17–20.

21. See especially his work, *Liturgia latinorum*, 2 vols. (Cologne, 1571).

22. The work of Ménard, *Divi Gregorii papae Liber sacramentorum nunc demum correctior et locupletior editus ex missali Mss. S. Eligii bibliothecae Corbeiensis* (Paris, 1642) [ms. 12051 of the Latin collection of the Bibliothèque nationale] was the edition of the Gregorian Sacramentary in use down to the twentieth century and the one found in *PL* 78, cols. 25–263.

23. See P. Jounel, "Saint Joseph-Marie Tomasi," *La Maison-Dieu* 167 (1986) 147–151.

24. Tomasi's complete work was published in 7 volumes by A. Vezzosi (Rome, 1717–1754); the fourth volume, dealing with the antiphonal, was reprinted (Farnborough, 1969).

25. This work in 2 volumes (Venice, 1748) was indexed by H. Wilson, *A Classified Index to the Leonine, Gelasian and Gregorian Sacramentaries* (Cambridge, 1892).

Finally, let us mention the work of F. A. Zaccaria (d. 1795) whose *Bibliotheca ritualis*[26] is replete with stimulating reflections, particularly in the domain of the typology of books.

2. RESEARCH ON LATIN LITURGICAL BOOKS OF THE MIDDLE AGES IN THE NINETEENTH AND TWENTIETH CENTURIES

The specialists in liturgical books of the late nineteenth and twentieth centuries followed, for the most part, the paths explored by their predecessors. The three principal domains where this research was most vigorously pursued are: the publication of the major texts dealing with the history of the liturgy, most notably the quest for their earliest form, the history of the books, and their typology. Overall, these three endeavors have greatly benefited from the contribution of disciplines that are necessary for liturgists, such as paleography, codicology, and even the history of illumination. Indeed, the publication of a text and the establishment of its critical apparatus, or else the determination of the typology of a specific liturgical book necessarily requires the handling of the "fresh documents"—as the sorely missed M.-D. Chenu[27] delighted in calling them—that medieval manuscripts are. This awareness of the demands of serious scientific research has not, however, transformed every liturgist into a specialist of medieval paleography or the ancient art of bookbinding,[28] but it has indubitably awakened a more discerning approach to the document itself.

A. Wilmart (1876–1941),[29] whose catalogue of the manuscripts in the Reginensis of the Vatican Library is a model,[30] remains an exception; a prominent liturgist, he is also considered one of the best paleographers of this century as well as a connoisseur of all aspects of

---

26. Published in Rome between 1776 and 1781, it was reprinted (New York, 1963).

27. M.-D. Chenu, *Une école de théologie: le Saulchoir*, 1st ed. (Paris, 1937; 2nd ed., 1985) 124.

28. The use of microfilm has favored a certain distancing of the liturgists, along with other specialists of ancient texts, from the manuscripts themselves; occasionally, this distancing has been at the root of gross errors in the establishment of the history of the text, precisely because of faulty codicological or paleographic evaluations.

29. On the career and work of Wilmart, one must consult J. Bignami-Odier, I. Brou, and A. Vernet, *Bibliographie sommaire des travaux du P. A. Wilmart*, Sussidi eruditi 5 (Rome, 1953); A. Ward, "Anniversary of a Liturgist: Dom André Wilmart, OSB (1876–1941)," *Ephemerides liturgicae* 105 (1991) 468–475.

30. *Codices Reginenses latini*, vol. 1 (Vatican City, 1937).

medieval manuscripts. A large part of his output (articles, books, and catalogues) has decisively contributed to the progress of the research on liturgical books, for either the typology or the history of the texts.

V. Leroquais (1875–1946),[31] whose catalogues of liturgical manuscripts in the public libraries of France are consulted by all medievalists, was a kindred spirit of Wilmart: neither one was a specialist in one single liturgical book, but both knew them all. Besides, it is probably no exaggeration to say that Leroquais is the undisputed master of the typology of liturgical books. Between 1924 and 1946, he successively published the descriptions of sacramentaries and missals, breviaries, pontificals, psalters, and books of Hours (this last only from the manuscripts of the Bibliothèque nationale). The descriptions contained in his different catalogues, which we will have occasion to mention again, very rarely end without his making a judgment, suggesting an idea, or stating a new opinion on the type of books to which a given manuscript belongs, as a conclusion to a paleographic, iconographic, and stylistic analysis, even if very brief. Along the same lines, it is worth mentioning that his opening lecture at the Division of Religious Sciences at the Ecole pratique des Hautes Etudes on November 13, 1931, commands admiration for being truly a little treatise on liturgical typology. All, or almost all, the important questions are broached: definition of the liturgical books, their diversity, their history, their role in the celebration, the ancient terminology. Lastly, it presents methodological orientations that are still valid today. Leroquais joined a thorough knowledge of constitutive elements of the liturgy (orations, chants, and so on) and their history to his ceaseless probing of the "fresh document." His personal notebooks, kept in the Bibliothèque nationale,[32] contain treasures that make possible the identification of the liturgical usages of the books of Hours.

This last point leads us to mention G. Beyssac (1877–1965),[33] a liturgist whose published work was minimal but whose files of notes are an inestimably rich mine for the historian of liturgical texts. Having spent his life poring over ancient manuscripts and printed books, he labored mostly in the fields of the history of the constitutive elements

31. See the eulogies given by F. Combaluzier, *Ephemerides liturgicae* 19 (1946) 389–395, and J. Leclercq, *Revue du Moyen Age latin* (1946) 126–128.

32. Mss. n.a.l. 3157–3173; plus his papers, n.a.f. 13083–13086.

33. See F. Combaluzier, *"In Memoriam Gabrielis Beyssac,"* *Ephemerides liturgicae* 82 (1968) 47–53; today, the "Beyssac holding" is kept at the Abbey of Bouveret in Switzerland.

of the liturgy. Furthermore, with his gifts as a paleographer, he deciphered difficult texts and reconstructed the history of many offices, without, for all that, becoming a specialist in manuscripts.

In contrast to the liturgists who became paleographers, few scholars conversant with medieval documents became liturgists. Only one person is an exception: L. Delisle (1826–1910). A forerunner in the study of medieval manuscripts,[34] he composed an excellent book on sacramentaries which encompasses the definition of the type of these manuscripts as well as their history, writing, and decoration.[35]

A Rapid Review of the Research on Different Books

In the domain of sacramentaries, several authors distinguished themselves; some of them focused their work on the history of the book, the search for and the establishment of the earliest texts; others studied the manuscript sources, their origin, their date, even their illustration. The pioneering work of A. Ebner (1861–1898)[36] is, along with Delisle's, the true point of departure for modern research on sacramentaries. Ebner had undertaken to trace the history of the missal on the basis of the ancient sacramentaries preserved in the rich collections of Italian libraries. The valid points of his book are, even today, the study of each manuscript, an attempt at a synthesis of the history of the book, and his ideas on the illustration of the sacramentaries and, later on, the missals. The catalogue of the sacramentaries kept in the French libraries, the first of the series written by Leroquais, is to be placed next to Ebner's work.[37] For the establishment of the texts of the different families of sacramentaries as well as for the history of the sacramentary and the attribution of the various pieces, one should consult the work of A. Stuiber (1912–1981) and even more, those of E. Bourque, J. Deshusses, to whom we are indebted for the best studies on the Gregorian Sacramentary,[38] and A. Chavasse, whose competence in the field of the reconstitution of

---

34. On the life and work of Léopold Delisle, who was the director of the Department of Manuscripts at the Bibliothèque nationale, see his "Souvenirs de jeunesse," published in the beginning of his book entitled *Recherches sur la librairie de Charles V* (Paris, 1907) 1:XI–XXVII.

35. L. Delisle, "Mémoires sur d'anciens sacramentaires," *Mémoires de l'Académie des Inscriptions et Belles-Lettres* 32 (1886) 57–423.

36. Ebner, *Missale Romanum.*

37. Leroquais, *Sacramentaires.*

38. See especially Deshusses, *Grégorien.*

liturgical books has spread into other fields.[39] We must also mention K. Gamber (1919–1989),[40] who devoted a large part of his work to sacramentaries. His *Codices Liturgici Latini Antiquiores* are without equal to this day; they offer a nearly complete catalogue of all the manuscript witnesses of the High Middle Ages through the eleventh century, all types of books indiscriminately listed, but with reflections and proposals on typology.[41]

The books of readings were studied principally by W. H. Frere (1863–1938),[42] T. Klauser, a great historian of the liturgy,[43] and Chavasse. While Frere was interested only in the history of the different books of readings, Klauser and Chavasse have pondered the earliest witnesses in order to reconstitute the lists of pericopes used in Rome between the sixth and eighth centuries[44] and to follow their evolution down to their definitive form in the lectionaries during the period from the ninth to eleventh centuries.

As regards the books of chant, the research was accompanied by a rediscovery of Gregorian Chant,[45] by the Benedictine monks of Solesmes in particular, among whom are some of the best specialists in medieval musicology and who have been publishing the important

39. On the life and career of A. Chavasse, see *Revue des Sciences religieuses* 58, Hommage à M. le Pr Chavasse (1984) in particular pp. 3–5; for his main works on the subject of sacramentaries, see the bibliography.

40. Gamber is the undisputed master of the German school of research on liturgical books. The part devoted to the high Middle Ages in the catalogue of the exhibit, *Liturgie im Bistum Regensburg von den Anfängen bis zur Gegenwart* (Regensburg, 1989), is the summation of nearly forty years of research done by Gamber on the earliest witnesses of the liturgy from southwestern Germany. On this catalogue and the work—often the object of controversy—of this liturgist, see the note in P.-M. Gy "Bulletin de liturgie," *Revue des Sciences religieuses et théologiques* 74 (1990) 114–115.

41. This work was published in two volumes in the Subsidia of the series *Spicilegium Friburgense* (1963 and 1968) with one volume of supplements (1988).

42. See C. S. Philipps, *W. H. Frere* (London, 1947) particularly pp. 204–213.

43. For the multifaceted work of this liturgist, see *Gesammelte Arbeiten zur Liturgiegeschichte, Kirchengeschichte und christlichen Archäologie*, Jahrbuch für Antike und Christentum, supp. 3 (Münster, 1974), where one finds his article on catalogues of liturgical manuscripts, based on the works of Leroquais, Delisle, and Ebner among others, "Repertorium liturgicum und liturgischer Spezialkatalog: Vorschläge zum Problem des liturgischen Handschriften," pp. 82–93 (first published in 1936).

44. See especially Klauser, *Capitulare evangeliorum*.

45. D. P. Combe, *Histoire de la restauration du chant grégorien d'après les documents inédits* (Abbey of Solesmes, 1969).

Paléographie musicale since 1889.[46] The main historian of books of liturgical chant is M. Huglo, whose competence covers many disciplines: the reconstitution of the melodies, the history of manuscripts (especially under their codicological aspect), musical paleography (notation), and finally the general history of the liturgy.[47] For his part, R.-J. Hesbert has established, also on the basis of the earliest manuscript sources,[48] the texts of the antiphonals of the Mass and Office. All these writings have become indispensable instruments for any research on this type of book.

The work M. Andrieu (1886–1956)[49] devoted to the *ordines* and then to the pontifical takes its place among the most remarkable studies on liturgical books.[50] His five volumes on the *Ordines Romani* are up to date on the manuscript sources and the textual tradition of each *ordo*. The critical edition of the Romano-Germanic Pontifical of the tenth century by C. Vogel and R. Elze continues Andrieu's *ordines*.[51] The link between the two preceding works is found in the work of N. K. Rasmussen (d. 1987) on the pontificals of the High Middle Ages;[52] it is a study of the genesis of the bishop's liturgical book, in other words, of the oldest forms of the pontifical before the Ottonian compilation in the tenth century. As an editor of texts and a historian of the liturgy, Rasmussen has chiefly contributed to the advancement of research concerning the typology of the bishop's book.

We owe our knowledge of other books of the Latin liturgy to liturgists like J. Dubois (d. 1991), whose name is intimately associated

46. Originally intended to justify the return to Gregorian chant, the *Paléographie musicale* gradually became one of the major published works of modern musicology, in particular for its contributions to the history of the liturgy. See J. Froger, "L'édition critique de l'Antiphonale Missarum romain par les moines de Solesmes," *Etudes grégoriennes* 1 (1954) 151–157, and "The Critical Edition of the Roman Gradual by the Monks of Solesmes," *Journal of the Plainsong and Mediaeval Music Society* 10 (1987) 1–14.

47. His contribution to the Louvain series of fascicles on typology, devoted to the books of chant, is the authoritative reference book in this field.

48. See Hesbert, *CAO* and *AMS*.

49. On the life and career of this great scholar, see *Revue des Sciences religieuses* 31, Mélanges en l'honneur de Mgr Michel Andrieu (Strasbourg, 1957) pp. v–ix; J.-M. Fabre and A.-G. Martimort, "Monseigneur Michel Andrieu," *Annales de l'Université populaire du Haut-Rouergue* 3 (1986–1987) 27–43.

50. See the Bibliographical Abbreviations and Part 4, I and III, the sections devoted to the *ordines* and pontificals.

51. Vogel and Elze, *PRG*.

52. Rasmussen, *Pontificaux*.

with research on the Roman Martyrology,[53] as well as H. Barré (1905–1968) and R. Grégoire for their studies on medieval homiliaries.[54] For the history of the breviary, we must mention P. Batiffol (1861–1929)[55] and P. Salmon (1896–1982).[56] Other scholars will be named in the following parts. But let us note here that all, or almost all, worked in different degrees, depending on the periods and the schools they belonged to, on manuscripts in order to elaborate a typology, to write the history of their documents, and to furnish a critical edition of them.

Theoreticians and New Orientations of Research

Other scholars are important as "theoreticians" of liturgical science and research on books. Highly reputable historians of the liturgy, they have labored unceasingly to bring about a renewal in the methods of approach and reflection proper to the study of books. Taking their place between technicians and historians, A.-G. Martimort,[57] P.-M. Gy,[58] Vogel (1919–1982),[59] and S. Van Dijk (1909–1971),[60] to cite only a few, have built bridges between liturgists and medievalists—whether historians, historians of art, or specialists in manuscripts. Often, they have made it possible for these last to have an easier access to the

53. See the collection of articles recently published, *Martyrologes, d'Usuard au martyrologe romain* (Abbeville, 1990).

54. On Barré, see the article in *Revue des Etudes augustiniennes* 15 (1969) 3–8.

55. See F. Cabrol, ed., *Dictionnaire d'Archéologie chrétienne et de liturgie [DACL]* (Paris) vol. 9, pt. 2, cols. 1744–1749.

56. Salmon, *Office divin;* he is also the author of the five catalogues of the liturgical manuscripts in the Vatican Library which replace the catalogue of H. Ehrensberger; see the eulogy in *Notitiae* 10 (1982) 386–387.

57. See the introductions to his volume of articles, *Mens concordet voci: Pour Mgr A.-G. Martimort à l'occasion e ses quarante années d'enseignement et des vingt ans de la constitution Sacrosanctum concilium* (Paris, 1983). We owe to this great scholar and theologian, an active participant in the liturgical reform of Vatican II, a recent book on the *ordines,* the ordinaries, and the ceremonials, part of the series Typologie des sources du Moyen Age occidental from Louvain, as well as a book on the liturgical readings and their books.

58. See the preface of Y. Congar in *Rituels: Mélanges offerts au P. Gy* (Paris, 1990) 9–11. Gy has for many years been particularly interested in rituals, see Gy, "Collectaire," and the section which is devoted to them in this book (Part 3, III).

59. See the eulogy in *Revue des Sciences religieuses* 57 (1983) 1–3. Besides his research on the Romano-Germanic Pontifical, Vogel is the author of numerous works, on penance and penitentials in particular.

60. This author is known especially for his research on the ordinaries of the Curia in the thirteenth century and the history of the Franciscan missal and breviary,

manuscript sources of the liturgy, their history, sometimes even their ecclesiology and theology. The recent collection of articles written by Gy[61] illustrates this productive approach to liturgical sources regarded as elements of a "total" history of the liturgy. For his part, Vogel, whom we have already mentioned in the general introduction, remains to this day the author of the sole compendium accessible to all medievalists on the subject of medieval liturgical books studied in their historical and ecclesiological contexts.

After having published the major texts necessary to the study of the liturgy, restored their original state, and written their history, the liturgists have turned to a kind of study that greatly interests historians in the wider sense. Two recent articles seem to me indicative of this new orientation; both concern liturgical books, the first, directly, the second, more peripherally.

Rasmussen approaches in a new way the problem of the typology of liturgical books and its implications for the different forms of celebration during the High Middle Ages.[62] Taking his point of departure from several medieval manuscripts, the author attempts to find a systematic approach to these according to a simple principle: the content and material aspect of a manuscript reveal what its use was. Therefore, there are as many forms of celebration as there are types of documents. For instance, sacramentaries were in use in monasteries and parishes as well as in episcopal ceremonies: in each of these cases, the external form and the content of the manuscripts are different. This approach permits us to establish the connection between the medieval liturgical book and the setting for which it was intended, and thus to determine the control it had on the liturgical practices of the monk, the parish priest, and the bishop. What is sought here is a true reconstitution of the living framework of the liturgy of the High Middle Ages, a difficult undertaking for which the documentation is fragmentary.[63]

Van Dijk, *Origins;* see the eulogy in *Archivum Franciscanum historicum* 64 (1971) 591–597.

61. *La liturgie dans l'histoire,* preface by J. Le Goff (Paris, 1990).

62. See N. K. Rasmussen, "Célébration épiscopale et célébration presbytérale, un essai de typologie," *Signi e riti nella chiesa altomedievale occidentale,* Settimane di studio del Centro Italiano di studi sull'alto Medioevo 33, 11–17 April 1985, 2 vols. (Spoleto, 1987) 1:581–603; see also his *Pontificaux.*

63. On what is known of the liturgical practices before the appearance of liturgical books, see P. De Clerck, "Improvisation et livre liturgique, leçons d'une histoire," *Communautés et liturgie* 60 (1978) 109–126.

Thanks to the contribution of various sources (literary texts, liturgical texts, archeological confirmations), V. Saxer has produced a stimulating study on the liturgical usages and fashions in Rome in antiquity and the High Middle Ages.[64] Although he does not deal directly with liturgical books, Saxer combines his sources in such a way that they shed a different light on his subject.

For a long time, liturgists stressed the importance, for the typology of the books, of labeling any manuscript as precisely as possible; this applies equally to the medieval and modern names. With few exceptions, this requirement received scant respect on the part of researchers.[65] Nowadays, we pay close attention to the terminology used in the Middle Ages to designate the books, a terminology often variable and fluctuating. But a whole field is open to research in this direction. The medieval library catalogues and the inventories of church treasuries prove extremely rich, a wealth completely ignored up to now. A preliminary inquiry on the terms used in medieval catalogues to designate the liturgical *libelli*[66] gave us an inkling of how beneficial it would be to extend this sort of study to all other liturgical books. In order to really profit from these catalogues and inventories, one must be attentive to the evolution of the meaning of each and every term as well as to the mixing of meaning between the words that designate the book as an intellectual unit and those which describe the books in codicological terms.[67]

At the same time, the "classical" approaches (publication of the books, elaboration of a typology) continue and seek to perfect their methods. Increasing attention given to codicological, paleographic,

64. V. Saxer, "L'utilisation par la liturgie de l'espace urbain et suburbain: L'exemple de Rome dans l'Antiquité et le haut Moyen Age," *Actes du 11e Congrès international d'Archéologie chrétienne, Lyon, Vienne, Grenoble, Genève, et Aosta, 21–28 septembre 1986* (Rome, 1989) 2:917–1031.

65. Concerning the names given to the different liturgical books, Gy has stressed that it was an insufficiently studied question, "Le vocabulaire liturgique latin au Moyen Age," *La lexicographie du latin médiéval et ses rapports avec les recherches actuelles sur la civilisation du Moyen Age*, Colloque international du CNRS [Centre national de recherche scientifique] (Paris, 1981) 295–301.

66. E. Palazzo, "Le rôle des *libelli* dans la pratique liturgique du haut Moyen Age: Histoire et typologie," *Revue Mabillon* 62, n.s. (1990) 9–36.

67. On this topic, see the study of F. Dolbeau, "Noms de livres," *Vocabulaire du livre et de l'écriture au Moyen Age: Actes de la table ronde, Paris, 24–26 septembre 1987*, ed. O. Weijers, Etudes sur le vocabulaire intellectuel du Moyen Age 2, CIVICIMA (Turnhout, 1989) 79–99.

and artistic data, characterizes a good number of the studies (especially those on the catalogues of manuscripts) undertaken by liturgists, specialists in cultic books. To cite but one example, the ordinaries are extremely useful to the archeologist—because the plan of a given building and its eventual repairs and restorations are described there—and to the topographer of the cities and villages of the Middle Ages—because the names of the streets and various places are sometimes mentioned in these books.[68]

68. See the remarks in Martimort, *Ordines,* pp. 82–85, and Part 4, V, of this manual.

Part Two

The Books of the Mass

STRUCTURE OF THE CELEBRATION OF A MASS

—Introit antiphon (cantor and *schola cantorum,* antiphonal)

—Kyrie

—Gloria in Excelsis (celebrant and *schola cantorum,* sacramentary and antiphonal)

—First oration:[1] collect (celebrant, sacramentary)

—Reading of the epistle (subdeacon, epistolary or lectionary)

—Gradual response and alleluia (cantor and *schola cantorum,* antiphonal and *cantatorium*

—Reading of the gospel (deacon, evangeliary, book of Gospels, or lectionary)

—Offertory antiphon (cantor, *schola cantorum,* antiphonal)

—Second oration: secret *(secreta or super oblata)* (celebrant, sacramentary)

—Preface

—Sanctus (celebrant and *schola cantorum,* sacramentary and antiphonal)

1. [In this book, the word "oration" refers to several sorts of prayers in the form of the Roman "collect" (from *oratio ad collectam,* "prayer upon assembly"), which contains an invocation, petition, and conclusion, such as the collect, secret, and postcommunion in the Latin Mass and the concluding collects of the Liturgy of the Hours. The word "prayer" refers to all other kinds of prayers. The English translation of the Latin terms and quotations which are enclosed in square brackets have been supplied by the translator. —*Ed.*]

—Canon of the Mass (celebrant, sacramentary)

—Our Father

—Agnus Dei (Cantor and *schola cantorum*, antiphonal)

—Communion antiphon (cantor and *schola cantorum*, antiphonal)

—Third oration: postcommunion (celebrant, sacramentary)

I. The Sacramentary, the Book of the Celebrant

During the High Middle Ages, the principal book for the celebration of the Mass is the sacramentary.[2] It contains all the texts of orations and prayers needed by the celebrant, whether a parish priest, a bishop, or the pope, for every day of the liturgical year. This material comprises an unchanging part (the canon of the Mass) and a part that varies from one day to the next (the formularies of the Temporal and Sanctoral Cycles, as well as votive Masses).

1. CONTENT OF THE SACRAMENTARY

Besides the canon of the Mass and orations grouped in formularies for each Mass, the sacramentaries have often a calendar, an *ordo missae, ordines* (rituals of baptism, funerals, penance, and so on), and blessings, these last in general for monastic use.

The Canon of the Mass

The canon of the Mass (today called the "Eucharistic Prayer") is made up of all the prayers which the priest says at each eucharistic celebration; it goes from the dialogue preceding the preface to the Our Father.[3] For its main part, the canon had in all likelihood been developed by the fourth century since St. Ambrose, bishop of Milan (374–397), already quotes some passages from it.[4] From the pontificate of Gregory the Great (590–604) on, one is on firmer ground for reconstructing its text. By then, it had already received various

2. For the history of the Eucharist, see Jungmann, *MS; CP,* 2; and especially H. B. Meyer, *Eucharistie: Geschichte, Theologie, Pastoral,* Gottesdienst der Kirche: Handbuch der Liturgiewissenschaft 4 (Regensburg, 1989). See the critical review of this work by A. Haussling, "Missarum Sollemnia und Eucharistie," *Archiv für Liturgiewissenschaft* 32 (1990) 382–393.

3. See *CP,* 2:85–106, and Meyer, *Eucharistie,* n. 1, pp. 177–181. See also B. Botte, *Le canon de la messe romaine,* critical ed., introduction and notes (Louvain, 1935).

4. *De Sacramentis* 4.21–27.

complements, of which the most important is the Sanctus, borrowed from the East—Jerusalem, perhaps—about the first third of the fifth century.[5] The variable prayers of the canon are also believed to have been written in the fifth and sixth centuries. Among these are the *Communicantes*[6] and the *Hanc igitur*,[7] in which the references to saints differ from one manuscript to the other, as do those in the *Nobis quoque* and the *Libera nos*. The study of these references directly concerns that of the sacramentary and enables researchers to determine in certain cases the origin of the manuscript and the place where it was used. It is therefore necessary to take into account the additions and corrections made to the original text. From the Carolingian period on, the text of the canon is usually placed in the beginning of the manuscripts, after the calendar, or else, in the missals of the second half of the Middle Ages, it is inserted in the body of the book in the vicinity of the feast of Easter.

Here follows the overall structure of the canon of the Mass:

—dialogue of introduction *(Per omnia secula seculorum, Dominus vobiscum)* followed by the common preface *Vere dignum* and the singing of the Sanctus;

—prayer of intercession *(Te igitur)*;[8]

—prayer for the living *(Memento)*;

—prayer of intercession with the saints (*Communicantes*, in which the Virgin, the twelve apostles, and the twelve Roman martyrs are always mentioned);

—prayer for the acceptance of the offering *(Hanc igitur* and *Quam oblationem)*;[9]

—story of the institution of the Eucharist *(Qui pridie,*[10] *Unde et memores)*;[11] anamnesis;

5. See P.-M. Gy, "Le Sanctue romain et les anaphores orientales," *Mélanges liturgiques offerts au R. P. dom Bernard Botte* (Louvain, 1972) 167–174; B. D. Spinks, *The Sanctus in the Eucharistic Prayer* (New York, 1991).

6. B. Botte, "*Communicantes*," *Questions liturgiques et paroissiales* 38 (1957) 119–123.

7. V. L. Kennedy, "The Pre-Gregorian *Hanc igitur*," *Ephemerides liturgicae* 50 (1936) 349–358, and *The Saints of the Canon of the Mass* (Rome, 1938); J. Dubois and J.-L. Lemaître, *Sources et méthodes de l'hagiographie médiévale* (Paris, 1993) 59–101.

8. L. Eizenhöfer, "*Te igitur* und *Communicantes*," *Sacris Erudiri* 8 (1956) 14–75.

9. W. Lallou, *The* Quam oblationem *of the Roman Canon* (Washington, 1943).

10. G. Morin, "Une particularité du *Qui pridie* en usage en Afrique au Ve–VIe siècle," *Revue bénédictine* 41 (1929) 70–73.

11. F. Manns, "L'origine judéo-chrétienne de la prière *unde et memores* au canon de la messe," *Ephemerides liturgicae* 101 (1987) 60–68.

—prayer for sanctification *(Supra quae,*[12] *Supplices);*
—prayer for fellowship with the saints *(Memento* of the dead, *Nobis quoque);*
—concluding prayers *(Per quem haec omnia, Pater noster,*[13] *Libera nos).*

The Calendar[14]

A great number of sacramentaries of the High Middle Ages have a calendar, usually placed in the beginning of the manuscript.[15] Mentioned in it are the universal feasts and the commemorations of the saints dear to a given community—this being a clue to the place where the manuscript was written or the place for which it was destined—commemorations which do not necessarily entail a Mass in the Sanctoral. It is important to ascertain that the calendar is part of the original manuscript and is not an addition (verification of the codicological and paleographic unity of the manuscript). Afterwards, one must examine whether the calendar and the Sanctoral of the sacramentary agree, for it frequently happens that they do not completely coincide. P. Jounel has rightly drawn attention to the fact that the calendars inserted in sacramentaries of the High Middle Ages are sometimes only summaries of the martyrologies.[16] Prudence is therefore in

12. B. Bagatti, "L'origine gerosolimitana della preghiera *Supra quae* del Canone Romano." *BeO* 21 (1979) 101–108.

13. J. A. Jungmann, "Das *Pater noster* im Kommunionritus," *Zeitschrift für Katholische theologie* 58 (1934) 552–571.

14. Concerning the visual organization and composition of calendars (ides, calends, nones), see Hughes, *Mass and Office,* pp. 275–279, and Dubois and Lemaître, *Sources et méthodes,* p. 48, n. 5, pp. 85–86 and 135–160. The calends always fall on the first day of the month whose name they bear (*Kalendis iunii* = June 1); the nones fall of the fifth day of the month (or the seventh in March, May, July, and October). Between the calends and the nones, the days are counted backwards: *Pridie nonas iunii* = June 4; *tertio nonas iunii* = June 3, *IV nonas iunii* = June 2. The ides fall on the thirteenth day of the month (on the fifteenth in March, May, July, and October). Between the nones and the ides, the days are counted backwards: *Pridie idus iunii* = June 12, *III id. iun.* = June 11, *VIII id. iun.* = June 6. Between the ides and the calends, the days are also counted backwards: *Pridie kalendis julii* = June 30, *III kal. iul.* = June 29, *XVIII kal. iul.* = June 14.

15. Calendars began to be integrated into liturgical documents as early as the ninth century, but they also continued to exist independently.

16. Concerning the martyrologies, see Part 3, devoted to the books of the Office, the section on the martyrology (V, 3). The first chapter of P. Jounel, *Le culte des saints dans les basiliques du Latran et du Vatican au XIIe siècle* (Rome, 1977), is a good summary of our knowledge of calendars in the Middle Ages.

order when it comes to using the calendar to determine the place of origin of a manuscript, even though the calendar often leads to reconstructing the history of the manuscript, thanks especially to the addition of obituaries (listings of dead persons, either contemporary with the manuscript or of a later period).

The Ordo Missae

It is in the Carolingian and particularly the Ottonian periods that the *ordo missae* developed in an important way; it contains all the prayers said by the priest during Mass, in general before the Eucharistic Prayer, in order to prepare himself to consecrate the bread and the wine. These prayers, variable in number according to the different manuscripts, are set in the beginning of the sacramentary, after the canon, or else at the end (and sometimes as additions). Rather than developing a true theology of the Eucharist,[17] these prayers dwell on the repentance for sins in the priest's personal prayer, so that he may be purified before celebrating the eucharistic mystery. Besides its interest for the theology of prayer, the study of the *ordo missae* often uncovers the liturgical geography proper to a specific sacramentary, demonstrating liturgical exchanges between important monasteries, as happened in the course of the ninth and tenth centuries.[18]

The Mass Formularies (Temporal, Sanctoral, Common of Saints, Votive Masses)[19]

Each Mass formulary, corresponding to one day of the year, comprises at least three orations (sometimes more when it is an important feast for which people want to "preserve" all the prayers related to

17. See P.-M. Gy, "La doctrine eucharistique dans la liturgie romaine du haut Moyen Age," *La liturgie dans l'histoire* (Paris, 1991) 187–204, and especially 189–190.

18. On this topic, see B. Luykx, "Der Ursprung der gleichbleibenden Teile der Heiligen Messe," *Liturgie und Mönchtum* 29 (1961) 72–119, which remains the basic article on the *ordo missae*. Many studies on particular points have since then completed and enriched Luyckx's conclusions. See especially J. O. Bragança, "O 'Ordo Missae' de Reichenau," *Didaskalia* 1 (1971) 137–162; B. Baroffio and F. Dell'Oro, "L' 'Ordo missae' del vescovo Warmondo d'Ivres," *Studi Medievali* 16/2 (1975) 795–823; N. K. Rasmussen, "An Early *Ordo missae* with a *litania abecedaria* ['alphabetical litany'] Addressed to Christ (Rome, Bibl. Vallicelliana, cod. B 141, eleventh century)," *Ephemerides liturgicae* 98 (1984) 198–211.

19. It would be useful to undertake a study on the names of orations in different medieval sources (liturgical books, customaries, episcopal capitularies, and so on).

it[20]), to which is added a proper preface replacing the common preface of the canon of the Mass. The collect, the first thing the celebrant says in the course of the ceremony, concludes the rite of entrance; after an address to God, it announces the theme of the day.[21] The secret[22] (also called *secreta* or *super oblata*) is placed at the end of the procession with the offerings. Terse in form, it asks God to accept and sanctify the offerings just brought to the altar.[23] The preface, whether proper or common, as the introduction to the canon of the Mass, is the richest piece from the literary point of view and the enunciation of the liturgical theology of a feast; it is often the place where a position on

20. The specialists disagree on the meaning to be given to the fact that the number of orations in a given formulary varies in the sacramentaries of the High Middle Ages. In the case of series of *aliae* ["others"] appended to the formulary, we are seeing in all likelihood the desire to preserve the treasury of the Church's prayers by writing them down, without implying that the priest should choose among the numerous orations set down in the book. The number of orations before the *Super oblata* (one, two, or three) is of much greater importance because it leads us back to the origins of the Roman liturgy (fourth to sixth centuries) and to the distinctions between the papal liturgy (one oration) and the priestly liturgy (two or three orations), a distinction which became meaningless when the Roman liturgical texts were adapted for Gallic use. See A. Massimo Martelli, "I formulari della messa con due o tre orazioni prima della segreta nei sacramentari romani," *Studia Patavina* 19 (1972) 539–579.

21. The word *collecta*, rarely found in the sacramentaries of the High Middle Ages, designated the place where people gathered before departing for the Roman stational liturgy; then the meaning was extended and applied to the oration pronounced at the time when the whole assembly is gathered. See K. Gamber *"Oratio ad collectam:* Ein Beitrag zur römischen Stationsliturgie," *Ephemerides liturgicae* 82 (1968) 45–47; V. Saxer, "L'utilisation par la liturgie de l'espace urbain et suburbain: L'exemple de Rome dans l'Antiquité et le haut Moyen Age," *Actes du 11ᵉ Congrès international d'Archéologie chrétienne, Lyon, Vienne, Grenoble, Genève, et Aosta, 21–28 septembre 1986,* 2 vols. (Rome, 1989) 2:917–1031, especially 952–958. In the oldest sacramentaries we still have (seventh to ninth centuries), the names of stations in the rubrics of the formulary (*ad sanctum laurentium, ad sanctam mariam majorem,* and so on) recall the topography of the Roman liturgy. As these references are worthless outside of Rome, they were progressively eliminated from the manuscripts of most of the western churches. Concerning the organization of the liturgical stations elsewhere than in Rome, see P. Saint-Roch, "L'utilisation liturgique de l'espace urbain et suburbain: L'exemple de quatre villes de France," *Actes du 11ᵉ Congrès international d'Archéologie chrétienne,* 1105–1115.

22. J. Brinktine, "Zur Deutung des Wortes *Secreta,*" *Ephemerides liturgicae* 44 (1930) 291–295.

23. See P. Tirot, "Histoire des prières d'offertoire dans la liturgie romaine du VIIᵉ au XVIᵉ siècle," *Ephemerides liturgicae* 98 (1984) 148–197.

a dogmatic or doctrinal[24] question is made expressly clear. In certain cases, such as the feasts of saints, the preface takes on the tone of a hagiographic panegyric. During Lent, it becomes a real catechesis, penitential in character. The postcommunion *(post communionem* or *ad complendum)* which concludes the celebration, is less a prayer of thanksgiving than a request for the fruitfulness in the believer's lives of the Communion and the eucharistic action in general.

This typical formulary, valid for the Temporal as well as the Sanctoral and the Common of Saints (undetermined formularies adapted to local circumstances) can be augmented, in particular during Lent, by an oration over the people *(super populum)*, a sort of final blessing, penitential in character.[25] The formularies for the votive Masses follow the same pattern as those of other Masses. The multiplication of votive Masses from the Carolingian period on is the consequence of the development of the practice of private Masses and of the new monastic spirituality, strongly penitential, that arises at the beginning of the ninth century.[26]

The "Ritual Ordines"[27]

In the High Middle Ages, the sacramentaries contained very few liturgical texts used in the performance of ritual acts, which today we call sacraments and sacramentals. It is only from the second half of the ninth century that complete texts of *ordines* (rubrics and orations) for the different sacraments begin to be a regular part of the sacramentaries. These *ordines* concerned a small number of rites, not reserved for bishops, which the priests could perform in their parishes with the help of their sacramentaries: penance, baptismal scrutinies

24. See E. Moeller, *Corpus Praefationum,* CCSL 159 (Turnhout, 1981), and the review of this work by A. Nocent, "L'édition critique des préfaces latines dans le 'Corpus Christianorum,'" *Revue bénédictine* 94 (1984) 245–256.

25. J. A. Jungmann, "*Oratio super populum* und altchristliche Büssersegnung," *Ephemerides liturgicae* 52 (1938) 77–96.

26. See the basic study by A. Angenendt, "*Missa specialis*: Zugleich ein Beitrag zur Entstehung der Privatmessen," *Frühmittelalterliche Studien* 17 (1983) 153–221. See also C. Vogel, "La multiplication des messes solitaires au Moyen Age: Essai de statistique," *Revue des Sciences religieuses* 55 (1981) 206–213, and "La vie quotidienne des moines-prêtres à l'époque de la floraison des messes privées," *Liturgie, spiritualité, culture: Conférences Saint-Serge, 30ᵉ Semaine d'Etudes liturgiques, Paris, 29 juin–2 juillet 1982,* ed. A. M. Triacca and A. Pistoia (Rome, 1983) 341–360; Th. P. Rausch, "Is the Private Mass Traditional?" *Worship* 64 (1990) 227–242.

27. See Part 4, II, the section on the rituals.

and baptism, anointing of the sick, funerals. In the manuscripts, the texts for baptism and penance are placed at the point when they are used in the liturgical year.

The Blessings

Blessings are short pieces proclaimed in connection with the ritual acts that occur in the course of Masses or other liturgical celebrations (consecration of a church, ordination to the priesthood, and so on). There are complete series of them in the monastic sacramentaries (blessings of all the parts of the monastery) or in the manuscripts used by bishops (episcopal benedictionals were often joined to pontificals)[28] in order to enable the bishops to bless the persons, places, and objects they had just consecrated. During the High Middle Ages, the benedictionals were disseminated particularly in Germanic countries, and even more particularly in monasteries.[29] In the manuscripts, these series of pieces are usually placed at the end of the book.

2. ANCIENT AND MODERN NAMES FOR THE SACRAMENTARY

In the contemporary typology of liturgical books, the sacramentary no longer exists as such because it is part of the missal. During the High Middle Ages, the progressive transition from sacramentary to missal, especially from the eleventh century on,[30] in no way caused the total disappearance of the former in favor of the latter. The terms used by people of the Middle Ages to designate either book reflect in large measure this typological evolution of the celebrant's book. From the paleo-Christian period until the end of the Middle Ages, the terms or names which are permanently encountered are *Liber sacramentorum, sacramentarium (sacramentorium), missale.* Of course, the terminology varies with the period and especially with the type of documents in which the book is mentioned; this is what we are about to verify through an exploration, rapid and not exhaustive, of diverse medieval texts.

28. See Part 4, III, the section on the pontifical.
29. See the study of A. Franz, *Die Kirchliche Benediktionen im Mittelalter,* 2nd ed., 2 vols. (Graz, 1960); this should be complemented by E. Moeller, *Corpus Benedictionum Pontificalium,* CCSL 162 (Turnhout, 1971).
30. See IV of this part, the history of the missal.

References in Liturgical and Other Texts

As a preliminary, general remark, few are the liturgical texts of the High Middle Ages that contain information on the names of books. Only the titles and the rubrics, in particular the practical regulations given in the *ordines*, occasionally supply this type of reference. As regards the sacramentary, we note first of all the title given to the Gregorian Sacramentary at the end of the eighth century:[31] *In nomine Domini hic sacramentorum de circulo anni exposito a sancto Gregorio papa Romano editum. Ex authentico libro bibliothecae cubiculi scriptum* ["In the name of the Lord. This sacramentary arranged according to the yearly cycle was published by Pope St. Gregory. This copy was written in a room of the library from the authentic book"].[32] Again in the Gregorian, the preface of the Supplement[33] adds, *Hucusque praecedens sacramentorum libellus* ["Here ends the preceding sacramentary"].[34] Likewise in the Old Gelasian Sacramentary,[35] the end of the book is clearly indicated: *Explicit liber sacramentorum. Deo Gratias* ["Here ends the Sacramentary. Thanks be to God"].[36] In three different places of ms. Paris, B. N., lat. 9433 (Sacramentary of Echternach, end of ninth century),[37] the scribe has written the following references respectively at the beginning and end of a part of the sacramentary, *Incipit sacramentorum liber* ["Here begins the sacramentary"] (canon of the Mass and the Temporal), *Explicit secundus sacramentorum liber* ["Here ends the second book of the sacramentary"] (Sanctoral and Common of Saints), *In honore sanctae Trinitatis incipit sacramentorum liber tertius* ["In honor of the Holy Trinity, here begins the third book of the sacramentary"] (votive Masses and *ordines*). These references identify not only the type of the book but also underline what its contents are. In the twelfth, thirteenth, and fourteenth centuries, inscriptions were placed on or inside the binding of a few manuscripts from the High Middle Ages; some of these inscriptions do not correspond to the actual contents of the sacramentary. This is the case for the sacramentary from

---

31. For the history of this book, see the section on the Gregorian below.

32. Deshusses, *Grégorien*, 1:85.

33. For the supplement to the Gregorian Sacramentary, see pp. 52–54.

34. Deshusses, *Grégorien*, 1:351.

35. See pp. 42–46.

36. Bibl. Vat., Regin. lat. 316, fol. 245; L. C. Mohlberg, ed., *Liber sacramentorum romanae ecclesiae ordinis anni circuli* (Rome, 1960) 248.

37. See C. Rabel and E. Palazzo, *Les plus beaux manuscrits d'Echternach conservés à la Bibliothèque nationale de Paris* (Paris, 1989) pls. 4 and 5.

Rheims (Paris, B. N., lat. 2294,[38] ninth century, which an inscription of the twelfth or thirteenth century (fol. 12) designates as a collectar,[39] probably because it does effectively contain collects.[40] In most *ordines* of the High Middle Ages, where the occasion presents itself, the sacramentary is also called *liber sacramentorum* (or a variant of this). As an example among many, let us single out the blessing of sacred objects at the time of the dedication of a church excerpted from the Romano-Germanic Pontifical of the tenth century, in which a large number of older *ordines* are collected: *benedicat ea pontifex sicut in sacramentario continetur* ["let the bishop bless these objects in the manner prescribed in the sacramentary"].[41] It is clear that during the High Middle Ages, the liturgical texts designate the sacramentary by *Liber sacramentorum*, a designation which gradually will disappear with the disuse of the sacramentary in favor of the missal, called *missale*.[42]

The references found in various texts of the High Middle Ages or even late antiquity confirm the testimony found in the liturgical books concerning the name of the sacramentary. At the end of the fifth century or beginning of the sixth, Gennadius of Marseilles (fl. 470), in a description of the works composed by the priest Musaeus (d. ca. 460), writes, *Composuit etiam sacramentorum egregium et non parvum volumen* ["He also wrote a remarkable sacramentary, and not a slim volume"];[43] in the same text, the author attributes to Paulinus, bishop of Nola (409–431), the composition of a sacramentary and hymnal *(fecit sacramentorum et hymnarium)*.[44] A little later, in the ninth century—a key period for the history of the sacramentary—Agnellus of Ravenna (805–c.846) states that Bishop Maximianus (sixth century) had written a missal with the Masses for the entire yearly cycle and all the feasts of saints, as well as for ordinary days and Lent.[45] Unfortunately, we

---

38. See Leroquais, *Sacramentaires*, 1:69–71.

39. For this type of book, see Part 3, on the Office, III.

40. The same sort of thing happened to St. Gall, Stiftsbibl. cod. 348: in the fifteenth century, someone wrote on the cover *Collectarium vetustum.*

41. Vogel and Elze, *PRG* 1:87; see also 1:173, 2:12, 55, 112, 148, 155; all these *ordines* are also found in the volumes of Andrieu, *OR*.

42. In the pontificals, the two terms coexist; see Andrieu, *Pontifical* 1:221 and 275, where the word *sacramentaria* is maintained; 2:349, 354, 365, 400, 440, 467, where the term *missale* is used.

43. *PL* 58, cols. 1103–1104.

44. *PL* 58, col. 1087.

45. *PL* 106, col. 610: *Edidit namque Missales per totum circulum anni, et sanctorum omnium; quotidianis namque et quadragesimalibus temporibus, vel quidquid ad ecclesiae*

do not know whether in this case the book is a sacramentary or a missal, two books with different contents. However, along with the writings of Alcuin (735–804), we possess references contemporary with Agnellus' testimony; they leave no doubt that it was a sacramentary and not a missal.[46] In a letter sent to the monks of St. Vaast in Arras, in which he describes a series of votive Masses he himself composed, Alcuin stipulates that they are excerpted from his own missal (*missas quoque aliquas de nostro tuli missale* ["I also took some masses from our own missal"]).[47] In fact, we know today that Alcuin had written a remodeled sacramentary with mixed contents (Gregorian and Gelasian).[48] The catalogue of the library of the Abbey of St. Riquier (831) attests to this: *Missalis gregorianus et gelasianus modernis temporibus ab Alcuino ordinatus I* ["One Gregorian and Gelasian Missal arranged by Alcuin for our modern times"].[49] Moreover, in another letter, Alcuin establishes clearly the distinction between the *libelli missarum*, small books of which certain ones are "embryos" of (or attempts at) missals, and the sacramentaries, which are much more extensive.[50] At the same period, the letter of Pope Hadrian I (772–795), accompanying the sacramentary, called Gregorian, he was sending to Charlemagne (reigned 868–814), specifies, *de sacramentario vero* ["from the authentic sacramentary"].[51] A little later, in the ninth century, Walafrid Strabo (c.808–849) confirms the attribution of the book to Gregory and insists he (Gregory) wrote a book called sacramentary as is indicated by its title.[52]

---

ritum pertinet, omnia ibi sine dubio ["He published mass formularies for the whole yearly cycle and all the saints' feasts; there are also the formularies for weekdays and the time of Lent; without any doubt, everything that pertains to the rites of the Church is included here"].

46. See especially H. Barbe and J. Deshusses, "A la recherche du missel d'Alcuin," *Ephemerides liturgicae* 82 (1968) 3–44.

47. *Ep.* 296, in MGH, *Ep.*, 4:455.

48. Concerning these two families of sacramentaries, see pp. 42–55.

49. Becker, *Catalogi*, n. 11.

50. *De ordinatione et dispositionem missalis libelli nescio cur demendasti; numquid non habes romano ordinatos libellos sacratorios abundanter? Habes quoque et veteris consuetudinis sufficienter sacramenaria majora* ["I don't know why you are inquiring about the ordering and arrangement of the Mass booklet; don't you have the booklets relating to sacred rites arranged in the Roman manner? You also have in sufficient number the major sacramentaries according to the old style"] (*Ep.* 226, MGH, *Ep.*, 4:370).

51. MGH, *Ep.*, 5:126.

52. . . . . *composui librum qui dicitur sacramentorum, sicut ex titulo ejus manifestis-*

In other texts of the High Middle Ages, such as episcopal capitularies and monastic customaries, among others, there are also allusions which demonstrate that the sacramentary was most often called *liber sacramentorum,* and sometimes *missale.* Given the period under consideration, the term *missale* never means a true missal complete with the sung parts and the readings of the Mass in addition to the orations. This is amply confirmed by the existence of *libelli missarum*— probably called *missalia*—during the ninth and tenth centuries and still more by the references, found in capitularies for instance, to the antiphonal or evangeliary (or even lectionary) placed side by side with the *missale.* In the episcopal capitularies, which are collections of rulings applying to the diocese,[53] there are sometimes lists of the liturgical books every priest was supposed to possess; one encounters the terms *liber sacramentorum,*[54] *sacramentarium,*[55] but most often *missale.*[56] On the contrary, the term *"liber sacramentorum"* predominates in the monastic customaries of the High Middle Ages. This word designates without any ambiguity—the liturgical and textual context leave no doubt on this point—the sacramentary, ubiquitous in the High Middle Ages, that is, the book of the celebrant, containing all the orations for the liturgical year.[57] It is interesting to note that even in the monastic customaries, the transition from the sacramentary to the missal is perceptible. Indeed, in the customaries of the eleventh to thirteenth centuries, and even more in those of the thirteenth and fourteenth centuries, the term *missale,* which by then designates real missals, takes over the term *liber sacramentorum* which, as a separate book, practically disappears from the typology.[58]

---

sime declaratur. . . ["I have written a book which is called a sacramentary, as is most clearly indicated by its title"] (*PL* 114, col. 946).

53. Brommer, *Cap. Ep.*

54. Capitulary of Waltcaud of Liège, ca. 812–814, ibid., 47–48.

55. Capitulary of Haito of Basel, ca. 613, ibid., 211 and 223.

56. Capitulary of Gherbald of Liège, ca. 809, ibid., 39; Capitulary of Rutger of Trier, between 915 and 939, ibid., 63; Capitulary of Gautier of Orléans, ca. 869–879, ibid., 189; Capitulary of Hildegar of Meaux, dated 868, ibid., 198; Capitulary of Ralph of Bourges, between 853 and 866, ibid., 237.

57. See, for example, the references drawn from the *Liber Tramitis,* containing the customs of the Abbey of Cluny in the eleventh century, Corpus Consuetudinum Monasticarum 10 (Siegburg, 1980) 39, 80, 121.

58. See the monastic customs collected in the volumes of the Corpus Consuetudinum Monasticarum.

Finally, the medieval library catalogues[59] and inventories of church treasuries[60] also reflect this evolution of the book of the celebrant from the sacramentary to the missal. In both cases, it usually heads the list of liturgical books. Sometimes, especially in the inventories of church treasuries, where the most precious books are kept, information is given on the richness of the binding (gold work, ivory) or the sumptuous gold calligraphy.[61] In general, the catalogues of the eighth and ninth centuries prefer to use *liber sacramentorum* (or just *sacramentorum*).[62] Sometimes, they specify the type of sacramentary (Gregorian, Gelasian, or the combination of the two) and in very rare cases, speak about the contents of the manuscripts (sacramentary with a lectionary part,[63] or with blessings proper to the bishop).[64] Details on the contents of the sacramentary were, for these periods, in no way necessary, since—save some rare exceptions—everybody knew that this book contained only orations, and eventually, blessings and *ordines*. Side by side with numerous mentions of *liber sacramentorum* in the catalogues of the eighth and ninth centuries, one finds some *missalia*, which could designate either *libelli missarum* or the first beginnings of missals (with juxtaposed parts?) more developed than the *libelli.*[65] In a good number of cases, the precise contents are specified (missal *with* lectionary; missal *with* lectionary and antiphonal). The library catalogues from the tenth and eleventh centuries—the period of gradual passage from sacramentary to missal—show a distinct predominance of *missale* over *liber sacramentorum,* which disappears almost com-

59. Concerning these documents, see A. Derolez, *Les catalogues de bibliothèques,* Typologie des sources du Moyen Age occidental 31 (Turnhout, 1979).

60. See Bischoff, *Schatzverzeichnisse.*

61. For instance, in the inventory of the Abbey of Prüm (1003): *missalem 1 cum auro et gemmis* ["one missal adorned with gold and precious stones"] (Bischoff, *Schatzverzeichnisse,* no. 74). See also in the same book, no.7 (second quarter of the twelfth century), *liber sacramentorum 1 ebure et argento ornatus* ["one sacramentary adorned with ivory and silver"], and nos. 5, 26, 36, 127.

62. See Becker, *Catalogi,* nos. 4, 5, 6, 7, and 16.

63. Ibid., no. 16 (Cologne, ninth century).

64. *Librum sacramentorum in quo continentur benedictiones ecclesiae et benedictiones sacrorum ordinum et cetera omnia quae ad ipsum ministerium episcopi pertinent* ["A Sacramentary in which are contained the blessings (for the consecration) of a church and the blessings (for the conferring) of the sacred orders and everything else which pertains to the episcopal ministry"] (Passow, 903); see ibid., no. 28.

65. See ibid., nos. 8, 11 16, 17, 22, 23, 27. On the rare use of the expression *Missale plenarium* ["plenary missal"], see Vogel, *Introduction,* p. 133, n. 287.

pletely. A sign of the internal evolution of the book is that from now on, the contents are itemized with exactness in the majority of cases (missal that *contains,* or *with,* the sung pieces and the readings, missal *with* epistles, gospels, and graduals, and so on).[66] After the eleventh century, the use of the term *missale* becomes general,[67] even though now and then, one notes a *liber sacramentorum,* probably referring to sacramentaries of the eighth and ninth centuries preserved in libraries but no longer in use for the actual liturgical celebrations.[68]

In contradistinction to the library catalogues, the references to sacramentaries in the inventories of church treasuries do not reflect the evolution of the book throughout the centuries. As early as the ninth century, one frequently and regularly encounters the term *missale* (without its being accompanied by *liber sacramentorum*) in the first place in a list enumerating the gradual, antiphonal, evangeliary, and epistolary, among others.[69] This leads us to suppose that the "missals" in question are rather sacramentaries (except in cases where the contents are described with exactitude). Indeed, from the time when the complete missals become the rule, their mention in the inventories of treasuries is no longer accompanied by that of other liturgical books, which are now incorporated into the missal. This uncertainty is still noticeable in the tenth and eleventh centuries in the earliest references in English and German, where the sacramentary is called "Mass book."[70]

66. See Becker, *Catalogi,* nos. 32, 36, 37, 42, 44, 48, 50, 51, 52, 58, 66, 69, 72, 74, 75. These specifications are important for the understanding of the history and formation of the missal. See section IV of this part.

67. See, for instance, nos. 87, 91, 106, 120, 122, 128, 132 in Becker's listing.

68. The library catalogues of the fifteenth and sixteenth centuries are full of references like *liber sacramentorum* and *missale,* which no doubt refer to ancient manuscripts no longer in use.

69. See Bischoff, *Schatzverzeichnisse,* nos. 1, 5, 6, 12, 13, 14, 15, 19, 21, 22, 26, 34, 36, 40, 44, 47, 49, 50, 58, 60, 63, 68, 70, 73, 74, 78, 89, 91, 97, 103, 106, 110, and 127. These references are important because they help scholars get a better knowledge of the history of the missal. See section IV of this part; see also the rare mentions of *liber sacramentorum,* in nos. 7, 108, and 111 in Bischoff.

70. *Maesseboc* ["Mass book"] appears in the Anglo-Saxon manuscripts of the tenth century. See H. Gneuss, "Liturgical Books in Anglo-Saxon England and Their Old English Terminology," *Learning and Literature in Anglo-Saxon England* (Cambridge, 1985) 91–141, especially 100–101. In German, one encounters the term *Messbuch;* see Bischoff, *Schatzverzeichnisse,* no. 42, an inventory of the treasury of the Abbey of Limburg (1065): *Ein Messbuch Helffenbeine und in Gold verfasst* ["a Mass book bound in ivory and written in gold"].

We must complete this overview with an allusion to the terminology used by researchers of the modern period to designate the sacramentary. First of all, we must point out that scholars of the sixteenth and following centuries had already established a clear distinction between missal and sacramentary. This is noteworthy because confusion still affects certain contemporary authors. For instance, about Paris, Arsenal, ms. 610 (Reichenau, end of tenth century), Mabillon, puzzled by its unusual contents, wonders whether this "manuscript . . . is a part of the sacramentary or a missal . . .";[71] in fact, it is a *libellus missae*, a completely different document with its own character.[72] All editors of the sacramentary between the sixteenth and the eighteenth centuries have chosen to mention in the titles of their works *liber sacramentorum, codex sacramentorum,* or *tria sacramentaria,* a decision demonstrating their historic sense and their familiarity with manuscripts.[73] Only Martène, who in any event was not an editor of the sacramentary, seems to have made some mistakes[74] in his *De antiquis Ecclesiae ritibus.* But overall, he seems to correctly designate manuscripts that are known for certain to be either sacramentaries or missals.[75]

71. Note in Mabillon's own hand on the flyleaf of the manuscript, February 1, 1707.

72. See N. K. Rasmussen and E. Palazzo, "Messes privées, livre liturgique et architecture: A propos du ms. Paris, Arsenal 610 et de l'église abbatiale de Reichenau-Mittelzell," *Revue des Sciences philosophiques et théologiques* 72 (1988) 77–87.

73. Pamelius in 1571, Rocca in 1593, Ménard in 1642, Tomasi in 1680, Mabillon and Germain in 1687–1689; see the summary proposed by Deshusses, *Grégorien,* 1:30–34.

74. As in nos. 24, 123, 205, 368, and 511bis in Martimort, *Martène,* called *missale,* whereas in each case the book in question is a sacramentary.

75. See Martimort, *Martène,* passim.

3. HISTORY OF THE SACRAMENTARIES
OF THE HIGH MIDDLE AGES

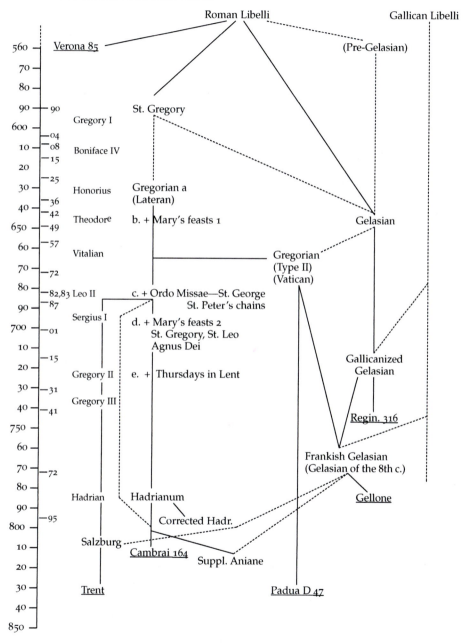

Stemma of Sacramentary Families (after A. Davril)

General Bibliography

E. Bourque. *Etude sur les sacramentaires romains.* 3 vols. Rome-Quebec, 1949–1958.

A. Chavasse. "Evangéliaire, épistolier, antiphonaire et sacramentaire: Les livres romains de la messe aux VIIe et VIIIe siècles." *Ecclesia Orans* 6 (1989) 177–225.

L. Delisle. "Mémoires sur d'anciens sacramentaires." *Mémoires de l'Académie des Inscriptions et Belles-lettres* 32 (1886) 57–423.

J. Deshusses. "Les sacramentaires: Etat actuel de la recherche." *Archiv für Liturgiewissenschaft* 24 (1982) 19–46.

J. Deshusses and B. Darragon. *Concordances et tableaux pour l'étude des grands sacramentaires.* 6 vols. Fribourg, 1982–1983.

K. Gamber. *Sakramentartypen.* Beuron, 1958.

V. Leroquais. *Les sacramentaires et les missels manuscrits des bibliothèques publiques de France.* 3 vols. and atlas. Paris, 1924.

The Sacramentaries before the Sacramentaries: At the Dawn of Liturgical Books

Liturgical books were not born overnight. In the early days of Christianity, before the progressive codification of texts occurred, improvisation was the rule.[76] Several factors contributed to this, each one in its own measure.[77] In the first place, we must mention that orthodoxy was defined through liturgical texts, especially orations. Very early, church leaders felt the need to check the contents of the prayers "improvised" by the priests, particularly in North Africa during the fourth and fifth centuries.[78] In the second place, it was not long before the ecclesiastical authorities (most notably Augustine, bishop of Hippo [396–430]), found fault with the quality of the clergy's improvisations; as a result, a selection of pieces drawn from the "treasury" of prayers was assembled in order to preserve the best ones as regards both

---

76. See C. Hanson, "The Liberty of the Bishop to Improvise Prayer in the Eucharist," *Vigiliae Christianae* 15 (1969) 173–176; L. Bouyer, "L'improvisation liturgique dans l'Eglise ancienne," *La Maison-Dieu* 111 (1972) 7–19.

77. P. De Clerck, "Improvisation et livres liturgiques: leçons d'une histoire," *Communautés et liturgie* 60 (1978) 109–126.

78. M. Vos, "A la recherche de normes pour les textes liturgiques de la messe (V^e–VIIe siècle)," *Revue d'Histoire ecclésiastique* 69 (1974) 5–37; M. Klockener, "Augustinus Kritteren zu Einheit und Vielfalt in der Liturgie nach Briefen 54 und 55," *Liturgisches Jahrbuch* 41 (1991) 24–39.

quality and orthodoxy.[79] The advent of liturgical books cannot be understood without taking into account the cultural mutation effected in the West by the emergence of the book in general. The passage from the *volumen,* the scroll, to the *codex,* the book as we know it, is indeed one of the major cultural phenomena of the first millennium; it had a considerable impact on the conditions of the oral culture then prevalent, especially in the liturgical domain.[80] Here, the book offers an important advantage over oral transmission, by fixing in a tangible and durable manner through its texts the memory of a culture, of a way of worship, of the liturgy. Finally, the advent of the liturgical book demonstrates an increasing codification of usages between the fifth and sixth centuries; it is part of a whole trend of that period: the setting down in writing of traditions and knowledge in many areas other than the liturgy, law for instance. In the study of the liturgical manuscripts of the High Middle Ages, one must always remember that they attest to only a minuscule part of the antique oral treasury from which the most beautiful pieces have been chosen (in general attributed to prestigious authors) and assembled into a stable corpus.

The Liturgical Libelli[81]

The liturgical *libellus* is the intermediary link in the evolution from the period of improvisation to the liturgical book properly so called. The *libelli* are small books, pamphlets with only a few pages, containing some liturgical texts: formularies for one or several Masses, a selection of various orations, the needed texts for a specific action (rituals, *ordines*). In many cases, the first liturgical books are nothing but the gathering of several *libelli* formerly independent from one another, which must be organized into a book with a more homogeneous content. Thus, *libelli* play an essential part in the elaboration of the

79. A. Bouley, *From Freedom to Formula: the Evolution of the Eucharistic Prayer from Oral Improvisation to Written Texts,* Studies in Christian Antiquity 21 (Washington, D.C., 1981).

80. See the unpublished doctoral thesis of Th. Elich, *Le contexte oral de la liturgie médiévale et le rôle du texte écrit,* 3 vols. (Paris: Paris IV–Sorbonne and Institut catholique de Paris, 1988); summary in J. Pierce, "Using Liturgical Texts in the Middle Ages," *Fountain of Life,* In Memory of Niels K. Rasmussen, O.P., ed. G. Austin (Washington, D.C., 1991) 69–83.

81. See P.-M. Gy, "The Different Forms of Liturgical *Libelli, Fountain of Life,* 22–34, and E. Palazzo, "Le rôle des *libelli* dans la pratique liturgique du haut Moyen Age: Histoire et typologie," *Revue Mabillon* 62/1 (1990) 9–36.

different medieval liturgical books; they are the ancestors of the sacramentary, the books of chant, the pontifical, among others. Furthermore, throughout the whole Middle Ages, the *libelli* were used to diffuse the text of a new office or Mass formulary. They will be found also in books of the "second generation" such as the missal. We must emphasize that the typology of the *libelli* sheds new light on the different forms of Christian worship because there are as many types of *libelli* as forms of celebration.[82]

The Leonine Sacramentary

APRIL:

Section VIII: (the beginning is missing) some forty Masses for martyrs (1–168).

MAY:

Section IX: Ascension (7 formularies, 169–186).

Section X: Vigil of Pentecost (6 formularies, 187–214).

Section XI: Pentecost (3 formularies, 215–225).

Section XII: June fast (1 formulary, 226–231).

JUNE:

Section XIII: St. John the Baptist (5 formularies, 232–256).

Section XIV: Sts. John and Paul (8 formularies, 257–279).

Sections XV and XVI: Sts. Peter and Paul (28 formularies, 280–379).

JULY:

Section XVII: The Seven Martyrs (9 formularies, 380–412).

Section XVIII: *Orationes et preces diurnae* (45 formularies, 413–670).

AUGUST:

Section XIX: St. Stephen (9 formularies, 671–703).

Section XX: Sts. Sixtus, Felicissimus, and Agapitus (8 formularies, 704–738).

Section XXI: St. Lawrence (14 formularies, 739–789).

Section XXII: Sts. Hippolytus and Pontianus (1 formulary, 790–799).

Section XXIII: Sts. Adauctus and Felix (6 formularies and one Preface of the Apostles, 800–823).

SEPTEMBER:

Section XXIV: Sts. Cornelius and Cyprian (2 formularies, 824–834).

Section XXV: St. Euphemia (3 formularies, 835–843).

82. See Palazzo, "Rôle des *libelli*."

Section XXVI: Dedication of the Basilica of St. Michael (5 formularies, 844–859).

Section XXVII: September fast and various Masses (15 formularies, 860–941).

Section XXVIII: Ordination of bishops, deacons, and priests (942–954).

Section XXIX: Episcopal anniversaries and various Masses (25 formularies, 955–1102).

Section XXX: Consecration of virgins (1103–1104).

Section XXXI: *Velatio nuptialis* (1105–1110).

OCTOBER:

Section XXXII: Masses *ad diversa* (for various intentions, 1111–1137).

Section XXXIII: Masses for the dead (5 formularies, 1138–1163).

Section XXXIV: St. Sylvester (2 pieces plus one oration for Pope Simplicius, 1161–1163).

NOVEMBER:

Section XXXV: The Four Crowned Martyrs (2 formularies, 1164–1170).

Section XXXVI: St. Cecilia (5 formularies, 1171–1187).

Section XXXVII: Sts. Clement and Felicity (7 formularies, 1188–1213).

Section XXXVIII: Sts. Chrysogonus and Gregory (1214–1218).

Section XXXIX: St. Andrew (4 formularies, 1219–1238).

DECEMBER:

Section XL: Christmas (9 formularies, 1239–1272).

Section XLI: St. John the Evangelist (2 formularies, 1273–1283).

Section XLII: Holy Innocents (2 formularies, 1284–1293).

Section XLIII: December fast (5 formularies) and blessing of the baptismal water (1294–1331).

History of the Book

Published for the first time in 1735 by G. Blanchini, it was immediately attributed to Pope Leo I (440–461); this first edition was entitled *Codex sacramentorum vetus Romanae ecclesiae a sancto Leone papa I confectus* ["Old Sacramentary of the Roman Church Composed by Pope St. Leo I"]. In 1749, J. Assemani rectified the erroneous title by calling his edition *Sacramentarium veronense* [Sacramentary of Verona] because the sole attestation to this sacramentary, called Leonine, is a manuscript in all likelihood written in Verona in the first quarter of the seventh century after a Roman model (now lost) and to this day preserved in Verona (Bibl. capit., cod. 85; 139ff.). The paleographic and codicological analysis of this manuscript, made by L. C. Mohlberg for his edition, clearly showed that a large portion of the beginning of the text is missing and that all visible traces of the collection of *libelli,* the origin of the book, have disappeared.[83]

Nature of the Book

Erroneously attributed to Pope Leo the Great,[84] this book is not an official one but a collection of Roman *libelli,* kept in the Lateran archives and later on adapted from papal to presbyterial use. The 1331 pieces (orations and prefaces) that comprise it are not organized to be used directly in the liturgical celebration. The plan of the book, if one can speak of plan for such a composite collection, follows the civil calendar without taking liturgical time into account. Each month (see the table above) is divided into sections which often include several formularies for the same feast. The book has the earmark of a careless compilation of *libelli;* several authors have detected two phases in this work of compilation: (1) the gathering of the formularies into collections; (2) the combination of these collections into a book. The medieval users of this work have visibly found it ill-suited to actual worship. The Verona manuscript has marginal notes—written during the tenth and eleventh centuries—that make it possible to put together new formularies out of pieces drawn from several disjointed formularies.[85]

Origin and Date

All authors agree on the Roman and papal origin of the book. The limited Sanctoral (only twenty-two saints have a feast, each with several formularies) is exclusively Roman and gives a particular place to Sts. Peter and Paul, as well as to St. Lawrence. According to Chavasse's[86] research, the book was composed at the time of Pope John

---

83. L. C. Mohlberg, ed., *Sacramentarium Veronense* (Rome, 1955); see also A. Stuiber, *Libelli sacramentorum romani* (Bonn, 1950), and the facsimile, *Sacramentarium leonianum,* introd. F. Sauer (Graz, 1960).

84. Concerning the liturgical work of St. Leo, see the numerous contributions of A. Lang and the article summarizing them by J. Pinell i Pons, "Teologia e liturgia negli scritti S. Leone Magno," *Ecclesia Orans* 8 (1991) 137–181.

85. The system of lowercase letters in red was worked out at the time; when read in order, they compose a "real" formulary; see the examples used by Mohlberg, *Sacramentarium Veronense,* 107–108; see also M. Andrieu, "Les signes du sacramentaire léonien," *Revue bénédictine* 42 (1930) 125–135.

86. See Chavasse's article summarizing the research, "Le sacramenaire dit léonien conservé par le Veronensis LXXXXV (80)," *Sacris Erudiri* 27 (1984) 151–190, with bibliography.

III (561–574)[87] from two documents dating from the fifth and sixth centuries. Chavasse demonstrated equally well that the joining of those two initial collections[88] occurred about 545–555, at the time of Pope Vigilius (537–555), who, moreover, is believed to be the author of certain formularies. By comparing different sources (*liber pontificalis*, accounts of contemporary historians, liturgical texts, and so on), Chavasse has determined, with strong probability, the historical circumstances that led Pope Vigilius to compose formularies for Sunday Masses especially (Section XVIII). He reused certain pieces composed by one of his prestigious predecessors, Pope Gelasius (492–496),[89] and worked principally during the siege of Rome by the Ostrogoths, under the leadership of Witiges, from July 537 to March 538.[90] Other researchers have shown that Formulary 13 (pieces 932–937) of Section XXVII (September fast and various Masses) often alludes directly to the famine, various grave situations, the blockade of the port of Rome, the consequences of the Goths taking the city.[91]

Descendants of the Book

The fact that there is only one manuscript of the Leonine Sacramentary proves that this type of sacramentary did not have any direct descendants. This remark does not come as a surprise since the Leonine Sacramentary was not a useful book for the actual celebration of the liturgy and since it was to be rapidly replaced by works carefully and thoughtfully organized, the Gelasian and the Gregorian. However, this does not detract from the historical and liturgical interest of the Leonine Sacramentary, first, because of the light it sheds on the history of the city of Rome, and second, because it is the only material witness we have of the passage from liturgical improvisation to codification through books.

87. Eleven saints out of twenty-two had lived in an area outside the walls of Rome, where John III resided for some years.

88. That is Section XVIII (45 formularies), *orationes et preces diversae*, and the block of Sections XXVII to XXXIV (*varia liturgica* ["various liturgical services"]).

89. B. Capelle, "Retouches gélasiennes dans le sacramentaire léonien." *Revue bénédictine* 61 (1951) 3–14; Gélase Ier, *Lettres contre les lupercales. Dix-huit messes du sacramentaire léonien*, ed. G. Pomarès, SC 65 (1959).

90. A. Chavasse, "Messes du pape Vigile dans le sacramentaire léonien," *Ephemerides liturgicae* 64 (1950) 161–213, and ibid. 66 (1952) 145–219. Finally, see also Chavasse, "Evangéliaire," 191–197.

91. A. Bastiaensen, "Un formulaire de messe du sacramentaire de Vérone et la fin du siège de Rome par les Goths (537–538)," *Revue bénédictine* 95 (1985) 38–43.

Nevertheless, we can detect an indirect lineage of the Leonine since the greater part of its contents was found again—differently arranged—in other types of sacramentaries whose beginnings are perceptible about the period John III's compilation was written down but whose completion was to be realized only in the seventh century.[92] Lastly, let us observe that certain "propositions" for formularies, noted in the Verona manuscript on the basis of marginal notations, were repeated in other manuscripts of the tenth and eleventh centuries.

The Gelasian Sacramentaries

The Old Gelasian (after Vat. Regin. 316)

BOOK 1: THE TEMPORAL

1–3	Vigil of the Nativity, 1–16 (3 formularies).
4–5	The Nativity, 17–29.
6–8	St. Stephen, St. John, Holy Innocents, 30–47.
9–10	Octave of the Nativity, 48–56.
11–12	Vigil of the Epiphany, Epiphany, 57–68.
13–17	Septuagesima, Sexagesima, Quinquagesima, 69–88.
18	First week in Lent, 104–133.
19	Fast of the first month (March), 134–139.
20–24	Ordination of priests and deacons, 146–162.
25	Second week in Lent, 163–192.
26	Third week in Lent, 193–224.
27	Fourth week in Lent, 225–253.
28	Fifth week in Lent, 254–282.
29–36	Pre-baptismal scrutinies, 283–328.
37	Palm Sunday, Passion of the Lord, 329–333; Monday, Tuesday, and Wednesday of Holy Week, 334–348.
38–40	Holy Thursday, 349–394.
41	Good Friday, Passion of the Lord, 395–418.
42–45	Holy Saturday, Easter Vigil, 419–462.
46	Easter Sunday, 463–467.
47–52	Week *in albis* [in white], 468–498.
53	Octave of Easter, 499–503.

92. Until recent times, historians believed that the types of sacramentaries had succeeded one another in time, whereas in fact they exchanged material, influenced one another, and appeared roughly at the same time within different celebration settings (papal, presbyterial).

BOOK 2: *ORATIONES ET PRECES DE NATALITIIS SANCTORUM*

93. [The expression "annotine Easter" refers to the custom of early Christians celebrating the first anniversary of their baptism. However, since Easter is a movable feast, the anniversary sometimes fell in Lent. To correct this inappropriate occurrence, the anniversary was fixed on the Saturday after Easter, called *Sabbatum in albis* ("Saturday in white") —*Trans.*]

BOOK 3: *ORATIONES ET PRECES CUM CANONE PER DOMINICIS DIEBUS*

1–16	16 formularies for Sundays, 1178–1214.
17	Canon of the Mass, 1242–1260; postcommunion and blessings, 1261–1287.
18–23	6 daily Masses, 1288–1312.
24–51	Various Masses and orations, 1313–1442.
52	Mass and blessing for weddings. 1443–1455.
53	Mass for birthdays, 1456–1460.
54	Mass for a barren woman, 1461–1470.
55	Blessing of a widow, 1471.
56–90	Various Masses and orations, 1472–1606.
91	Office for funerals. 1607–1627.
92–105	Masses for the dead, 1628–1695.
106	Mass for the salvation of the living, 1696–1700.
107	*Ordo* for the reconciliation of a sinner, 1701–1704.

History of the Book

This type of sacramentary appears to be the first true liturgical book organized as such, together with evangeliaries (see III, 5, of this part). Its attribution to Pope Gelasius (492–496), author of certain pieces in the Leonine, goes back to the heading of the *Liber Pontificalis* dedicated to the pope: *fecit sacramentorum praefationes et orationes cauto sermone* ["he composed a sacramentary with carefully worded prefaces and orations"]. Since then, we have learned that orations composed by Gelasius have been preserved in sacramentaries but that he is not the author of the type that bears his name.[94] Published for the first time in 1680 by Cardinal Tomasi, the Old Gelasian has since then been the object of numerous translations, all of them from the unique witness of this type, the Regin. 316 of the Vatican Library (245 folios plus two sections now inserted in Paris, B. N., lat. 7193; fols. 41–56). This manuscript was written in the eighth century in the scriptorium of Chelles.[95]

94. In his important work, *Sakramentartypen*, Gamber thought he could attribute the Gelasian to Maximianus of Ravenna; this hypothesis, along with many others proposed by the German scholar, has not withstood criticism. See in particular the review of Gamber's work by B. Botte, *Revue d'Histoire ecclésiastique* 55 (1960) 516–517.

95. See Mohlberg, *Liber sacramentorum*; the study of A. Chavasse, *Le sacramentaire gélasien* (Tournai, 1958); the note in *Liturgica Vaticana*, 64–67, n. 3. On the scriptorium of Chelles, see B. Bischoff, "Die Kölner Nonnenhandschriften und das *Scriptorium* von Chelles," *Mittelalterliche Studien: Ausgewahlte Aufsatze zur Schriftkunde und Literaturgeschichte*, vol. 1 (Stuttgart, 1966) 16–34.

Nature of the Book and Date of Composition

The Gelasian is a liturgical book in the full sense of the term and it appears to be Roman through and through. Its title, *Incipit liber sacramentorum romanae ecclesiae ordinis anni circuli* ["Here begins the sacramentary of the Roman Church ordered according to the yearly cycle"], and its Sanctoral confirm this origin. (There are vigils for the feasts of Sts. Gervase and Protase, John and Paul, Cecilia; octaves for the feasts of Sts. Lawrence and Andrew.) We are in presence of a sacramentary of the presbyterial type because it contains everything needed by a priest in charge of a "titular" church [one of the older churches of Rome] or a parish church and only that material. Chavasse supposes that the archetype of this book could have been written for the church of St. Peter in Chains in Rome. In all likelihood it was written in the middle of the seventh century, because it features modifications introduced by Gregory the Great (590–604) in the canon of the Mass (notably the insertion of the prayer *Hanc igitur*), but does not yet contain either the Masses for the Thursdays in Lent added by Gregory II (715–731) or the Agnus Dei made official by Sergius I (687–701).

Content of the Book

The 1704 pieces of the Old Gelasian are divided into three distinct books (or sections). The first book comprises the celebrations of the Temporal from the Nativity to Pentecost. The second is devoted to the Sanctoral and one Common of Saints, as well as to the Advent Masses. The third comprises the Masses for ordinary Sundays, the canon of the Mass, and a series of votive Masses. The typical formulary of this sacramentary is made up of two collects, one secret, a proper preface, a postcommunion, and one oration *ad populum* (or *super populum*, "over the people"); the two collects in the beginning of the formulary are traces of the presbyterial usage in the Old Gelasian because the second one serves as a conclusion to the general intercessions, that is, a conclusion before the canon.[96]

Descendants and Historical Importance of the Book

The Gelasian Sacramentary appears as the earliest agent of the romanization of the Frankish liturgy before the reform of Pepin the Short (751–768). It was in use in the presbyterial churches of Rome in the seventh and eighth centuries; it must have reached Gaul in the course of the

---

96. See A. Chavasse, "A Rome, au tournant du Ve siècle, additions et remaniements dans l'ordinaire de la messe," *Ecclesia Orans* 5 (1988) 25–42, especially 30–40.

eighth century through the intermediary of pilgrims returning from a visit to the Eternal City. Once received beyond the Alps, it was gallicanized by the insertion of five sections which are Frankish in origin; these are attested in the writings documenting the liturgy in Gaul before the introduction of the Roman books. These five sections form compact blocks easy to detect within the structure of the Old Gelasian. They concern the ritual for ordinations (derived from a complete Romano-Gallican ritual for ordinations), the ritual for the consecration of virgins (same origin as the preceding), the ritual for the dedication of a church (essentially focused on the dedication of the altar, in contradistinction to the Roman usage), the ritual for the blessing of the lustral water, and the ritual for funerals. The descendants of this book can be properly evaluated only if one takes its "successor" into account.

The Eighth-Century Gelasian or Frankish Gelasian

History of the Book

For a long time historians of the liturgy confused the Old Gelasians and the Eighth-Century Gelasians (also called Frankish), which the Middle Ages did not distinguish, as can be seen by entries in library catalogues. Modern scholars have distinguished the two types of Gelasians, and we owe to the English liturgist E. Bishop the expression "Roman Sacramentary of King Pepin" to designate the Eighth-Century Gelasians. There exist a dozen manuscript witnesses, all of Frankish origin, reflecting in different degrees the archetype now lost. However, this archetype can be recovered through its most faithful witness, the book called the Gellone Sacramentary (Paris, B. N., lat. 12048), written about 790–800, perhaps in Meaux.[97] The other Eighth-Century Gelasians are the result of a systematic revision of the Gellone Sacramentary. Their history is well known today, thanks especially to the work of Chavasse.[98]

97. A. Dumas and J. Deshusses, eds., *Liber sacramentorum Gellonensis*, CCSL 159–159A (1981). Two other important witnesses of the Eighth-Century Gelasian are St. Gall, Stiftsbibl., cod. 348 (ca. 795–796; L. C. Mohlberg, ed., *Das fränkische Sacramentarium Gelasianum in alamanischer Überlieferung*, 2nd ed. [Münster, 1939]), and Paris, B. N., lat. 816, from Angoulême (P. Saint-Roch, *Liber sacramentorum Engolismensis*, CCSL 159C [1987]).

98. For additional details, one must consult Chavasses's studies, "Le sacramentaire gélasien du VIIIe siècle: Ses deux principales formes," *Ephemerides liturgicae* 73 (1959) 249–298, and particularly, *Le sacramentaire dans le groupe dit "gélasien" du VIIIe siècle*, 2 vols. (Steenbruges, 1984). See the review of A. Davril, *La Maison-Dieu* 165 (1986) 147–152. Concerning Chavasses's writings on the Eighth-Century

The monastic connections of the Eighth-Century Gelasians are beyond doubt. Many rites for the monastics' exclusive use are found in
them; St. Benedict is called *patronus* in the formulary for his feast day
Mass on July 11 (the date of the transfer of his relics to Fleury, today
St.-Benoît-sur-Loire) and his name appears in the prayers of the canon
of the Mass together with saints of the Frankish world (Hilary, Martin).
Several clues prove the Frankish origin of the archetype: the Sanctoral,
overall identical with that of the Old Gelasian, makes room for Gallican saints (Mass of St. Prix, bishop of Clermont, d. 674); there are
mentions of specifically Gallican customs, such as the Rogation Days
(sections 131–136), established by St. Mamert, bishop of Vienne (or
Clermont) in 470, and extended to the whole of Gaul by the Council
of Orléans in 511. It is probable that the compilation was undertaken
by monks at the prompting of King Pepin. Opinions converge to lo-
calize the execution of this project in the monastery of Flavigny (in
Burgundy), founded in 742 in memory of St. Prix, whose relics were
transferred to Flavigny in 760. Pepin the Short would have wanted to
exemplify the ambitious movement of liturgical unification in his kingdom by the composition of a sacramentary intended for use throughout its territory. The number of copies that have survived proves the
rapid success of this book, with local adaptations, and its suitability
for serving the king's unification program. However, the success was
short-lived because this new sacramentary, probably completed about
760–770, was almost immediately supplanted by the Gregorian Sacramentary which Charlemagne—with the same intention as that of his
father—obtained directly from Rome (see p. 30). Nevertheless, it remains true that the Eighth-Century Gelasian is the first major attempt
at liturgical unification undertaken by royal authority. The Gelasian
failed to gain authority for two reasons: first Pepin's enterprise, contrary to Charlemagne's, was not accompanied by a policy of liturgical
unification vigorous enough to impose the book; second, even though
the contents of this sacramentary reveal the serious work of a team of
competent liturgists,[99] the Gelasian lacked the prestige of a famed

---

Gelasian, it will be helpful to consult the critical article of M. Klockener, "Sakra-
mentarstudien zwischen Fortschritt und Sackgass," *Archiv für Liturgiewissenschaft*
32 (1990) 207–230.

99. Despite the absence of decisive proof, this book has for a long time been attributed to Chrodegang, bishop of Metz between 742 and 766, a fervent admirer

author like Pope Gregory for the sacramentary that bears his name. However, the Eighth-Century Gelasian will have important descendants since it will be used in the first decades of the ninth century to remedy the deficiencies of the Gregorian (see pp. 52–54).

Nature and Content of the Book

The structure of the Eighth-Century Gelasian reveals a meticulous and well-thought-out work on the part of the liturgist-monks. They used the two types of Roman sacramentaries which were in circulation in Gaul since the first half of the eighth century: the Old Gelasian and the Type 2 Gregorian (*Paduense*, see p. 54), that is, a papal sacramentary modified for presbyterial use. The Eighth-Century Gelasian is the result of the fusion of these two types with the addition of Gallican sources. The analysis of the contents (in particular when working with the Gellone Sacramentary, perhaps executed for the cathedral of Cambrai at the time of Bishop Hildoard and later on used in Gellone—St.-Guilhem-le-Désert—as early as 804[100]) betrays a basic frame that is Type 2 Gregorian and a structure of formularies proper to the Old Gelasian (two collects, one secret, one proper preface, one postcommunion, and one oration *super populum* in Lent). The Gallican sources are visible in the episcopal blessings, the votive Masses placed after the Common of Saints, and the Gallican prefaces absent from the Roman books. The Gellone Sacramentary comprises 3,024 pieces divided into two parts: part 1 (sections 1–328), the sacramentary properly so called in which the Temporal and Sanctoral are arranged into one series, according to the Gregorian type (the canon of the Mass is placed at Easter), instead of three books; part 2, rituals and "pontifical," episcopal blessings, orations for monastic use, the *ordo* of baptism, the "pontifical" (pieces for the exclusive use of the bishop), and the summary of the Hieronymian Martyrology.

What we have here is a very rich book that marks the onset of the "era of the complete liturgical books."

The Gregorian Sacramentaries

Content (*Hadrianum* and *Paduense* types); Temporal and Sanctoral combined. The parts common to the two books are in bold type.

---

of the Roman liturgy. But today it seems more likely that this book was composed by a team of liturgists working in the monastery of Flavigny.

100. Essential for the history of the illustration of sacramentaries (see pp. 56–61), this manuscript is one of the treasures of the Bibliothèque nationale of France.

Ordo of the Roman Mass.

Blessing of a bishop.

Ordinations of the priest and deacon.

Formularies from the Vigil of the Nativity to the octave of the Lord (January 1).

Orations for Sundays.

Epiphany, followed by the Sundays after Epiphany.

Feasts of the saints from January 14 to March 25.

Septuagesima, Sexagesima, and Quinquagesima.

Daily Masses from Ash Wednesday to Wednesday in Holy Week.

Formularies from Holy Thursday to the Sunday following the octave of Easter.

Feasts of saints from April 14 to May 13.

Sundays after the octave of Easter.

Ascension, followed by the Sunday after Ascension.

Formularies from the Vigil of Pentecost to the first Sunday after Pentecost.

Feasts of the saints from June 1 to September 16.

Formularies for the five Sundays after Pentecost.

Formularies for the six Sundays after the octave of the Apostles [Sts. Peter and Paul].

Formularies for the five Sundays after the feast of St. Lawrence.

Week of the Ember Days of September.

Feasts of the saints from September 27 to November 30.

Formularies for the nine Sundays after the Holy Angel [St. Michael].

First and second Sundays of Advent.

Third and fourth Sundays of Advent.

Orations for Advent.

Various Masses.

Mass of the ordination of a pope and a priest.

Blessing for a wedding.

Orations for [the forgiveness of] sins.

Daily orations.

Common of Saints.

Daily Masses, votive Masses.

Morning and evening orations.

Ordines for the sick.

Orations for penitents, the poor, the [giving of] the tonsure.

Blessing of a deaconess, a virgin, an abbot or abbess.

Orations for various needs (fair weather, needed rain, and so on).

Orations for the funeral of a bishop and other deceased persons. Oration for the ordination of a pope.

History

The people of the Middle Ages were aware of the distinction between the Gelasian and Gregorian types of sacramentaries, as the titles given to those books in library catalogues attest. The attribution of a sacramentary to Pope Gregory rested on a sounder tradition than that concerning Gelasius. A letter from Egbert of York, about 735–736,[101] attributes the authorship of the sacramentary and the antiphonal then in use in the British Isles to Pope Gregory. Responding to Charlemagne's request for a sacramentary (see pp. 51–54), Pope Hadrian assures him that he is sending a copy of the book composed by his predecessor Gregory. The title of the book that was going to be disseminated opens with an attestation of authenticity, *In nomine Domini. Hic sacramentorum de circulo anni exposito a sancto Gregorio papa romano editum. Ex authentico libro bibliothecae cubiculi scriptum* ["In the name of the Lord. This sacramentary arranged according to the yearly cycle was published by Pope St. Gregory. This copy was written in a room of the library from the authentic book"]. Since 1571, the date of the first edition of the Gregorian by Pamelius, a good number of scholars have believed that they could retrieve the very text written by Gregory, but most often through documents that did not favor the search for the archetype.[102] Decisive progress was made in the twentieth century by historians of the liturgy who approached the problem from a different angle than that of their celebrated predecessors. H. A. Wilson (1915), then H. Lietzmann (1921), and especially J. Deshusses (1971)[103] have attempted to reconstitute the text Charlemagne received from the pope, rather than the work of Gregory, because we know today that even if that pope played an important role in the liturgical renovation undertaken in Rome between the sixth and the seventh centuries, he did not necessarily compose an actual sacramentary but principally orations which all agree are his work.[104]

101. *De Institutione catholica*, PL 89, cols. 441–442.

102. First Pamelius, then A. Rocca in 1593, H. Ménard in 1642, L. A. Muratori in 1748, all have used manuscripts from the ninth and tenth centuries already extensively modified in comparison with the basic Gregorian.

103. Deshusses, *Grégorien*.

104. See a summary of the problems concerning the attribution of orations to Saint Gregory in J. Deshusses, "Grégoire et le sacramentaire grégorien," *Grégoire le Grand: Chantilly, Centre culturel Les Fontaines, 15–19 septembre 1982: Actes*, CNRS:

This approach has proven to be more productive than that adopted by historians of the liturgy up to these recent decades; their vision was clouded by questions of authorship and archetype, less fruitful than attention to the history of texts.

Nature and Origin of the Book

The Gregorian Sacramentary is a book intended for the exclusive use of the pope. It is perfectly organized according to the liturgical year (it comprises 83 formularies for the Temporal and 79 for the Sanctoral, which total nearly 565 pieces). It was probably written in the first half of the seventh century under the pontificate of Honorius I (625–638).[105] In the second half of the seventh century, this papal sacramentary developed in three distinct directions, each one leading to a different type of Gregorian Sacramentary.

The Gregorian of the Hadrianum Type[106] (see the stemma, p. 35)

This title designates the text sent by Pope Hadrian to Charlemagne between 784 and 791; the greatest part of the manuscripts that have survived derive from this text. The best among these is Cambrai, B. M., ms. 164, written about 811–812 upon orders from Bishop Hildoard; it is believed to be a direct copy of the book received by Charlemagne.[107] Its contents are very close to those of the book composed in the first half of the seventh century under Pope Honorius. The fusion of the Temporal and Sanctoral into one liturgical year

---

International Colloquies (Paris, 1986) 637–644 (with references to and discussion of the important work of H. Ashworth). The same author was kind enough to share with me—for which I thank him very much—an unpublished study, "Quelques remarques sur les oraisons de saint Grégoire," 13 typewritten pages which I hope will be published. The ivories of Cambridge and Frankfurt am Main (second half of the ninth century) represent Gregory as celebrant and liturgist, and visually confirm the fact that the two main books of the time, that is, the sacramentary and the antiphonal, were attributed to Gregory (E. M. Knop, "Der Liturgiker als Liturge: Zu den Elfenbeintafeln mit Darstellungen der Messfeier in Cambridge und Frankfurt," *Ecclesia Orans* 7 (1990) 23–42.

105. See principally Chavasse's important contributions, "L'organisation générale des sacramentaires dits grégoriens," *Revue des Sciences religieuses* 56 (1982) 179–200 and 253–273; also *Revue des Sciences religieuses* 57 (1983) 50–56; "Le sanctoral et le temporal grégoriens vers 680: Distribution et origine des pièces utilisées," *Ecclesia Orans* 3 (1986) 263–288.

106. See Deshusses, *Grégorien*.

107. See the note in *La Neustrie: Les pays au nord de la Loire de Dagobert à Charles le Chauve (VIIe–IXe siècle)* (Rouen, 1985) 121, n. 18.

distinguishes it from the Old Gelasian. Throughout the book, the formularies present the following structure: one collect, one *super oblata*, and one *ad complendum*, with very rare proper prefaces. The term used to designate the different orations *(super oblata, ad complendum)* as well as the absence of a second collect are the fundamental differences between the Old Gelasian (presbyterial type used in Roman parishes) and the Gregorian, very spare (festive type in use at the papal court). The Gregorian of the *Hadrianum* type had been used in the papal liturgy during the whole of the High Middle Ages so that it had been steadily augmented by the additions to the liturgical year made by the popes, notably Sergius I (687–701) and Gregory II (715–731), to whom we owe the introduction of the Masses for the Thursdays in Lent (see the stemma).

In the context of the liturgical unification of the Empire implemented by Charlemagne—thus renewing his father's undertaking—this sacramentary arrived at the court of Aachen to be preserved there as the "standard" of the text attributed to Pope Gregory, and copies of which were to be disseminated throughout the whole Empire.[108] However, this sacramentary soon proved unsuited to the Emperor's unification policy. The court liturgists promptly understood that they were dealing with a festive sacramentary intended to be used on certain feasts only and clearly ill-adapted to the daily liturgical needs of a parish. Whereupon Charlemagne complained to Pope Hadrian who answered that he chose from the Lateran library what seemed to him the authentic sacramentary of St. Gregory. It is easy to realize how embarrassed the Pope was if one remembers that there was no uniformity in the Roman liturgical practice at that time when there was no mandatory use of any one sacramentary, whatever its authority. Nevertheless, wishing to satisfy the request of the Frankish sovereign, Hadrian simply picked out from the papal library the book that appeared to him endowed with the literary and religious authority desired by Charlemagne. But after crossing the Alps, this sacramentary acquired a new status: from ancient collection it became an official book although it had not been written for that purpose. Recognizing the obvious unsuitability of the book, the liturgists

---

108. C. Vogel. "Les échanges liturgiques entre Rome et les pays francs jusqu'à l'époque de Charlemagne," *Le chiese nei regni dell'Europa occidentale e i loro rapporti con Roma sino all'800, 7–13 aprile 1959,* Settimane del Centro italiano di studio sull'alto medioevo 7 (Spoleto, 1960) 229–246.

decided to correct the text (especially the rather mediocre Latin), then to augment it with a supplement so that it could serve for the daily liturgy. The result is what is called the supplemented *Hadrianum*. In the past, it was attributed to Alcuin, a masterful Carolingian liturgist to whom we owe the composition of many votive Masses and even a sacramentary[109] (see pp. 54–55). However, nearly all historians agree that it was Benedict of Aniane (c.750–821), the principal reformer of monastic life at the Council of Inden-Aachen in 816–817, who was the mastermind of the supplement to the *Hadrianum*.[110] At first appended to the pure Gregorian, later on reorganized and incorporated into the liturgical year, the supplement opens with a preface (called *Hucusque* from the first word of the text) explaining the work accomplished and the very character of the supplement. This preface disappeared, a logical step, when the contents of the supplement were distributed throughout the *Hadrianum,* from the year 850 on. The supplement itself contains two parts: (1) many formularies, arranged according to the liturgical year, that were missing from the *Hadrianum* (Sundays after Christmas, after Epiphany, after Easter, after Ascension, after Pentecost, Common of Saints, certain votive Masses; various blessings, consecrations, and ordinations for the use of monastics; the *ordo* of baptism; the whole of ordinary Sundays, and so on); (2) 221 proper prefaces, a series of blessings given by the bishop, and the ritual for the ordinations to minor orders. The principal sources consulted for this work of revision are the Old Gelasian Sacramentary, the type II Gregorian (for use by priests, see p. 54), and the Eighth-Century Gelasian which in a certain way took its revenge over the Gregorian

109. J. Deshusses, "Les anciens sacramentaires de Tours," *Revue bénédictine* 89 (1979) 281–302; J. Deshusses and H. Barré, "A la recherche du missel d'Alcuin," *Ephemerides liturgicae* 82 (1968) 3–44; J. Deshusses, "Les messes d'Alcuin," *Archiv für Liturgiewissenschaft* 14 (1972) 7–41.

110. See J. Deshusses, "Le supplément au sacramentaire grégorien: Alcuin ou saint Benoît d'Aniane?" *Archiv für Liturgiewissenschaft* 9 (1965) 48–71. Recently, J. Décréaux, *Le sacramentaire de Marmoutier (Autun 19bis) dans l'histoire des sacramentaires carolingiens du IXᵉ siècle,* 2 vols. (Vatican City, 1985), thought he was on solid ground in attributing to Helisachar (d. 836), the chancellor of the Empire under Louis the Pious (reigned 814–840), the second part of the supplement and the oversight of the completion of the work begun under Benedict of Aniane. The arguments advanced by Décréaux to support his hypothesis do not withstand criticism: his supposition that Pope Leo III (795–816) sent a second book to the court, questionable use of the date found in manuscripts, and so on; review by E. Palazzo in *La Maison-Dieu* 171 (1987) 120–123.

(see pp. 46–48). Other sources also contributed to enriching the contents of the book: Alcuin's votive Masses, various Gallican documents, some Visigothic pieces (such as nos. 1400–1414 of the ritual for the liturgy of the dead).

The descendants of the *Hadrianum* are numerous since this book was the point of departure for the evolution from sacramentary to modern missal.[111] As early as the middle of the ninth century, it was the sacramentary used in a large part of the West, and the constant additions and remodelings it received answered the needs of the local liturgies. The impressive number of its manuscripts attests to the success of the *Hadrianum*.[112]

The Type 2 Gregorian (Paduense)

We know this sacramentary through one single manuscript copied in the middle of the ninth century, perhaps in northern Italy (Padua, Bibl. Cap., cod. D.47). Its contents suggest a revision of the Gregorian executed between 659 and 681 in order to adapt the papal sacramentary to presbyterial use.[113] Its direct descendants are practically nonexistent, but we have seen in what manner the medieval compilers used it to compose the Eighth-Century Gelasian and, later on, the supplement to the *Hadrianum*.

The Pre-Hadrianic Gregorian

Deshusses has proved the existence of a pre-Hadrianic Gregorian side by side with the *Hadrianum*; it was composed about 685 on the foundation of the primitive Gregorian and reached Gaul at the end of the eighth or beginning of the ninth century, along with the *Hadrianum*.[114] Its contents reveal the state of the *Hadrianum* before the pontificate of Sergius I, and the only witness to this text is the manuscript of Trent, Museo Nazionale (Castel del Buon Consiglio), probably written about 825 for the bishop of Salzburg, Arno, who was a close friend of Alcuin. Like the *Paduense*, this manuscript did not have any

111. On this topic, see P. Bruytlants, *Les oraisons du missel romain*, 2 vols. (Louvain, 1952), and the well-documented article of A. Dumas, "Les sources du nouveau missel romain," *Notitiae* (1971) 37ff.

112. See Gamber, *CLLA*, 325–367.

113. See the study by A. Chavasse, "Le sacramentaire grégorien: Les additions et remaniements introduits dans le témoin P," *Traditio et Progressio: Studi liturgici in onore Prof. Adrien Nocent, OSB*, Studia Anselmiana 95 (Rome, 1988) 125–148.

114. J. Deshusses, "Le sacramentaire grégorien pré-hadrianique," *Revue bénédictine* 80 (1970) 213–237.

direct descendants except in Tours in the beginning of the ninth century when Alcuin used it to compose a sacramentary (called Alcuin's Missal) to be used in his abbey of St.-Martin. It has been possible to reconstruct Alcuin's work thanks to two Sacramentaries of Tours dating back to the ninth century[115] and the Sacramentary of Trent.[116] In spite of all this, many obscure areas remain concerning the exact character of this sacramentary and the type (ecclesial) to which it belongs. This difficulty is due to the uncertain reconstitution of Alcuin's sacramentary, given the many contaminations undergone by the manuscripts utilized for this reconstitution.

Evolution of the Main Types of Sacramentaries between 850 and 1000: The Composite Sacramentaries

The great success of the Gregorian of the supplemented *Hadrianum* type is not the final stage in the evolution of this sacramentary during the Middle Ages. For the historian of the sacramentary, the tenth and eleventh centuries mark both the progressive disappearance of this book in favor of the missal (see IV in this part) and the clearly affirmed will to preserve it in the face of potential rivals in the domain of liturgical preeminence, such as the pontifical.

From the second half of the ninth century on, the fusion of the *Hadrianum* with its supplement entailed rearrangements whose result was the gradual addition of pieces to this type, most of which were present in the Eighth-Century Gelasian but had not been kept at the time when the supplement was put together. The expression coined by historians to designate the manuscripts having been thus modified shows well the textual remodeling that took place: they speak of "gelasianized Gregorians." In the course of the tenth century, the Gelasian proportion in the structure of the manuscript became so prevalent that the Gregorian vestiges are sometimes difficult to detect in a precise way. This process led to the creation of a true Gelasian based on the Gregorian of the supplemented *Hadrianum* type. For instance, the structure of a fair number of formularies follows that of the Old Gelasian, whereas others remain faithful to that of the Gregorian. These books are sometimes called "composite sacramentaries,"

---

115. Deshusses, "Sacramentaires de Tours," 281–302.

116. See J. Deshusses, "Le sacramentaire grégorien de Trente," *Revue bénédictine* 78 (1968) 261–282, and the edition *Monumenta liturgica Ecclesiae Tridentinae saeculo XIII antiquiores*, vol. 2, Fontes liturgici; Libri sacramentorum (Trent, 1985).

an appropriate expression to designate this new kind of sacramentary. These did not have any descendants to speak of because as early as the year 1000, they were quickly supplanted by the new books produced at that time, opening the way to a fresh period in the history of the liturgy and its books.[117]

The main witness to the composite sacramentaries is indisputably the Sacramentary of Fulda (Göttingen, Universitätsbibl., cod. theol. 231), composed in the scriptorium of Fulda about 975.[118] It is the first of a series of sacramentaries copied and decorated in Fulda for export, and it is a true liturgical "monument" to the glory of the Carolingian past and its sacramentaries. The overabundance of prayers proves that people wanted simply to gather together into an organized whole all the great Carolingian creations in this domain. Certain formularies have an extravagant number of orations, much too large for normal liturgical use: what we have here is a liturgical anthology focused on the Carolingian period. This exceptional undertaking, the only one of its kind, can be explained by the liturgical rivalry between the pontifical composed in Mainz about 960–961 on the orders of Otto I (936–973) with a view to unifying the Empire and the sacramentary as such, which had also served this same plan of unification in Charlemagne's time. Feeling the sacramentary was threatened by the pontifical and supported by the Ottonian rulers, the monks of Fulda somehow wanted to remind their society of the religious and political authority of a book already in decline. However, it was a false rivalry between the two liturgical books since their characters were radically different and excluded any competition.

4. ILLUSTRATION OF SACRAMENTARIES DURING THE HIGH MIDDLE AGES

In the research on the illustration of liturgical books, sacramentaries always occupied a special place. The reasons for this particular treatment are to be sought in the importance of the sacramentary for the typology of liturgical manuscripts and in the fact that it was one of the earliest books to be adorned, at first by a simply ornamental dec-

117. In addition to some works on particular points of the manuscripts, a complete study of the composite sacramentaries is still lacking. In the meantime, one will benefit from consulting Ebner, *Missale Romanum*, 362–394, and Vogel, *Introduction*, 102–105.

118. See E. Palazzo, *Les sacramentaires de Fulda: Etude sur l'iconographie et la liturgie à l'époque ottonienne*, LQF 77 (1994).

oration and later on by iconographic cycles. Besides the many monographs, we owe to German scholars the best syntheses published on this topic.[119] In France, Leroquais' catalogues, though already dated, remain a mine of information for art historians, and their introductions are still very precious as a summary of each type of book under study, including the sacramentary.[120]

The first illustrated sacramentaries appeared during the Carolingian period. In spite of an unparalleled decorative richness, they did not yet have a fixed iconography. Indeed, in the beginning, liturgical books were not meant to receive any narrative illustration. Let us recall that in the eighth and ninth centuries, the manuscripts which painters abundantly decorated were mostly non-liturgical. The Bible was treated with particular care in this respect in conformity with the paleo-Christian tradition.[121] The illustration of the Bible (the Gospels in particular) played a major role in the establishment of iconographic cycles which were later on integrated into the sacramentaries.[122]

Among the many sacramentaries of the eighth and ninth centuries that have been preserved to our day, a rather small number are illustrated in an iconographic or merely ornamental manner. Only some have the monogram VD (*Vere Dignum*) of the common preface and the T of the *Te igitur* in the canon of the Mass adorned with interlacings and various vegetable motifs. The Gellone Sacramentary (Paris, B. N., lat. 12048) is an exception with its anthropomorphic and zoomorphic letters and the representation of the crucifixion inserted in the canon of the Mass.[123] It is only from the second half of the ninth century on, and especially in the tenth century, that the textual stability progressively acquired by the sacramentaries is accompanied by a trend of systematization in the manner of illustrating them. Those sacramentaries of the ninth century which are the most richly decorated present

119. There is great profit to be derived from consulting the ancient but fundamental studies of A. Springer, "Der Bilderschmuck in Sacramentarien des frühen Mittelalter," *Abhandlungen Philologisch-Historischen Classe der Königl. Sächsischen Gesellschaft der Wissenschaften* (Leipzig, 1889) 339–378, and Ebner, *Missale Romanum*, 429–453, to which one must add O. Pächt, *Buchmalerei des Mittelalter* (Munich, 1984) 32–44, and *Liturgica Vaticana*, 32–34.

120. Leroquais, *Sacramentaires*, 1:XXXII–XLI.

121. See H. Kessler, *The Illustrated Bibles from Tours* (Princeton, 1977).

122. On the illustration of the Bible, see W. Cahn, *Romanesque Bible Illumination* (Ithaca, N.Y., 1982).

123. B. Teyssèdre, *Le sacramentaire de Gellone et la figure humaine dans les manuscrits francs du VIIIe siècle* (Toulouse, 1959).

a diversified iconography without fixed rules. The Sacramentary of Marmoutier (Autun, B. M., ms. 19 *bis*), written in Tours about 850, mixes christological themes with liturgical scenes (Abbot Raganaldus blessing the monks, the conferring of minor orders).[124] The incomplete (or fragmentary) Sacramentary of Charles the Bald, perhaps written in Metz about 869, of which only a part of the canon of the Mass remains (Paris, B. N., lat. 1141),[125] presents a particularly developed iconography (illustration of the Sanctus with an image of the heavenly hierarchy) which will not become the rule in all subsequent sacramentaries. Much to the contrary, in the tenth and eleventh centuries, the painters will be content with interlacings or vegetable motifs for the common preface and the representation of Christ crucified before the *Te igitur*; a certain number of these representations become a strong theological[126] statement. Lastly, let us cite the Sacramentary of Drogo (Paris, B. N., lat. 9428), written in Metz in the middle of the ninth century; its ornamental decoration and christological, hagiographic, and liturgical cycles lodged in the initials make it one of the gems of medieval illumination.[127] Often, the images of these manuscripts greatly influenced the illustration not only of the sacramentaries of the tenth and eleventh centuries,[128] but also those of many other liturgical books.

The iconography of sacramentaries can be classified into four main thematic categories: (1) the illustration of the calendar with the signs of the Zodiac and eventually the works of the months, (2–3) the cycle of the New Testament and hagiographic representations for the great feasts of the Temporal and the Sanctoral, and (4) the scenes with liturgical significance for the ritual part of the sacramentary. In some rare cases—in general, royal or imperial commissions—one finds illustrations developing themes of political theology. One good example of

124. See R. E. Reynolds, "The Raganaldus Sacramentary and Its Liturgico-Canonical Significance," *Speculum* 46 (1971) 432–442.

125. See the facsimile of this manuscript (Graz, 1974) with an introduction by F. Mütherich.

126. See the exhaustive study by R. Suntrup, complete with a good repertory of the works under study, *"Te igitur*: Initialen und Kanonbilder in mittelalterlichen Sakramentarhandschriften," *Text und Bild* (Wiesbaden, 1980) 278–382.

127. See the facsimile (Graz, 1972) with an introduction and commentaries by W. Koehler and F. Mütherich.

128. See, for instance, the series of sacramentaries written in Fulda at the end of the tenth and beginning of the eleventh centuries in Palazzo, *Sacramentaires de Fulda.*

this is the Warmund Sacramentary (Ivrea, Bibl. capit., cod. 86), made for the bishop of Ivrea (969–1011); in several places it glorifies the person of Otto III (reigned 983–1002) through images stressing the divine origin of the emperor's power.[129] In the manuscript, one of the pictures of the coronation of Otto represents two ampullae for the anointing—whereas the text of the *ordo* mentions only one—thus expressing the theology of the *rex* and *sacerdos* (king and priest) by closely associating the anointing of baptism with the anointing of the coronation. The two ampullae, also shown in the representations of the baptism of Christ and that of Constantine in the same manuscript signify that the sovereign (Otto) is invested with a twofold power, priestly and royal. The explanation for these representations is found in the desire of the Ottonian emperor to restore the connection with the Carolingian tradition and to establish himself as the legitimate heir of the Roman Emperor.

How were the different images of a cycle organized? What was the placement of iconographic representations within the textual structure? Is there a direct relation between the text and the illuminations? Among the many themes forming the iconographic cycle, some are transmitted together (this is the case in particular for the scenes of the New Testament, having in general originated in the illustration of Bibles); others come from isolated images (most often those of ivory and gold work); still others are entirely new creations to fit a particular text, such as those illustrating a ritual (baptism, anointing of the sick, and so on). One of the major functions of the decoration of sacramentaries was to underscore the very structure of the liturgical year through the succession of the Mass formularies, to accent the structure of the ritual by setting off the texts of the *ordines*. The decoration, ornamental or figurative, visually emphasizes the salient points of the liturgical year, above all the most important feasts of the Temporal and Sanctoral; in addition, it is tailored to the needs and circumstances of the place where the manuscript was to be used. Through an original treatment of the subject, the decoration can even

---

129. R. Deshman, "Otto III and the Warmund Sacramentary: A study in Political Theology," *Zeitschrift für Kunstgeschichte* (1971) 1–20. In the same vein, see the iconographic study of the miniature representing King Canute and Queen Emma in the *Liber vitae* (London, B. L., Stowe 944, fol. 6), and in the manuscript produced in England in the eleventh century; J. Gerchow, "Prayers for King Cnut: The Liturgical Commemoration of a Conqueror," *England in the Eleventh Century: Proceedings of the 1990 Harlaxton Symposium,* ed. C. Hicks (1992) 219–238.

propose a theological interpretation of the feast, as, for instance, the paintings accompanying the formularies of the Mass of All Saints in the Fulda Sacramentaries, whose iconography is very innovative and rich. In the same manuscripts, there are other themes not belonging to the classical iconographic cycle, such as, for example, the representation of Popes Gregory and Gelasius in the process of writing their respective sacramentaries;[130] this illustration at the beginning of the book shows that the monk-compilers were fully aware of producing a liturgically composite sacramentary.

The relationships between the orations and the iconographic representations are tenuous. The content of the orations and of the non-narrative texts lend themselves poorly to illustration. Consequently, side by side with the strictly liturgical text, the different images of the christological cycle offer a narrative and linear reading of the story of Christ in parallel with the texts of the prayers. This same "visualization" of the gospel narratives will reappear in the evangeliaries (see III, 5, of this part). The hagiographic story is not linear, but the connection between the images and the texts is as elusive as for the images from the life of Christ. Only the scenes with a liturgical character (description of actions) have some relation with the text—the text of the rubrics in the *ordo*, not that of the prayers—that they accompany. This absence of direct correlation between text and illustration in sacramentaries partly explains why all the paintings are done within frames which are set in the overall layout, sometimes occupying a full page, sometimes inserted within the text, sometimes placed inside ornamented initials. The liberation of the image from the text and its subsequent autonomy are a phenomenon which developed in conjunction with the diffusion of the codex during antiquity, and is not peculiar to religious books.[131]

Apart from the decorative aspect, one may wonder whether such illustrations, joined to the text which the celebrant must speak, played any role in the act of praying itself. It is fitting to be prudent on this point because we know nothing of the eventual stimulating effect

130. Authors' portraits are encountered more commonly in the psalters with the figure of King David or in the evangeliaries with representations of the four evangelists at work.

131. See the masterly study of K. Weitzmann, *Illustrations in Roll and Codex: A Study of the Origin and Method of Text Illustration* (Princeton, 1947); also, H. Tourbet, "Formes et fonctions de l'enluminure," *Histoire de l'édition française: Le livre conquérant: Du Moyen Age au XVIIe siècle*, 2nd ed. (Paris, 1989) 108–146.

produced on the theological discourse by these images. During the celebration itself, they probably served only as visual landmarks, a sort of instantaneous reminder—the very nature of images is to quickly suggest—of the theme of the liturgy of the day.[132] Nonetheless, it is possible that certain illustrations may have been the occasion for the creation of a theological discourse through images, but this remains exceptional in liturgical manuscripts. We must not forget that these illuminations contributed to the beauty of the sacred books (including the sacramentary) and that they were subject to aesthetic criteria in order to worthily honor the word of God. Many medieval texts insist on the material value of the liturgical books because since St. Jerome, peoples deemed that nothing was too beautiful when it came to the praise of God. With this attitude, it is not surprising that the liturgical books are by far the most numerous among the books that have received sumptuous bindings with gold work, ivory work, and precious stones.[133] The famous binding of the Drogo Sacramentary has scenes describing, among other things, the celebration of the Eucharist in Metz in the ninth century after the introduction of the *ordines romani*[134] into Gaul; it is the most striking example of the effort made by clerics of the Middle Ages to adorn in a fitting manner the book of worship par excellence, the sacramentary.

132. See J.-C. Bonne, "Rituel de la couleur: Fonctionnement et usage des images dans le sacramentaire de Saint-Etienne de Limoges," *Image et signification,* Rencontres de l'Ecole du Louvre (Paris, 1983) 129–139.

133. See F. Steenbock, *Der kirchliche Prachteinband im Mittelalter* (Berlin, 1965).

134. On these ivories, see the very stimulating work of R. E. Reynolds, "Image and Text: A Carolingian Illustration of Modifications in the Early Roman Eucharistic *Ordines,*" *Viator* 14 (1983) 59–75.

II. The Books of Chant

1. HISTORY OF LITURGICAL CHANT
IN THE HIGH MIDDLE AGES

The history of liturgical chant in antiquity and the High Middle Ages interests not only musicologists but also liturgists and historians. Numerous studies by musicologists especially make it possible to reconstruct the history of the liturgico-musical forms of the High Middle Ages through the different families of liturgical chant. Nowadays there is a better appreciation of the importance of oral transmission in the practices of antiquity and the High Middle Ages because for all those centuries the transmission of pieces and their melodies relied entirely on oral memory.[135] In the seventh century, Isidore of Seville (c.560–636) wrote about this, "If people do not retain the sounds in their memories, the sounds perish because they cannot be written."[136] And yet, the eighth and ninth centuries saw the rise of the codification of liturgical chant in the West, thanks to the creation of a notation system and the multiplication of books whose purpose was to help cantors memorize the repertories of melodies (see pp. 68–69). During antiquity, the first forms of chant were very close to the way the readings were proclaimed in churches. Cantillation, a way of reading verging on melody, and responsorial chant, the alternation of a cantillated psalm with a short response by the assembly, are at the origin of liturgical chant properly so called.[137] Later on, the chants of the liturgy—Mass and Office—fall into two categories found throughout

135. See Elich, *Contexte oral,* 1:44–125; Pierce, "Using Liturgical Texts" (summary on Elich).

136. *Nisi enim ab homine memoria teneantur, soni pereunt, quia scribi non possunt,* M. Gerbert, ed., *Sententiae de Musica,* no. 1: *Scriptores Ecclesiastici de Musica: Sacra Potissimum,* 3 vols. (Hildesheim, 1963) 1:20.

137. M. Huglo. *Les livres de chant liturgique,* Typologie des sources du Moyen Age occidental, fasc. 52 (Turnhout, 1988) 17–19.

the Western churches: antiphons and responsories.[138] Sung at different moments of the celebrations (see the table of the structure of the celebration of a Mass, pp. 19–20), the pieces were generally performed from memory by the soloist and the *schola cantorum*.

From the eighth century on, especially under the reign of Pepin the Short (751–768), Roman liturgical usages reached Gaul, first through individual initiatives, mostly those of pilgrims, later on through the official action of the state. As a result of its transfer from Rome to Gaul,[139] the repertory of liturgical chant used in Rome for several centuries was submitted to modifications. It was also at that time that the repertories proper to different rites became individualized and were sung to their own particular melodies.[140] At that time, Gregorian chant was taught by cantors in a large part of Gaul on the basis of a classification of the antiphons in a special book, the tonary, in which the antiphons are arranged under the eight tones of the Gregorian chant.[141] The Carolingian period was also marked by the appearance and development of neumatic notation, a true memory aid for the cantors, but not yet in any way a true musical notation in the strict sense. The neumes (from the Latin *neuma*[142]) are graphic signs written above the words of liturgical texts (antiphons, responsories, and so on), *a campo aperto* ["in an open field"], that is to say, without staves; these signs helped cantors remember the melody appropriate for a given text.[143] Regarding liturgical chant, the neumatic notation that developed in the ninth century was in some way a support of

138. Concerning the history and technical characteristics of antiphons and responsories, see Huglo, ibid., 23–27.

139. See H. Hueck, "Die Einführung des Gregorianischen Gesanges im Frankenreich," *Römische Quartalschrift* 49 (1954) 172–187; Ph. Bernard, "Sur un aspect controversé de la réforme carolingienne, 'vieux-romain' et 'grégorien,'" *Ecclesia Orans* 7 (1990) 163–189.

140. See, for example, the repertory of the Benevento liturgy, M. Huglo, "L'ancien chant bénéventain," *Ecclesia Orans* 2 (1985) 265–293.

141. See M. Huglo, *Les tonaires: Inventaire, analyse, comparaisons* (Paris, 1971).

142. In the Middle Ages, the word *neuma* had a broader meaning than the one we are used to—a group of notes sung on one syllable: it could designate a melody, a melisma, a responsory of the choir, among other possible meanings. See A.-M. Bautier-Régnier, "A propos des sens de *neuma* et de *nota* en latin médiéval," *Revue belge de Musicologie* 18 (1964) 1ff.; J. Hourlier, "L'origine des neumes," *Ut mens concordet voci: Festschrift E. Cardine zum 75. Geburtstag* (St. Ottilien, 1980) 354–360.

143. See M. Huglo, "Les noms des neumes et leur origine," Etudes grégoriennes 1 (1954) 53–67.

the oral tradition; at the same time, by producing a chant book, it gave concrete expression to the effort at codification-through-writing of liturgical practices, an effort characteristic of the Carolingian period. The chant manuscripts were not yet systematically provided with neumes; only in the tenth century, would the neumes occupy all the spaces between the lines of text.[144] Since the end of the nineteenth century, with the publication of the *Paléographie musicale* of Solesmes, musicologists have stressed the importance of a sound knowledge of the different traditions of neumatic notation, a knowledge necessary from the historical and liturgical viewpoints and equally needed for the reconstitution of ancient melodies.

2. THE CHANTS OF THE ROMAN MASS[145]

In the celebration of a Mass, the orations and canon belonged to the celebrant using his sacramentary; the readings were reserved for the deacon and subdeacon equipped with their own books (see III, 5–6, in this part); finally, the lyrical component of the Mass was the province of the soloists and the *schola cantorum*. In the course of a eucharistic celebration (see the table of the structure of the celebration of a Mass, pp. 19–20), cantors had their several parts to play in perfect synchrony with the other actors in the celebration. Among the chants at Mass, it is necessary to distinguish those which change from day to day (the chants of the proper of the Mass) and those which are invariable, whatever the feast (the chants of the ordinary of the Mass).

The Chants of the Proper

The five chants of the proper vary throughout the year and are, with very few exceptions, biblical, and most often, psalmic. They are designated by the generic term of antiphon *(antiphona)*.[146] The introit antiphon, usually sung with one or several psalm verses, accompanied the entrance procession into the church at the beginning of the celebration.[147] The offertory and communion chants also accompanied

144. During the High Middle Ages, one also often finds chant pieces with neumes in non-liturgical manuscripts; frequently this is because of additions. See D. Escudier, "Des notations musicales dans les manuscrits non liturgiques antérieurs au XIIe siècle," *Bibliothèque de l'Ecole des Chartes* 129 (1971) 27–48.

145. See especially A. Ekenberg, *Cur cantatur? Die Funktion des liturgichen Gesanges nach den Autoren der Karolingerzeit* (Stockholm, 1987).

146. See Huglo, *Livres de chant*, 23–25.

147. J. Froger, "Le chant de l'introït," *Ephemerides Liturgicae* 21 (1948) 248–255; J. A. Jungmann, *MS*, 2:72–87; Ekenberg, *Cur cantatur* 34–46.

processions, the first one during the presentation of the gifts, before the consecration of the bread and wine, the second, during communion. This last, the final sung piece of the Mass, which immediately followed the Agnus Dei and the breaking of the bread, has a structure close to that of the introit.[148] The offertory chant could last as long as was necessary during the preparation of the bread and wine; this is why the antiphon is followed by a large number of verses.[149] The gradual, placed after the reading of the epistle, is the oldest of the chants of the proper of the Mass. Made of a gradual antiphon (response) and its verse, it used to be sung by the soloist at the ambo, standing not quite at the top—a place reserved for the gospel—but on a lower step, the *gradus,* hence the term "gradual" to designate this chant.[150] The gradual was immediately followed by the alleluia, sung before the gospel and still having one psalm verse attached to it. The alleluia was introduced into the Roman Mass about the seventh century as a prelude to the reading of the gospel; it announced the coming glory of Christ the Savior and accompanied the entrance procession of the holy book.[151]

The Chants of the Ordinary

The Kyrie eleison, the Sanctus, and the Agnus Dei are the three main chants of the ordinary, to which one can add the Gloria and the Credo,[152] sung on certain occasions during the High Middle Ages. The first three are groups of acclamations.

The Kyrie, at first purely christological, comes directly after the introit and has taken the form of a threefold supplication addressed to the Father, a threefold supplication addressed to the Son, and again a threefold supplication addressed to the Father.[153] In all likelihood, it

148. See Jungmann, *MS,* 3:325–335; Ekenberg, *Cur cantatur,* 105–109.

149. Jungmann, *MS,* 2:298–304; Ekenberg, *Cur cantatur,* 85–89.

150. R. J. Hesbert, "Le graduel: Chant responsorial," *Ephemerides liturgicae* 95 (1981) 316–350; Jungmann, *MS,* 2:188–211; Ekenberg, *Cur cantatur,* 61–68.

151. A.-G. Martimort, "Origine et signification de l'Alleluia de la messe romaine," *Mens concordet voci: Pour Mgr A.-G. Martimort à l'occasion e ses quarante années d'enseignement et des vingt ans de la constitution Sacrosanctum concilium* (Paris, 1983) 95–122; Ekenberg, *Cur cantatur,* 68–75.

152. Concerning the Greek versions of these chants encountered in the manuscripts of the ninth century, see C. Atkinson, "Zur Entstehung und Überlieferung der 'Missa graeca,'" *Archiv für Musikwissenschaft* 39 (1982) 113–145.

153. Concerning the history of the Kyrie and its function in the ancient Mass, see P. De Clerck, *La prière universelle dans les liturgies latines anciennes,* LQF 62 (1977) 282–314; Ekenberg, *Cur cantatur,* 46–53.

was introduced into the Roman Mass before 529.[154] As for the Gloria (Luke 2:13-14), immediately following the Kyrie, it was originally restricted to the pontifical Christmas liturgy. Because it is a hymn of praise, it was not sung during times of penance or preparation, such as Advent, Lent, the feast of the Holy Innocents.[155] The Sanctus, strongly focused on the Trinitarian faith, immediately follows the preface introducing the canon of the Mass, and was sung by the priest;[156] it was not part of the primitive eucharistic liturgy but was introduced into the Mass about the fifth or sixth century as an address to Christ.[157] The biblical text (threefold Sanctus from Isaiah 6:3) was combined with the exclamation "Hosanna. . . ," a reminiscence from Matthew's Gospel (21:9). The Agnus Dei, sung at the moment of the breaking of the bread, is a threefold christological supplication and was adopted by the Roman liturgy only about 700. Fundamentally, it is praise directed to Christ.[158] The Credo, during the celebration of Mass, appeared first in the East in the sixth century; in the West, it soon took the form of an expression of faith said before Communion. From the end of the eighth century, it was sung after the gospel reading, but just occasionally; it became an integral part of the Latin Mass only in 1014.[159]

The Gloria, Sanctus, and Credo were included in the sacramentary but were solemnly sung by cantors. Only the Kyrie was always included in the antiphonal (also called the gradual). From the tenth century on, these chants were frequently regrouped into the books intended for the cantors and the *schola cantorum*; they had musical notation according to several repertories, along with other chants that came to enrich the Latin Mass.

Enrichment of the Chant at Mass

Among the principal creations of the High Middle Ages in matter of liturgical chant, one must mention the tropes, proses (or sequences),

154. Chavasse, "A Rome," 25–44.

155. J. Magne, "*Carmina Christo*, 3: Le *Gloria in excelsis*," *Ephemerides liturgicae* 100 (1986) 368–390; Ekenberg, *Cur cantatur*, 54–61.

156. Concerning the history of the Sanctus, see I, the section on the sacramentary, in this part, as well as G. Iversen, ed., *Tropes de l'ordinaire de la messe: Tropes du Sanctus*, Corpus Troporum 7 (Stockholm, 1990) 17–24; Ekenberg, *Cur cantatur*, 89–93.

157. Magne, "*Carmina Christo*: 1: Le *Sanctus* de la messe latine," *Ephemerides liturgicae* 100 (1986) 3–27.

158. G. Iversen, ed., *Tropes de l'Agnus Dei*, Corpus troporum 4 (Stockholm, 1980) 195–201; Ekenberg, *Cur cantatur*, 94–100.

159. See *CP*, 2:131–132, 145; Jungmann, *MS*, 2:233–247.

and prosules. A specifically monastic phenomenon, the tropes are text-based or melody-based[160] chants, extra-biblical in origin, that are interpolated into the texts or melodies of certain liturgical chants of the proper or ordinary of the Mass in order to offer an exegetical interpretation of these chants.[161] Owing to their theological richness, the tropes have in recent years been studied by liturgists, historians, philologists, musicologists, art historians, who have called attention to their historical interest.[162] Certain great monastic centers, Cluny principally, were opposed to this kind of composition since their spirituality did not correspond to the prevalent liturgical sensibility of the time.[163] The sequence is a melody-based trope of the alleluia; the prosule is inserted at the end of the concluding responsories of each nocturn[164] in the office of Matins. Finally, in all these pieces of the High Middle Ages, the literary and poetic aspects are of prime importance. The most beautiful Latin versification harmoniously allies with the richness of the liturgical melodies, respecting both metrical and musical rules; one does not melodize just any text or textualize (*Textierung*) just any melody.

Liturgical and Codicological Preliminaries

In the beginning, the sole function of the books of chant was simply to transmit the liturgical texts because the melodies were part of the oral repertory. From the Carolingian period on, the liturgical repertory for the Mass and Office was established and was disseminated principally by means of the book, at first without notation.

160. The text-based tropes were entirely new compositions, text and melody, grafted onto a pre-existing liturgical text, whereas, in the melody-based tropes, the text was generated by the liturgical melody.

161. See, for instance, the interpretations of Amalarius of Metz (c.750–780) for the tropes of the Kyrie in R. Johnson, "Amalaire de Metz et les tropes du *Kyrie eleison*," *Classica et mediaevalia: Francisco Blatt septuagenario dedicata* (Gyldendal, 1973) 510–540.

162. The team of the *Corpus Troporum* of Stockholm University has already published seven volumes of the great edition of the tropes of the High Middle Ages. The proceedings of several conferences have also been published. See the recent *La tradizione dei tropi liturgici, atti dei convegni sui tropi liturgici*, Paris (15–19 October 1985), Perugia (2–5 September 1987), ed. E. Menesro (Spoleto, 1990).

163. See P.-M. Gy, "Les tropes dans l'histoire de la liturgie et de la théologie," *Research on Tropes* (Stockholm, 1983) 7–16, and D. Hiley, "Cluny, Sequences and Tropes," *La tradizione*, 125–138.

164. Concerning these pieces and others that appeared after the ninth century, see Huglo, *Livres de chant*, 29–35.

However, the book, even in its final form of codex was not the only channel. In order to set down in writing new musical compositions, the *rotulus* (see pp. 78–79) and the *libellus*, both older than the book properly so called, played an important role. Like the sacramentary and missal, the early books of chant[165] were often made up of the collections of several *libelli* (see the tropers, II, 6, of this part). From the ninth century on, and throughout the whole of the Middle Ages, the *libellus* was also used to circulate a new office, or a new Mass, notably as far as chant was concerned.[166]

On the codicologic plane, the manuscripts of chant of the High Middle Ages show two peculiarities that distinguish them from other liturgical books. Their format is smaller than average; this is partly explained by the way they were used at that time: in general, only the soloist conducting the *schola* was in possession of the book, as a memory aid. The book of chant is often oblong with narrow pages because the soloist had to be able to hold it with one hand, contrary to the celebrant, whose book rested on the altar, and the deacon, who read the gospel from the book placed on the ambo. Only in the thirteenth century, would the large choir lecterns allow the *schola* to follow the chant in the big antiphonals (60 to 70 centimeters long) written in especially large characters.[167]

3. THE ANTIPHONAL OF THE MASS OR GRADUAL[168]

The masculine noun *antiphonarius,* or the neuter noun *antiphonale* derive from *antiphona* ["antiphon," "sung piece"]. With the antiphonal's appearance in the eighth century, either word designated the antiphonal of the Office, the antiphonal of the Mass, or else the manuscripts that contain both repertories. The ancient library catalogues as well as the inventories of the treasuries kept in cathedrals demonstrate that the people of the Middle Ages used *antiphonarius* to mean indistinctly any type of antiphonal.[169] In the second half of the

165. See Palazzo, "Rôle des *libelli.*"

166. See Huglo, *Livres de chant,* 64–75.

167. See Huglo, ibid., 75–78, and D. Escudier, "Les manuscrits musicaux du Moyen Age (du IXe au XIIe siècle): Essai de typologie," *Codicologica* 3 (1980) 34–35.

168. See Huglo, *Livres de chant,* 99–108; H. Möller, "Research on the Antiphonar: Problems and Perspectives," *Journal of the Plainsong and Mediaeval Music Society* 10 (1987) 1–14.

169. An exhaustive study on the medieval vocabulary pertaining to chant books (also taking account of this vocabulary in customaries) ought to be undertaken.

eighth century, the pieces of the Office on the one hand and those of the Mass on the other were progressively separated into two different books: the Office antiphonal and the Mass antiphonal. The latter is more commonly called gradual (a term rather frequent in the second part of the Middle Ages), after the chant of the proper of the Mass introducing the alleluia.

History

Throughout the Middle Ages, people attributed to St. Gregory (590–604), besides the sacramentary, the composition of the chants of the Mass. In his life of Gregory, John the Deacon (825–880) writes at the end of the eighth century that the pope composed an antiphonal for the Roman *schola cantorum*.[170] Modern criticism easily explains this attribution within the perspective of the Carolingian reform, which even in the liturgical domain, needed an argument drawn from authority in order to impose a document.[171] Be that as it may, the prologue *Gregorius praesul* ["Bishop Gregory"], which is found in the earliest graduals and was probably composed about 800, attests to the medieval belief in Gregory's authorship. As for the modern editors of the Mass antiphonal, they for the most part showed no hesitation about writing the pope's name in the title.[172] We are indebted to Hesbert for the critical edition of the six oldest manuscripts (from the eighth and ninth centuries)[173] of the Mass antiphonal; it is a work indispensable to all research in the history of the book and the pieces it contains.[174]

Nature and Content of the Book

The gradual comprises the chants of the proper of the Mass and secondarily (at least during the High Middle Ages) those of the ordinary. It presents the Temporal and the Sanctoral combined (except after

---

See Becker, *Catalogi,* and Bischoff, *Schatzverzeichnisse;* see also the distinction made by Amalarius between the different chant books, J. M. Hanssens, ed., *Amalarii episcopi opera liturgica omnia,* vol. 1: *Liber de ordine antiphonarii,* Studi e testi 138 (Vatican City, 1948) "Prologus 17," p. 363.

170. *Vita Gregorii* 2.6. (*PL* 75, col. 90).

171. See the recent update by M. Huglo, "L'antiphonaire: archétype ou répertoire originel?" *Grégoire le Grand,* 661–669.

172. See, for instance, J. M. Tomasi, *Antiphonarius ordinatus a S. Gregorio Opera omnia* (Venice, 1750).

173. See the list of manuscripts with bibliography in Vogel, *Introduction,* 359–360.

174. R.-J. Hesbert, ed., *Antiphonale Missarum sextuplex,* according to the Gradual of Monza and the Antiphonaries of Rheinau, Mont-Blandin, Compiègne, Corbie, and Senlis (Brussels, 1935).

Easter and Pentecost) into one homogeneous liturgical year where Easter falls on April 3. It begins with the first Sunday of Advent (whereas the sacramentaries and evangeliaries open with the vigil of the Nativity) and ends with the feast of Saint Andrew on November 30. It contains more than 560 pieces, of which 70 are introit antiphons, 118 are gradual responsories, 100 alleluia verses, 18 tracts (chants replacing the alleluia on certain penitential days), 107 offertories, and 150 communion antiphons.

Origin, Date of Composition, and Evolution

Learned works have clearly shown that the "Gregorian" gradual has its roots in the Roman liturgy as celebrated in the basilicas.[175] However, the manuscript tradition has transmitted to us a liturgical and musical revision undertaken about 780 in the Frankish realm, on the basis of a Roman model of the second half of the eighth century. It is therefore difficult to go further back in the search for the original repertory (a notion to be preferred to that of archetype)[176] and for the oldest forms of the Mass antiphonal. The studies of Chavasse have nonetheless shown that on the whole, the repertory of the Mass chants took shape at the same time as the repertories of the books of readings and the sacramentaries, that is, in Rome between the fifth and seventh centuries.[177]

From the Carolingian period on, the evolution of the Mass antiphonal was determined by two facts: elements that were originally movable became fixed and texts increased in number. Among the different chants of the proper, some (like the alleluia verses and the graduals) were, more often than others, either fixed or subject to variation in the course of centuries. Many changes also occurred in the Sanctoral, especially through the creation of Masses for patron saints

175. See in particular A. Chavasse, "Les plus anciens types du lectionnaire et de l'antiphonaire de la messe," *Revue bénédictine* 62 (1952) 3–94; "La formation de l'*Antiphonale missarum*," *Bulletin du Comité des Etudes de Saint-Sulpice* 32 (1961) 29–41; "*Cantatorium et Antiphonale missarum:* Quelques procédés de confection, dimanches après la Pentecôte, graduels du sanctoral," *Ecclesia Orans* (1984) 15–55; and Chavasse, "Evangéliaire," especially 230–237.

176. See M. Huglo, "L'édition critique de l'antiphonaire grégorien," *Scriptorium* 39 (1985) 130–138.

177. One must be prudent with regard to recent attempts to attribute certain precise parts of the Gregorian repertory to Popes Damasus I (366–384) and Celestine I (422–432); see P. Jeffery, "The Introduction of Psalmody into the Roman Mass by Pope Celestine I (422–432)," *Archiv für Liturgiewissenschaft* 26 (1984) 147–165.

and the formation of a Common of Saints, whereas the Temporal remained rather stable. Let us note also that from the eleventh century on, five chants of the ordinary were inserted into the Gradual; formerly, they were most often written in the sacramentary, because of their place and role in the celebration, or less often in books like the troper when they were ornamented with tropes (see II, 6, of this part).

Historical Importance of the Antiphonal of the Mass

Like the sacramentary, the antiphonals (of the Mass and of the Office) were destined to become the official book serving the politics of liturgical unification undertaken by the Carolingian rulers. We have seen that the adoption of the gradual in Gaul went hand in hand with the knowledge and diffusion of Gregorian chant, then used in Rome, by bishops and monastics in their liturgies.[178] But in contradistinction to the Office antiphonal, the gradual was not remodeled either in its texts or in its repertory. Huglo has remarked that the division of the repertory of the antiphonal into two groups (lands of Germanic languages in the east and lands of Romance languages in the west), which evolved in separate ways from the middle of the ninth century, very probably results from the division of the Carolingian Empire in 843 at the Treaty of Verdun.[179]

Let us end by looking at one of the manuscripts of the ninth century, the Antiphonal of Compiègne (Paris, B. N., lat. 17436), whose origin is still debated by specialists; written about 860–880, it was in use at St. Cornelius of Compiègne, imperial chapel of Charles the Bald (reigned 840–877).[180] Gy has aptly demonstrated that it was perhaps an exact copy of the antiphonal in use at Charlemagne's court in Aachen at the beginning of the ninth century, a document which has been lost to us.[181] This manuscript is made up of two parts (gradual in fols. 1v–30v, antiphonal in fols. 31v–107v), probably originally distinct. Both parts

178. See the testimony of Paul the Deacon (c.720–c.800), *Gesta episcoporum Mettensium*, MGH, *Sc.* 2:268.

179. See Huglo, *Livres de chant*, 84.

180. See especially J. Froger, "Le lieu de destination et de provenance du *Compendiensis*," *Ut mens concordet*, 353; Hesbert, *AMS*, nos. 17–19.

181. P.-M. Gy, "Le *Corpus Antiphonalium Officii* et les antiphonaires carolingiens," *Grégoire le Grand*, 645–648; on the liturgy in the chapels of the Carolingian sovereigns, see J. Fleckenstein, *Die Hofkapelle der deutschen Könige*, vol 1: *Die Karolingische Hofkapelle* (Stuttgart, 1959); D. A. Bullough and L. H. Corréa, "Texts, Chants and the Chapel of Louis the Pious," *Charlemagne's Heir: New Perspectives on the Reign of Louis the Pious (814–840)* (Oxford, 1990) 489–508.

are adorned with a frontispiece-prologue, richly decorated, ascribing the composition of the books to St. Gregory. Written with great care in gold letters and embellished with ornate initials, this sumptuous manuscript, used at the imperial court, acquires for this reason a particular importance for historians of liturgy because it is the sole witness to the official character of the antiphonal.[182]

4. THE GRADUAL OUTSIDE THE GRADUAL (OR ANTIPHONAL OF THE MASS)

Some rare medieval manuscripts juxtapose into a perfect codicological and paleographic unity the sacramentary properly so called and the gradual, or a table of the incipits in the gradual.[183] These are the first sketches of missals with juxtaposed parts, such as those which were developed from the eleventh to thirteenth centuries and contain the Mass readings in a third section. The fact that both books, sacramentary and gradual, were believed to be the work of Pope Gregory is without doubt at the root of the juxtaposition of the two books, for as far as the celebration is concerned, nothing was changed in the usual practices of the High Middle Ages: the celebrant with his "missal" (in fact a sacramentary with the gradual appended to it) pronounced only the orations, while the cantors and choir executed the sung parts contained in the gradual. On the contrary, the fact that in the sacramentary, the incipits of the sung pieces are added in the margin by the collect of each formulary, or else are inserted at the beginning of the formularies, even sometimes with notation, attests to an intermediary stage in the elaboration of the missal (see IV of this part) and in the changes in eucharistic practice.

One encounters a gradual table [of incipits] in one of the sacramentaries of St. Amand (Paris, B. N., lat. 2291; fols. 9–15), written about

182. Concerning the other pertinent manuscripts of the High Middle Ages, see Vogel *Introduction,* 350–362 (with a list of the principal manuscripts of the non-Roman liturgies); Gamber, *CLLA,* 503–518. Gamber's typology for the gradual, as for other documents, is dubious in a certain number of cases. However, a detailed discussion of the validity of his classification would be far beyond the scope of this manual.

183. See, for instance, the fragments of a gradual table without musical notation, written in Fulda in the ninth century, in B. Offermann, "Un frammento liturgico di Fulda del IX secolo," *Ephemerides liturgicae* 50 (1936) 207–223; one finds there the incipits of the sung pieces from December 27 to Ash Wednesday, and from the fourth Sunday after Easter to August 9.

875–876,[184] and also in Paris, B. N., lat. 12050 (fols. 3–16v), coming from the scriptorium of Corbie (shortly after 853).[185] Examples of the incipits of sung pieces in the margins of the Mass formularies are found, for instance, in Paris, B. N., new acq. lat. 1589 (Tours, second half of ninth century);[186] Paris, B. N., lat. 9432 (Amiens?, ninth or tenth century);[187] and Rheims, B. M., 213 (St. Amand, about 869).[188]

Rarer still are the lectionaries (with epistles and gospels) combined with a gradual.[189] This kind of composite book completely disappeared after the twelfth century.

5. THE *CANTATORIUM*

"After the reading of the epistle by the subdeacon, the cantor ascends the ambo with his *cantatorium* and says the responsory."[190] This text, taken from an *ordo*, gives the definition and purpose of the *cantatorium*: it was the soloist's book, containing only the chants intercalated between the readings at the beginning of the Mass (gradual responsory and alleluia), with sometimes the verses of the offertory. Practically absent from the ancient nomenclature of liturgical books, the *cantatorium* had, in the Middle Ages a function more honorific than real in the celebration. On this topic, Amalarius writes, "The cantor, [at the ambo], without being obliged to read his text, holds in his hands [the *cantatorium* whose cover is decorated with ivory] plaques";[191] thus the purely honorific character of the book is emphasized. Some documents attesting this liturgical book are still extant; the oldest is the *Cantatorium* of Monza (Monza, Tesoro della basilica S. Giovanni, cod. CIX), made about 800, probably in northern Italy.[192]

184. See J. Deshusses, "Chronologie des grands sacramentaires de Saint-Amand," *Revue bénédictine* 87 (1977) 230–237.

185. The gradual table was perhaps added to the main manuscript in the tenth century; see Hesbert, *AMS*, nos. 21–22.

186. See Deshusses, "Sacramentaires de Tours."

187. Leroquais, *Sacramentaires*, 1:38–43.

188. See Deshusses, "Chronologie des sacramentaires."

189. Like St. Omer, B. M., ms. 252 (tenth–eleventh centuries); see Huglo, *Livres de chant*, 122.

190. *Postquam (subdiaconus) legerit, cantor cum cantatorio ascendit et dicit responsum*, *Ordo romanus* I, Andrieu, *OR*, 1:86.

191. *Cantor, sine aliqua necessitate legendi, tenet tabulas in manibus*, Hanssens, *Amalarii opera*, vol. 3: *Liber officialis*, Studi e testi 139 (Vatican City, 1950) 303.

192. See Vogel, *Introduction*, 359; for other *cantatoria* of the High Middle Ages, see Gamber, *CLLA*, 500–503.

A text from Amalarius of Metz (c.780–c.850) suggests that from the eighth and ninth centuries on, the lists of chant books for the Latin liturgies were on the whole patterned on the model of the Roman usages of the eighth century.[193] In Rome they used an antiphonal without the intercalary chants of the first part of the Mass (gradual responsory and alleluia), which were written in the *cantatorium*. Consequently, when the Roman liturgy was introduced into Gaul, the Mass antiphonal became the official book of the Romano-Frankish liturgy, completed by the *cantatorium*, in imitation of the Roman practices. Later on, the *cantatorium* disappeared rather quickly from the typology of chant books; it was first absorbed by the antiphonal and afterward, in the second part of the Middle Ages, by the missal.

6. THE TROPER

The collections of tropes with notation for the chants of the proper and/or the ordinary have for several years been the subject of numerous studies thanks to the assiduous work of the team of the *Corpus Troporum* of the University of Stockholm. We owe to this team the publication of several volumes and four books of articles dealing with particular aspects of the trope genre.[194] In these publications, the most significant manuscripts of the High Middle Ages occupy an important place.[195] The oldest tropers we know go back only to the tenth century,[196] but without doubt, the tropes existed already in the eighth century.[197] Originally, they were written in the empty spaces (margins, blank sheets) of other liturgical manuscripts, principally and logically in the antiphonals of the Mass and Office.

193. Hanssens, *Liber antiphonarii, "Prologus de ordine antiphonarii,"* 363; on this point, see the translation and comments of Huglo, *Livres de chant,* 97–98.

194. Seven volumes have already been published, in particular tropes of the proper of the Mass (cycle of Christmas and cycle of Easter), tropes of the Agnus Dei, tropes of the Sanctus.

195. For an overall view of these manuscripts, see H. Husmann, *Tropen- und Sequenzhandschriften,* International Inventory of Musical Sources 5 (Munich, 1964).

196. As for the manuscripts St. Gall, Stiftsbibl., 381 and 484 (perhaps dating back to 965), and Verona, Bibl. Capit., cod. XC (Monza, mid-tenth century), see C. Zivelonghi and G. Adami, *I codici liturgici della Catedrale di Verona* (Verona, 1987) 86–87.

197. It seems certain today that the tropes appeared in the course of the ninth century and developed very rapidly. See P.-M. Gy, "La géographie des tropes dans la géographie liturgique du Moyen Age carolingien et postcarolingien," *Tradizione dei trope,* 13–24. The earliest trace of the existence of tropes seems to be a canon of the Council of Meaux in 845; see G. Silagi, *Liturgische Tropen,* Münchener Beiträge zur Mediävistik und Renaissance-Forschung 36 (Munich, 1986) nos. 7–10.

At the root of the tropers, we encounter anew, as Huglo demonstrated, *libelli* which allowed for the circulation of the pieces and the making of collections; these were the point of departure for the creation of a book homogeneous in its contents and material form.[198] Tropers reveal with particular clarity the process of the formation of a liturgical book in general because in a large number of manuscripts, the different liturgical sections which they comprise (tropes of the Sanctus, tropes of the Gloria, and so on) begin with a new fascicle, an obvious sign of the compilation of *libelli*. These manuscripts attest to the intermediary stage between the *libellus* and the final book. In the latter, every trace of the grouping of the original *libelli* has been erased: the text has been made a single whole on the codicological level. Tropers fell in disuse before being officially suppressed by the Council of Trent; this elimination naturally entailed their disappearance. The manuscripts which survived date for the most part from between the tenth and twelfth-thirteenth centuries. They were produced in many parts of Europe;[199] however, the greatest concentration of places of composition was in northern Italy, the southwestern part of France, and the Alpine region (today's Switzerland and Austria). Another characteristic trait of the history of the tropers is that since tropes were an essentially monastic phenomenon, the majority of manuscripts we possess were written in the scriptoria of abbeys, among which St. Gall and St. Martial of Limoges are the principal, and in cathedral centers such as that of Winchester in England.[200]

There is no set pattern to the contents of the troper even though certain tropes, like the celebrated dialogue *Quem qaeritis* of Easter Sunday, are found in the majority of manuscripts. This remarkable variety results from several factors. One of the most important is the specialization, often extreme, of the productions of the different places where the pieces were composed. The contents of the manuscripts often reflect the type of pieces that were favorites in one center or

198. M. Huglo, "Les *libelli* de tropes et les premiers tropaires-prosaires," *Pax et Sapientia: Studies in Text and Music of Liturgical Tropes and Sequences in Memory of Gordon Anderson* (Stockholm, 1986) 13–22.

199. The question of the place of origin of tropes and of their diffusion throughout Europe is still discussed; today, scholars agree that there was not just one place where tropes arose, but that there were several in different regions. See Gy, "Géographie des tropes," and M. Huglo, "Centres de composition des tropes et cercles de diffusion, *Pax et Sapientia*, 139–144.

200. See Husmann, *Tropen*, 124.

another. The composition of a troper was subject to no strict rule. The book may contain either a great number of tropes (for the proper and the ordinary of the Mass) or pieces intended to be used exclusively, or almost exclusively, with introit or offertory antiphons. Things become still more complicated when a sequentiary, or even in certain cases a *cantatorium*[201] is appended to the troper. A cursive review of the lists of sources used by the *Corpus Troporum* shows that this kind of composite book was not rare between the tenth and twelfth centuries. Other examples, such as Paris, B. N., lat. 1118 (Gascony, tenth–eleventh centuries), a troper-sequentiary from St. Martial of Limoges, even include a tonary (Paris, B. N., lat. 1118; fols. 104–114).[202]

The great variety in the contents of the tropers is no obstacle to the uniformity of their presentation on the page. In general, visual preeminence is given to the neumatic notation. The neumes seem to "crush" the written texts which employ very small letters and form an extremely narrow ribbon. In the case of the long melismas on the final *a* of the Alleluia, for instance, the neumes occupy practically the whole page, whereas only two or three alleluias are written out. Obviously, the tropers were utilitarian books used in the actual worship services. With no pretense of luxury as a rule, they were simply liturgical books filling the practical need of regular use.

Finally, two principal groups of tropers must be distinguished: monastic and cathedral. Most manuscripts belong to the first group, within which several categories are defined according to the repertories (either specialized or general) and the codicological aspect of the manuscripts. The tropers of the cathedral type are much rarer and contain a repertory proper to the liturgical use of cathedrals (festive calendar, tropes for the ordinary of the Mass). They also present certain particularities absent from monastic tropers, such as the *Laudes regiae* ["praises of the king"] (see Paris, Bibl. de l'Arsenal, ms. 1169; Autun, 1005/1006–1024),[203] which suggest that the manuscript was written for a special occasion (visit of the sovereign to the cathedral, as was perhaps the case in Autun).

201. See Huglo, *Livres de chant*, 123–126.

202. See Husmann, *Tropen*.

203. E. Palazzo, "Confrontation du répertoire des tropes et du cycle iconographique du tropaire d'Autun," *Tradizione dei trope*, 95–123.

7. OTHER FORMS OF BOOKS

Besides the many possible combinations of chant books,[204] there exist odd kinds that cannot be classified in any category; such is the case of the *Exultet* scrolls.[205] The use of a scroll, a *rotulus*, for a liturgical text was not restricted to the Easter *Exultet* and was certainly a current practice before books, under the form of *codices*, became common in the West.[206] In general, in the Middle Ages, the text of the *Exultet*, the deacon's chant at the time the Easter candle is lit during the Easter Vigil, was included in the sacramentary among the Holy Week texts. In southern Italy, probably from the second half of the tenth century on, the custom arose of making scrolls of the text of the *Exultet* with musical notation alternating with paintings illustrating the main passages of the *laus cerei* ["praise of the candle"] (see p. 81). During Easter night, the deacon, holding his liturgical *rotulus*, ascended the ambo, sang of the resurrection of Christ, symbolized by the lighted candle, and unrolled the scroll at the same time so that the gathered faithful could see one by one the images illustrating the chant. The *Exultet* scroll—whose production was concentrated in the Benevento region in the eleventh and twelfth centuries—is the sole representant of its kind and seems to be a peculiar liturgical book. Indeed, it was clearly intended for the assembly of the faithful, who saw the paintings right side up as it was unrolled,[207] whereas the text with notes was written in the other direction so that the deacon

204. See Huglo, *Livres de chant*, passim.

205. See Huglo, ibid., 63–64, and *Liturgica Vaticana*, 37–40.

206. See the examples cited by R. E. Reynolds, "The Liturgy of Clerical Ordination in Early Medieval Art," *Gesta* 22 (1983) 27–38, especially p. 31. For instance, Pope Zacharias (741–752) sent to St. Boniface (680–754) a scroll with the canon of the Mass: *votis autem tuis clementer inclinati, in rotulo dato praedicto Lul religioso presbitero tuo, per loca signa sanctae crucis quante fieri debeant infiximus* ["Kindly yielding to your desire, we have marked the sign of the cross at the appropriate places where it must be made, in the the scroll given by the above-mentioned Lul, your religious priest"] (MGH, *Ep.*, 3:372). The famous *rotulus* of Ravenna (Lugano, Archivio dei Principe Pio (no number), from the seventh or eighth century, contains orations for Advent; see S. Benz, *Der Rotulus von Ravenna, nach seiner Herkunft und seiner Bedeutung für die Liturgiegeschichte kritisch untersucht*, LQF 45 (1967). For the Byzantine East, see, among others, A. Grabar, "Un rouleau liturgique constantinopolitain et ses peintures," *Dumbarton Oaks Papers* 8 (1954) 161–199 (text reproduced in *L'art de la fin de l'Antiquité et du Moyen Age*, vol. 1 [Paris, 1968] 469–496).

207. Even though one may reasonably wonder how the crowd assembled in the church could possibly see these rather small paintings.

might read it.[208] The twofold function of this book is clear: liturgical and catechetical since it was directly destined for a liturgical action in which the assembly takes an all-important part. Pastoral concern and liturgical decorum meet here to worthily celebrate the highest point of the liturgical year, the resurrection of the Lord.

8. ILLUSTRATION OF THE CHANT BOOKS
OF THE HIGH MIDDLE AGES[209]

In contradistinction to the sacramentary and evangeliary, the books of liturgical chant were never truly decorated with ample iconographic cycles highlighting through images the structure of the liturgical year. This is probably due to the secondary place they occupy in the hierarchy of liturgical books. The sacramentary, containing the sacred prayers (especially the canon of the Mass), and the evangeliary, the holy book par excellence from which the word of God is proclaimed, occupy the first two places in the ecclesiological system of liturgical books in the High Middle Ages. In view of their eminent positions, the sacramentary—placed on the altar and used by the priest for the Eucharistic Prayer—and the evangeliary—processionally carried for the readings—are essential elements of the liturgical decorum of the eucharistic celebration. This is why their material aspect (calligraphy, binding, mode of illustration, all unsystematized) were treated with special care. By contrast, the chant manuscripts, beginning with the Mass antiphonal, are practical books, playing only a secondary role on the liturgical stage. The general aspect, and in particular the ornamentation of these books, reflect their lower status. Among the many precious bindings described and analyzed by F. Steenbock, only six belong to chant books[210] and in most cases were not originally intended for these but are bindings of antique ivories reused as covers. For example, the Troper of Autun (Paris, Bibl. de l'Arsenal, ms. 1169; beginning of eleventh century) inherited as its cover an ivory of the fifth century representing an allegory of secular music;[211] the *Cantatorium* of Monza (Monza, Tesoro della basilica S. Giovanni, cod. CIX;

208. In fact, the deacon knew by heart this chant, sung but once a year, and probably had no need for his scroll. Here again we see the fundamental role played by the oral tradition in the medieval liturgy.

209. See especially *Liturgica Vaticana*, 35–37.

210. F. Steenbock, *Der Kirchliche Prachteinband im frühen Mittelalter* (Berlin, 1965) nos. 1, 3, 7, 40, 41, 84.

211. See ibid., no. 1 and fig. 1.

eighth–ninth centuries) is protected by two consular diptychs dating from the beginning of the sixth century.[212] Thus, the appearance of the *cantatorium* fully corresponds to the description supplied by *Ordo romanus* I from the eighth century, confirmed by Amalarius' comment emphasizing its honorific function (see p. 74). A few rare mentions (such as *antiphonarium I cum tabulis eburneis* ["one antiphonal with ivory covers"]) found in the inventories of church treasuries confirm the witness of the manuscripts.[213] Other ivories, today separated from their manuscripts, may have served as covers for chant books. This is the probable hypothesis that one can formulate for the two famous pieces from Frankfurt am Main (Liebighaus, cod. Barth. 181) and Cambridge (Fitzwilliam Museum) dated to the second half of the ninth century; both are oblong in shape and represent clerics, especially cantors, engaged in a liturgical celebration.[214] Overall in the Middle Ages, one encounters in various manuscripts or on the ivories of bindings[215] scenes of liturgical singing, but in these scenes, the books used by singers are not necessarily clearly shown. By invoking the new practice in the domain of liturgical chant which came about in the second half of the Middle Ages and the use of a lectern for the large choir books, T. Elich has given a convincing explanation of the appearance in breviaries and psalters of the thirteenth century of the representation of cantors at the lectern.[216]

When one examines the contents of the chant books, one sees that although the ample iconographic cycles are lacking (with few exceptions), a large number of manuscripts were decorated with many

212. See ibid., no. 7 and fig 9.

213. A first sampling of the inventories of church treasuries was made possible by the Bischoff, *Schatzverzeichnisse*, which offers only a partial overview, nonetheless significant, of the conditions in the West. A similar but exhaustive work ought to be undertaken on the subject of library catalogues and treasury inventories of countries other than Germany.

214. On the meaning of these ivory plaques and the hypothesis identifying the central figure of the liturgical scenes on the plaques as St. Gregory, see Knop, "Litugiker als Liturge."

215. As on one of the small plaques on the back cover of the Drogon Sacramentary (Paris, B. N., lat. 9428, mid-ninth century), showing a Communion scene. To the left, the members of the *schola* are singing with hands open and extended, and above them, the choir master leads them by gestures. Reynolds, on the strength of the comparisons made with the *ordines romani* used in Metz at that time, thinks that the singers are executing the Agnus Dei, "Image and Text," 73–74.

216. Elich, *Contexte oral*, 2:235–245; Pierce, "Using Liturgical Texts" (summary of Elich).

ornamented initials, from the simple colored letter to the richest compositions intermingling zoomorphic and vegetable motifs. In a fair number of manuscripts, the painted initials lack artistry; but there are exceptional works such as the Antiphonal of Compiègne (Paris, B. N., lat. 17436; see pp. 72–73). The official character of this manuscript explains the care lavished on its calligraphy and ornamentation. The latter exhibits initials with foliated bands of color and gold, as well as frontispieces written in gold letters on a purple background for the titles of the two parts of the manuscript.[217] Throughout the Middle Ages, the richness and sumptuousness of the initial letters increase.

As a conclusion to this section, let us tarry on some chant manuscripts decorated in an exceptional manner. The illustration of the *Exultet* scrolls of southern Italy during the eleventh and twelfth centuries rank among the most beautiful creations of medieval illumination.[218] Intended for the assembly of the faithful gathered on Easter night (see p. 78), the illustrations, literal in character, are inserted between the passages of the text. At the beginning of the scroll, the deacon is represented at the ambo, with the Easter candle in one hand and the scroll in the other; he is facing the assembly, each member of which is holding a lighted candle. This scene is followed by a variable number of others entirely focused on the glory of Christ (*Majestas Domini*, angelic choir adoring the Lord). Occasionally, this cycle is interrupted by liturgical scenes (blessing of the baptismal font because baptism follows the lighting of the candle during the Easter Vigil) or anecdotal scenes (beekeeping because of the praise of bees in the text of the *Exultet*).

Only four tropers, out of all the manuscripts that have been preserved,[219] present iconographic cycles mostly borrowed from other

217. See F. Mütherich and W. Koehler, *Karolingische Miniaturen*, vol. 5 (Berlin, 1982) 127–131.

218. G. Cavallo and C. Bertelli, *Rotoli di "Exultet" dell'Italia meridionale* (Bari, 1973).

219. Paris, B. N., lat. 9448 (Prüm, c.990–995): J. Marquardt-Cherry, *Illustration of Troper Texts: The Painted Miniatures in the Prüm Troper-Gradual* (Los Angeles, 1986); "Ascension Sundays in Tropers: The Innovative Scenes in the Prüm and Canterbury Tropers and Their Relationship to the Accompanying Texts," *Essays in Medieval Studies*, Proceedings of the Illinois Medieval Association 6 (1989) 68–78; and "Ottonian Imperial Saints in the Prüm Troper, *Manuscripts* 33 (1989) 129–136. Bamberg, Staatsbibl., lit. 5 (Reichenau, 1001): P. K. Klein, "Zu einigen Reichenauer Handschriften Heinrichs II, für Bamberg," *Bericht des Historischen Vereins Bamberg* 120 (1984) 417–422. London, B. L., Cotton Caligula A XIV (Canterbury [?], c.1050): E. Temple, *Anglo-Saxon Manuscripts 900–1006* (London, 1976) 113–115 (while waiting

liturgical manuscripts like the sacramentary and the evangeliary. Certain subjects, especially the hagiographic ones, are not necessarily found in other types of books; in this case, the images are directly inspired by the text of the tropes. Except for that of Prüm (Paris, B. N., lat. 9448), the illustrated tropers were written for cathedral use or else adapted for it. The liturgical purpose of these manuscripts, meant for episcopal celebrations, certainly explains the high quality of their execution.

Lastly, let us mention the superb figures personifying the eight tones of Gregorian chant; their linear and very colorful style is typical of southwestern France in the tenth and eleventh centuries.[220] They were placed in the part of Paris, B. N., lat. 1118 (fols. 104–114),[221] which deals with tones and represent musicians and jugglers carrying various musical instruments.[222]

for the publication of the thesis of E. Teviotdale, *The Cotton Troper*, University of North Carolina at Chapel Hill, 1990). Paris, Bibl. de l'Arsenal, ms. 1169 (Autun, 1105/1006–1024): Palazzo, "Confrontation du répertoire."

220. This style is characteristic of the decoration of another troper originating in southwest France (Aurillac, eleventh–twelfth centuries), Paris, B. N., lat. 1084.

221. See *Tropaires de la Bibliothèque nationale* (Paris, 1985) 8.

222. T. Seebass, *Musikdarstellung und Psalterillustration in Früheren Mittelalter* (Berne, 1973).

III. The Books of Readings

1. HISTORY OF THE LITURGICAL READINGS FOR THE MASS

Among the three essential actions of the liturgy, prayer, chant, and reading, this last occupies a predominant place because of its well-established role in the cultic practices of the early Christians. The reading of the Scripture goes back to the very beginning of Christian worship, thus setting the Liturgy of the Word at the heart of the whole *actio liturgica* ["liturgical action"].[223] From the earliest time of Christianity, the Bible was read during the different assemblies of the faithful. The principle then was to read the sacred text in its entirety *(lectio continua)* so that the whole of Scripture could be food for meditation. However, according to general opinion, texts (or biblical passages) were chosen rather early (as early as the second century?) to be read during the eucharistic celebration[224] of a specific feast because they were particularly fitting. The yearly recurrence of the important events of Christian history rapidly led to a choice of readings whose themes corresponded to the meaning of the feasts or the liturgical time (principally Easter, Ascension, Pentecost, Christmas). It quickly became customary to read a given pericope[225] on a precise day, but prior to the fifth and sixth centuries, there were no strict rules in this area. Dominated by liturgical improvisation,[226] the first centuries left

223. This is not the place to discuss the complex origins of the Liturgy of the Word in the West and the East; see the well-documented survey of Vogel, *Introduction,* 291–304 (with bibliography); *CP,* 2:59–68; A.-G. Martimort, *Les lectures liturgiques et leurs livres,* Typologie des sources du Moyen Age occidental, fasc. 64 (Turnhout, 1992) 15–20.

224. The same is true of the Liturgy of the Hours, although to a lesser degree; see Part 3 in this book and Taft, *Liturgy of the Hours;* Martimort, *Lectures liturgiques,* 19.

225. This term is used by liturgists to designate the part of a scriptural text used as a liturgical reading; see Martimort, *Lectures liturgiques,* 16.

226. See I, on sacramentaries, in this part.

a great deal of freedom to the bishop (or the leader of the community) as to the choice of Mass readings.

Although the passage from Greek to Latin occurred progressively during the first four Christian centuries, most authorities select the middle of the third century as the time when Latin began to replace Greek in the liturgy. This was the period during which people began to compose liturgical pieces in Latin and made translations of the Greek versions of the Bible.[227] In view of this, it is believed that the readings were translated earlier than other liturgical texts.

No document before the sixth century attesting to the existence of a system of readings has reached us. But there is no doubt that such a system existed owing to the influence of the Jewish custom of reading the Law and the Prophets in the synagogues.[228] The testimony of authors like Tertullian (c.160–c.225), Ambrose of Milan (374–397), and Augustine of Hippo (396–430) support this hypothesis.[229] The oldest attestation to the existence of a book of readings is found in Gennadius (fl. 470), according to which Musaeus of Marseilles (d. c.460) composed, at the request of his bishop Venerius (d. 452), *ex sanctis scripturis lectiones totius anni festis aptas diebus; responsoria etiam psalmorum capitula temporibus et lectionibus congruentia* ["(a book containing) the readings from sacred Scripture appropriate to the feast days for the whole year, and also responsories and even lists of psalms appropriate to (liturgical) times and (the contents of) the readings"].[230] In addition, several documents, that is, the writings of St. Cyprian (d. 258) and the *Apostolic Tradition* (composed about 215), mention a category of clerics entrusted with the readings during the assemblies and therefore attest to the existence of liturgical readings.[231] For the ecclesiology of the liturgy, the emergence of the function of reader is important because for the duration of the High Middle Ages, two types of readers will have their respective books for their part in the

227. See Vogel, *Introduction*, 293–297; there is a good treatment of all the questions connected with Latin as a liturgical language in C. Mohrmann and B. Botte, "Le latin liturgique," *L'ordinaire de la messe*, Etudes liturgiques 2 (Louvain, 1953) 29–48.

228. See Vogel, *Introduction*, 378–379.

229. See the texts quoted by Vogel, ibid., 301–302.

230. *PL* 58, cols. 1103–1104; see K. Gamber, "Das Lektionar und Sakramentar des Musaeus von Massilia," *Revue bénédictine* 69 (1959) 198–315.

231. The passage from the *Apostolic Tradition* is lapidary: "One is instituted reader when the bishop hands one the book because there is no laying on of hands," B. Botte, ed., *The Apostolic Tradition*, SC 11 bis (1968) 67.

celebration of the Mass, the deacon and the subdeacon (see III, 6–7, of this part). The two oldest "lectionaries" that have been preserved are the manuscripts at Wolfenbüttel (Herzog-August Bibl., cod. Weiss. 76; beginning of sixth century, Gaul) and at Fulda (Hess. Landesbibl. cod. Bonif. 1; about 645, Capua).[232]

As to the number of readings at Mass, it is necessary to distinguish the Roman rite from the other Latin rites of the West.[233] The usage common to the Gallican, Milanese, Visigothic, and other rites was to have three readings in the course of the eucharistic celebration (Old Testament, epistle, and gospel), with pericopes which varied from rite to rite. In contrast, the Roman rite had only two readings (the epistle and gospel).[234] From the seventh and eighth centuries on, the custom of having two readings was widely adopted in Gaul when the Roman rite made its way beyond the Alps.

Since the important surge in learning in the sixteenth and seventeenth centuries, liturgists have shown interest in the liturgical readings and their organization into lists and systems. Before the second half of the nineteenth century, great scholars like Pamelius, Tomasi, Martène published lists of pericopes rather than occupying themselves with their origins and history.[235] The works of E. Ranke[236] and S. Beissel[237] in the nineteenth century and then of W. H. Frere,[238] T. Klauser,[239] and A. Chacasse[240] in the twentieth have made possible

232. See Vogel, *Introduction*, 320–321 and 335–336.

233. See A.-G. Martimort, "A propos du nombre des lectures à la messe," *Revue des Sciences religieuses* 58 (1984), Hommage à M. le Pr Chavasse, 42–51; Martimort, *Lectures liturgiques*, 6–18. Without taking into account the "reading" of the psalms, under the form of verses attached to the gradual and alleluia, see Martimort, "Fonction de la psalmodie dans la liturgie de la Parole," *Liturgie und Dichtung: Ein interdisziplinäres Kompendium*, vol. 2 (St. Ottilien, 1983) 837–856.

234. See A. Chavasse, "Le calendrier dominical romain au VIe siècle," *Recherches des Sciences religieuses* 41 (1953) 96–122.

235. For a historiography of these studies, see Klauser, *Capitulare evangeliorum*, XXII–XXVI.

236. E. Ramke, *Das Kirchliche Pericopensystem aus den ältesten Urkunden der römischen Liturgie* (Berlin, 1847).

237. S. Beissel, *Entstehung der Perikopen des römischen Messbuches* (Freiburg-im-Breisgau, 1907).

238. W. H. Frere, *Studies in Early Roman Liturgy*, vol. 2: *The Roman Gospel Lectionary*, vol. 3: *The Roman Epistle Lectionary* (Oxford, 1934–1935).

239. Klauser, *Capitulare evangeliorum*.

240. See the compendium of his numerous studies in Chavasse, "Evangéliaire," 177–258 and especially 177–189.

the reconstitution of the history of the different systems of readings and the ascertainment of their "archetypes."[241]

2. THE LISTS OF PERICOPES BEFORE THE BOOKS OF READINGS

The liturgical year was gradually established in the course of the first centuries of Christianity and had become very stable[242] by the seventh century. This evolution fostered, in Rome especially, the development of systems of Mass readings which became fixed at the same time, as demonstrated by the lists of pericopes in medieval manuscripts.[243] For the preceding period, liturgists avail themselves first of all of the references to books and of the lists of readings, very brief references which yield only scant information on the contents of the readings. Although indirect, other testimonies furnish more details and certain of them allow us to determine the contents of a list and to deduce what the system of readings was. This has been masterfully demonstrated by Chavasse in his research on the city of Rome, whence, once more, comes the most weighty documentation.[244] Chavasse's conclusions are as follows: under different forms, the lists of Mass readings existed before the appearance of the first sacramentaries even though no document before the end of the sixth century proves this. By going back in time from the first attestations in the seventh century, it is possible to picture what the lists of the fifth and sixth centuries were like. For example, the homilies *in evangelia* ["on the gospel"] which Gregory the Great delivered in the years 590–592 and published in 593, are the first written testimonies of a list of readings organized according to a system.[245] Every homily is preceded by a pericope which is then commented upon, and the

241. Here, the notion of archetype is not identical with the notion of liturgical book in the strict sense, the sacramentary for instance. What is sought is the recovery of the lists of pericopes as they were composed and circulated; see Martimort, *Lectures liturgiques*, first part.

242. See T. J. Talley, *The Origins of the Liturgical Year* (New York, 1986).

243. See Vogel, *Introduction*, 304–314.

244. Chavasse, "Evangéliaire," 177–179. For the documentation concerning the Gallican, Iberian, Ambrosian, and other rites, see Martimort, *Lectures liturgiques*, 47–51.

245. A. Chavasse, "Aménagements liturgiques à Rome au VIIe et au VIIIe siècle," *Revue bénédictine* 99 (1989) 75–102, especially 83–102, and "Les célébrations eucharistiques à Rome, V[e]–VIIIe siècle: Une double ossature *in urbe*," *Ecclesia Orans* 7 (1990) 69–75.

list pertains to the cycle of readings in use at that time in the church of Rome. Despite the particular historical circumstances at the time this list[246] originated, we have here an intermediary link between the ancient lists, before Gregory, and the extensive revision undertaken in the seventh century.[247] The continuity or, on the contrary, the divergences observed by Chavasse between this list and those of the seventh century support the idea that a progressive rearrangement of the readings took place; from time to time, attempts at a more thorough reorganization had consequences of greater import for the establishment of a true system than mere rearrangements. The marks of the antiquity of Gregory's list are seen in the structure of Advent (with six Sundays) and Eastertide, and also in the length of certain pericopes. Other features appear already as elements which will remain stable throughout the whole Middle Ages and even beyond: nineteen pericopes out of the total are already those which will remain assigned to certain feasts of the Temporal and Sanctoral.

In another sort of document, historians derive precious information from the detailed lists of the liturgical objects and books given as endowments to churches newly founded. For instance, in a chart of 471, relating to the foundation of a rural church in the vicinity of Tivoli, liturgical books are mentioned after objects such as chalices and patens.[248] In this list, one encounters biblical books (Gospels, epistles, Psalter) accompanied by a *comes.* As will be seen shortly, in the High Middle Ages, this term often designated a list of readings of variable length that could serve for a good portion of the liturgical year. Such mentions are rare in the first Christian centuries but are significant clues suggesting that quite early there was a distribution of pericopes over the liturgical year.

3. THE EARLY FORMS OF THE BOOKS OF READINGS

As early as the fifth and sixth centuries, the principal forms of the books of readings made their appearance; we must therefore abandon the idea that they would have succeeded one another in a progressive manner. Before the ninth century, the most common usage was to

---

246. Chavasse, "Evangéliaire," 179, thinks that the forty homilies commented upon by the pope are not the result of a choice, but of a preaching program interrupted by Gregory's state of health.

247. A. Chavasse, "Après Grégoire le Grand: L'organisation des évangéliaires au VIIe et au VIIIe siècle," *Rituels: Mélanges offerts au P. Gy, OP* (Paris, 1990) 125–130.

248. Quoted by Chavasse, "Evangéliaire," 177–178.

write marginal notes in the books of Gospels and even the whole Bible.[249] Theodor Klauser has recorded,[250] from among the extant manuscripts antedating the year 800,[251] twenty-five samples with marginal notations,[252] fourteen lists of pericopes,[253] three evangeliaries,[254] and two sacramentaries with pericopes.[255] These notations were various signs (for instance, crosses placed in the margin just before the pericope) in order to assist the reader in locating the gospel passage proper to a given feast. No particular sign marked the end of the passage. As early as the ninth century, the great success of the lists of pericopes *(capitulare)* and the evangeliaries did not entail the radical disappearance of the marginal notes, which would continue to be used on occasion in Bibles until the fourteenth century.[256]

It was also in the eighth century, and especially in the ninth, that a multitude of graphic signs (similar to punctuation) arose and developed in order to facilitate the reading, in particular during the liturgy; these signs continued the attempts of St. Jerome, among others, in that domain. [257] In the same spirit as Isidore of Seville, Alcuin gave his readers advice on the proper way of reading a text, by taking into

249. See Martimort, *Lectures liturgiques* 22–26; Klauser, *Capitulare evangeliorum;* also, for an overall view of the graphic systems invented for the use of the gospel books in the Middle Ages, see J. Vezin, "Les divisions du texte dans les Evangiles jusqu'à l'apparition de l'imprimerie," *Grafia e interpunzione del latino nel Medioevo,* International Seminar, Rome, 27–29 September 1984 (Rome, 1988) 53–68.

250. Klauser, *Capitulare evangeliorum,* XXX–XXXV.

251. On the corpus of the oldest sources dealing with the books of readings, without any distinction among rites, see Klauser, *Capitulare evangeliorum,* XXX–XXXV; Gamber, *CLLA,* vol. 1, nos. 240–247, 360–376, 401–407, 540–549. On the numerous manuscripts attesting to the Gallican rite—in fact the lectionaries of the Merovingian period (like the famous Luxeuil Lectionary, Paris, B. N., lat. 9427; see P. Salmon, *Le lectionnaire de Luxeuil,* Collectanea biblica latina 9 (Rome, 1953)— see the summary in the article by Salmon, "Le texte biblique des lectionnaires mérovingiens," *La Biblia nell'alto Medioevo, 26 aprile–2 maggio 1992,* Settimane di studio del Centro italiano di studi sull'alto Medioevo 10 (Spoleto, 1963) 491–517.

252. The distribution of these twenty-five manuscripts by centuries is the following: sixth: 2; seventh: 11; eighth: 10; about the year 800: 2.

253. With the following distribution: sixth: 2; seventh: 3; eighth: 5; about the year 800: 4.

254. One manuscript from the seventh century and two from the eighth.

255. Both are from the seventh century, including the Missal of Bobbio, Paris, B. N., lat. 13246.

256. See Vogel, *Introduction,* 314–316.

257. See Vezin, "Divisions du texte," 107; A.-V. Gilles, "La ponctuation dans les manuscrits liturgiques au Moyen Age," *Grafia,* 113–135. For a general treatment of

account the oratorical punctuation and the divisions of the text according to the meaning: *Quisque legat hujus sacrato in corpore libri lector in ecclesia verba superna Dei, distinguens sensus, titulos, cola, commata voce dicat, ut accentus ore sonare sciat. Auribus ecclesiae resonet vox vinula longe, omnis ut auditor laudet ab ore Deum* ["Let any reader who reads the exalted words of God from the sacred body of the book make clear distinctions between meanings, titles, periods, and commas so that he may enunciate the accents with his mouth. May his pleasant voice carry far, so that everyone may hear and praise God through the reader's mouth"].[258] These words of advice from the Carolingian master bore fruit because the graphic and material presentation of the manuscripts improved in order to facilitate reading and comprehension. One proof of this is the preface of Paris, B. N., lat. 9452 (fol. 126–126v, ninth century, St. Amand), which contains the lectionary compiled by Alcuin himself (see pp. 98–99).[259]

4. THE LISTS OF PERICOPES OR CAPITULARIES

First of all, it is necessary to distinguish three types of lists of pericopes or capitularies: the lists of epistles (entitled *capitula lectionum,* either with readings from the Old Testament or without these), the origin of the epistolary; the lists of gospel readings (*capitularia evangeliorum*), the origin of the evangeliary; and the lists uniting the two, the origin of the lectionary. In all three cases, the entries indicate for each feast the day and the month; the liturgical day with, eventually, the Roman station (that is, the Roman stational church); the biblical book with, for the Gospels, the number of the Eusebian section;[260] the incipit and the *explicit* ["here ends"] of the pericope joined by *usque*

---

these questions, see M. Banniard, *Viva voce: Communication écrite et communication orale du IVe au IXe en Occident latin* (Paris, 1992).

258. *Carm.* 69, lines 185–188, MGH, *Po.,* vol. 1: *Aevi Karolini,* 292; he gives similar advice to scribes; see *Carm.* 94, lines 1–2, MGH, *Po.,* vol. 1; (this is quoted by Gilles, "Ponctuation dans manuscrits," 121).

259. Gamber, *CLLA,* vol. 2, no. 1040.

260. See Martimort, *Lectures liturgiques,* 26ff. The division into pericopes of the four Gospels in use during the High Middle Ages was the one established by Eusebius of Caesarea (260–340): 355 sections for Matthew, 233 for Mark, 342 for Luke, and 232 for John. In order to easily find the parallel passages, Eusebius compiled lists of concordance containing side by side the pericopes common to different Gospels. The division into chapters we are used to was elaborated only in the thirteenth century and the division into verses, the work of Robert Estienne, goes back only to the sixteenth century.

["up to"]. For example, on the feast of the Nativity, one reads: *In natale Domini ad sanctam Mariam maiorem. Scd. [secundum] Luc. cap. III. Exiit edictum a Caesare Augusto usq. [usque] pax hominibus bonae voluntatis* ["On the Nativity of the Lord at St. Mary Major, according to Luke 2:1-14. 'In those days a decree went out from Caesar Augustus' up to 'peace among those whom he favors'"]. Another example, the feast of St. Stephen: *In natale sci Stephani. Scd. Matth. cap. CCXL. Dicebat Jesus turbis Iudaeorum usq. benedictus qui venit in nomine Domini* ["On the day of the birth into heaven of St. Stephen, according to Matt 23:34-39. 'Jesus said to the crowds of the Jews' up to 'Blessed is the one who comes in the name of the Lord'"].

The generic term *capitulare* appears in the eighth century in certain *ordines romani: legitur lectio una sicut in capitulare commemorat* ["one reading is read as is indicated in the capitulary"] (*Ordo romanus* XXIV, *ordo* of the offices from Ash Wednesday to Holy Saturday);[261] or else, *Et inde leguntur lectiones duae quas in capitulare commemorat* ["And at this point two readings are read as is indicated in the capitulary"] (*Ordo romanus* XV, *capitulare ecclesiastici ordinis*).[262] This term perhaps designates, as early as the fifth century, any type of list of pericopes intended for the liturgical readings. The term *comes* (or *liber comitis*) is used with a meaning equivalent to that of *capitulare* but is never applied to a list of gospel pericopes. Thus *comes* sometimes replaces the term *capitulare lectionum* and, in certain cases, can designate the lectionary (epistles and gospels) (see III, 7, of this part).

One can understand the history of the capitularies only by clearly distinguishing the texts on the one hand and the manuscripts which are their material vehicle on the other. For most of the cases we shall examine, we possess only "late" manuscripts in comparison with the date of the composition of their contents. We have already seen the same problem in the history of the sacramentary and antiphonal. For the books of readings, the problem is aggravated by the fact that neither the evangeliary nor epistolary were ever preceded, and therefore prepared, by *libelli*, independent at first, then gathered into collections, a sort of rudimentary book. This difference is explained by the simple fact that for the books of readings, the texts used already existed since they were biblical texts, whereas for the sacramentaries and certain books of chant, the texts were progressively created for

261. Andrieu, *OR*, 3:289.
262. Ibid., 118.

the different feasts of the liturgical year. Reasons both practical and ecclesiological led to the composition of books of readings, compiled from marginal notes in Bibles and from capitular lists which somehow played for the evangeliary the same role as the *libelli* for the sacramentary and the chant books.

An additional piece of information will help to understand the history of the evangeliary, the epistolary, and the lectionary. As the works of Klauser[263] and Chavasse[264] have shown well, the gradual organization of liturgical time, in particular of the Temporal, and to a lesser degree that of the local setting where the liturgy was enacted (especially in Rome) have in a large measure determined the history and the writing down of the lists of readings (the *capitularia*), which are the ancestors of the evangeliary, the epistolary, and the lectionary.[265] From the viewpoint of both time and space, we find once more the Roman liturgy to be the point of departure for the history of the books used for Christian worship in the West.

Thus, in a general manner, the choice of readings and the organization of the calendar are most often the best clues to the identity of a list of readings. Moreover, let us add that in the High Middle Ages, since each church had its own Sanctoral and Masses for various circumstances, the study of these two groups of celebrations allows us to discern the individuality of a given church's system of readings; in most cases, at least in Gaul in the eighth century, churches had adapted one of the Roman systems of the sixth and seventh centuries.[266]

5. THE BOOK OF GOSPELS WITH THE *CAPITULARE EVANGELIORUM*; THE EVANGELIARY[267]

The *capitulare evangeliorum* ascribes one pericope excerpted from one of the Gospels to most days of the liturgical year. In general, these lists are written at the beginning or, more often, at the end of the manuscripts containing the complete text of the four Gospels. Thus equipped, the book of Gospels could be used directly at the eucharistic liturgy for the proclamation of the word of God by the deacon, for

263. Klauser, *Capitulare evangeliorum*.

264. Among Chavasse's many contributions to the history of the books of readings, let us mention the summary in Chavasse, "Evangéliaire," especially 177–189 and 249–255.

265. See Martimort, *Lectures liturgiques*, 51ff.

266. This is a vast domain, still unexplored.

267. See Martimort, *Lectures liturgiques*, 28–30 and 36–37.

whom this reading was reserved. The evangeliary was the result of the transformation of the *capitulare evangeliorum*—up to then added to the book of Gospels—into a book. Its structure followed that of the capitulary, and this time the complete pericopes were written. These characteristics made the evangeliary an exclusively liturgical book in which the thread of the narrative was broken, whereas the books of Gospels, even with the addition of the *capitulare* or marginal notations, were not purely liturgical because the stories of Matthew, Mark, Luke, and John were not used in their entirety for divine worship. Two principal reasons explain this progressive passage from book of Gospels with *capitulare* to evangeliary. First, an obvious practical consideration led the scribes to facilitate the reader's task: it is much simpler to follow the liturgical year by turning pages on which the pericopes succeed one another in order than to manipulate, even with a certain dexterity, a book of Gospels for which the continual consulting of the *capitulare* is necessary to find the appropriate pericope.[268] Second, the ecclesiology of the liturgy was determinative: it tended more and more to attribute a specific book to each person having an official role in the celebration of the Mass.[269]

Klauser's census, although not exhaustive, is representative and allowed him to establish a typological classification of the books of readings. On this basis, one can make a fruitful comparison, throughout the Middle Ages, between the books of Gospels with *capitulare evangeliorum* on the one hand and the evangeliaries and lectionaries on the other:

	Books of Gospels with *capitulare*	Evangeliaries and lectionaries
8th century	2	1
9th century	140	14

268. Martimort, ibid., 28, has a theory to explain the high number of gospel books with *capitulare evangeliorum* in comparison to the number of evangeliaries during the Middle Ages; in fact, one should specify the High Middle Ages because the reverence shown to the Gospel in the celebration led people to prefer a book containing the complete Gospels to one comprising only the pericopes read at Mass. Martimort's argument does not appear to me solidly supported for antiquity and the High Middle Ages and does not take into account the "natural" evolution of the books owing to the desire of the liturgists to compose books which were as appropriate as possible to the liturgical actions.

269. See P.-M. Gy, "Typologie et ecclésiologie des livres liturgiques médiévaux," *Liturgie dans l'histoire*, 75–89.

	Books of Gospels with *capitulare* (cont'd)	Evangeliaries and lectionaries (cont'd)
10th century	96	30
11th century	101	72
12th century	63	91
13th century	13	65
14th century	6	45
15th century	8	53

These figures clearly reveal the predominance of the books of Gospels with *capitulare* during the High Middle Ages. Then in the twelfth century, one notes the reversal of the tendency: the first book becomes less frequent. Furthermore, the second becomes rarer from the thirteenth century on because of the rapid ascent of the missal, which combines all the books necessary for the celebration of the Mass, up to then distinct.

In several types of medieval documents (library catalogues, inventories of church treasuries, monastic customaries, and so on), the terms used to designate the books of readings do not vary much as a rule and do not seem to reflect either their typological variety or their evolution through the centuries. The title does not have the same symbolic importance as for the sacramentary and the antiphonal, for which the authority of their presumed author (Gregory the Great, for instance) imposed their contents in the whole, or almost whole, West. Because biblical texts do not need any literary or religious authority, the evangeliary never bore any official title, and the formula *incipit capitulare evangeliorum*[270] at the beginning of the capitularies is strictly practical in character. Besides, until very late in the Middle Ages, the expression *liber evangeliorum* can designate any book used for readings, whatever its kind. In spite of this lack of lexical accuracy, one encounters with the passage of time, especially from the eleventh century on, such terms as *evangelium, lectionarium, epistolarium, evangeliorum,* whose exact meaning often remains rather blurred because the sort of

270. Occasionally, one encounters the following terms, much rarer than *capitulare evangeliorum: breviarium lectionum evangelii, breviarium quattuor evangeliorum, tituli evangeliorum, ordo evangeliorum per annum, capitulatio, quotationes evangeliorum* ["summary of the gospel readings," "summary of the four Gospels," "titles of the gospel readings," "order of the gospel readings throughout the year," "summary," "incipits of the gospel readings"].

documents in which these terms appear (library catalogues, inventories of church treasuries, customaries, and ordinaries) does not favor the typological accuracy that historians would wish to find. Unfortunately for them, literary texts do not shed more light on this field. However, it seems that in the second half of the Middle Ages, the diversification of the books of readings is accompanied by a certain increase in the vocabulary that designates them. Let us note that the word *evangeliorum* is very rare and is not in use before the twelfth century, which proves that the people of the Middle Ages distinguished between the *liber evangeliorum cum capitularia* and the *evangeliarium*, the evangeliary.[271] The books of readings, especially the books of Gospels richly adorned and decorated, are often described by the expressions *textus aureus, liber aureus,* or else *comes (liber comitis),* deriving from *comma,* that is, "section of a pericope" and not "companion," as has too often been believed.[272]

Content of the Capitularies and Evangeliaries

Thanks to the work of Klauser,[273] which refined that, a trifle older, of Frere, the organization of the gospel pericopes used in Rome in the seventh and eighth centuries and later in a large part of the West from the second half of eighth, is well known to liturgists. Klauser distinguishes four great types of gospel books: (1) Type Pi (about 645 in Rome), representing the oldest system of readings; this type was established on the basis of the *capitulare* transcribed in a manuscript going back to about the year 700 (Würzburg, Universitätsbibl., cod. M.p.th.f. 62; fols. 10v–16v);[274] (2) Type Lambda (about 740)[275] and (3) Type Sigma (about 755),[276] both Roman in origin and later varieties of

---

271. Andrieu, *Pontifical,* 1:255: *Tunc diaconus progrediens de altari, sacra veste industus precedentibus cereostatis cum ceresis et incenso, portat evangeliorium usque ad ambonem qui constitutus est in medio conventus* ["Then the deacon, leaving the altar, wearing the sacred vestment, preceded by candle-bearers with candles and incense, carries the evangeliary to the ambo which is placed in the middle of the assembly"]. With the exception of a few studies, lexical research is lacking in the domain of liturgical books; the books of readings are a case in point.

272. See Vogel, *Introduction,* 318–319 and 392, for the different terms used in the Middle Ages to designate the books of readings.

273. Klauser, *Capitulare evangeliorum.*

274. Ibid., 1–46; see Martimort, *Lectures liturgiques,* 31–32; G. Morin, "L'évangéliaire de Würzbourg," *Revue bénédictine* 28 (1911) 296–330.

275. Klauser, *Capitulare evangeliorum,* 47–92.

276. Ibid., 93–130.

the first type, they differ from Type Pi in the Sanctoral and in the Temporal because of the presence of pericopes for the Thursdays in Lent, introduced at the time of Gregory II (715–731);[277] (4) Type Delta (about 750), which is the Romano-Frankish adaptation of the 645 list.[278] In this last case, as for the Frankish Eighth-Century Gelasian Sacramentary, it was necessary to adapt the Roman gospel readings of the liturgical year to the needs of the Frankish churches.[279] Compared to the three purely Roman types, the Sanctoral of Type Delta is swollen by local Gallican feasts corresponding to the contents of the Eighth-Century Gelasian Sacramentary.

The origin and manner of composition of Type Pi from 645 are not yet entirely clear; its very complex composition can only be the end product of a protracted period during which liturgical time was being constituted. Each pericope is indicated by the number it carries in the Eusebian numeration, as well as by its incipit and explicit, and preceded by the day of the year. Chavasse has shed light on several points which explain the list of 645.[280] This Roman[281] "evangeliary" proposes a classification of feasts and their gospel pericopes on the basis of the liturgical year, combining the Temporal and the Sanctoral. The liturgical year, following the Julian calendar, is the undisputed temporal frame of reference for the system of readings. In this, there is a striking correspondence between the organization of the evangeliary of 645 and that of the sacramentaries, especially those of the Gregorian type. For these books, as in a lesser measure for the antiphonal,

277. See Martimort, Livres liturgiques, 52–53, on the oldest manuscripts of these two types.

278. Klauser, Capitulare evangeliorum, 131–172.

279. The oldest source of type delta is Besançon, B. M., ms. 184 (end of eighth century, in all likelihood composed in Murbach); the readings from the epistles and the gospel pericopes are together (fols. 57–73), thus forming a regular little lectionary (see pp. 99–100); on the manuscript and its publication, see Martimort, Lectures liturgiques, 32ff.; A. Wilmart, "Le comes de Murbach," Revue bénédictine 30 (1913) 25–69.

280. See especially Chavasse, "Plus anciens types"; "L'évangéliaire romain de 645, un recueil: Sa composition (façons et matériaux)," Revue bénédictine 92 (1982) 33–75; "Aménagements liturgiques"; "Après Grégoire le Grand." I have not had the opportunity to consult the two unpublished studies of Chavasse [since published —Ed.], Les lectionnaires romains de la messe au VIIe et au VIIIe siècle, sources et derivés, vol. 1: Procédés de confection, vol. 2: Synoptique général, tableaux complémentaires, Spicilegii friburgensis Subsidia 22 (Fribourg, 1993).

281. To take up the term used by Chavasse, "evangeliary" means here a series of gospel pericopes and does not mean a book as such, a manuscript.

the intent of the Roman liturgists was one of the main factors that produced the system of readings of Type Pi; this intent was to structure a liturgical year more and more filled with a formulary, chants, and readings proper to each day. Chavasse has also shown that whereas the temporal frame was all-important, the local setting of the celebration of the feasts played no part in the establishment of this list. The stational churches are mentioned, but these references do not affect either the date or the succession of the formularies. The sixty-eight feasts of the Sanctoral of Type Pi would be incorporated into Types Sigma and Lambda, with a few additions, and into the Romano-Frankish Type Delta, which also has the feasts of local saints and ends up having a Sanctoral identical with that of the Eighth-Century Gelasian Sacramentary. The Romano-Frankish "Evangeliary" of 750, in addition to the epistolary of the same type (see pp. 97–98), will be the authoritative one in the majority of Western churches during the whole of the Middle Ages, even though the Sanctoral presents specific local variations. The character of an evangeliary is determined above all by its Sanctoral, which must be studied first in order to detect particularities proper to a specific church, classify manuscripts, discern the influence of one church upon another, and so on.[282]

On the codicological plane, the books of Gospels with *capitulare* and the evangeliaries (see the comparative list, pp. 92–93) do not present a typological variety as rich as other books, the sacramentaries for instance. As a rule, they are complete copies, often decorated with particular care both on the inside and the binding because of their use in church worship and their place of destination (monastery, cathedral, parish, and so on)[283] Festive samples are rare, for instance the *libellus* of Fulda (a quire of 10 folios) (Aschaffenburg, Hofbibl., ms. 2) from the end of the tenth century which contains only a series of pericopes for certain big feasts: Christmas, Circumcision, Epiphany, Purification, Easter Vigil, Easter Sunday, and some feasts of the local Sanctoral,

282. The study of the feasts of saints in the evangeliaries of the Middle Ages is still a domain under-exploited by liturgists and historians. There exists, however, a number of editions of gospel lists or particular evangeliaries, chiefly from the Carolingian period; see, for instance, R. Amiet, "Un *capitulare evangeliorum* carolingien en relation avec le sacramentaire de Gellone," *Revue des Sciences religieuses* 58 (1984) 280–289.

283. See Gamber, *CLLA*, for an exhaustive list of the manuscript-sources of the High Middle Ages. See 8 below, the section on the illustration of the books of readings.

like St. Martin. Its carefully executed decoration and its restricted contents prove that this *libellus evangeliorum* was reserved for festive use,[284] which is an exception in the Middle Ages. This small degree of typological variety noted for the books of readings in general is explained by the uniformity of customs, except for some feasts of the Sanctoral; thus, the bishop or the priest were spared the need of securing a special copy when they traveled to celebrate the liturgy in a different diocese or parish.

6. THE *CAPITULARE LECTIONUM* AND EPISTOLARY

Whether combined with the pericopes from the Old Testament or not, the lists of the epistles ascribed to each day of the liturgical year were formed roughly at the same time as the systems of gospel readings. The *capitula* indicate here also the liturgical use of the pericopes, the biblical book, the incipit and explicit. In the same way as the gospel capitularies, the lists of epistles were progressively made into books, thus becoming epistolaries properly so called. The eleventh century appears here also as the hinge[285] between the two. According to the work of the specialists,[286] the Roman model of the *capitulare lectionum*, at the root of the epistolary when it was made into a book, would have been organized at the end of the sixth century and, in its medieval form, would go back to the seventh century. Its overall plan corresponds rather well to that of the ancient Gelasian Sacramentary, although the Temporal and Sanctoral are combined. Its structure is as follows: readings for the yearly liturgical cycle, readings for the celebrations independent of the cycle, and lastly, without precise day, a list of the forty-two readings from Paul's letters in their order in the biblical text. Overall, its mode of composition is identical to that of the evangeliary although its details are more difficult to make out.

284. Palazzo, *Sacramentaires de Fulda.*

285. See the lists of manuscripts established by Klauser, *Capitulare evangeliorum,* LXXI–XC. For the *capitularia lectionum,* the distribution by century is the following: eighth: 1; ninth: 1; tenth: 1; eleventh and twelfth: 1; thirteenth: 83; fourteenth: 53; fifteenth: 40. For the epistolaries: ninth: 5; tenth: 6; eleventh: 10; twelfth: 26; thirteenth: 27; fourteenth: 20; fifteenth: 32. Concerning the oldest three manuscript-sources of the lists of epistles, Fulda, Landesbibl., cod. Bonif. 1 (middle of the sixth century); Bibl. Vat., Regin. lat. 9 (seventh–eighth century); and Bibl. Vat., Vat. lat. 5755 (palimpsests from the sixth and eighth centuries), see Martimort, *Lectures liturgiques,* 27–28.

286. In particular Frere, *Roman Epistle Lectionary,* and Chavasse, "Evangéliaire."

Again the temporal frame of the liturgical year is preeminent, with Temporal and Sanctoral combined. As for the evangeliary, the system of readings in the epistolary was established on the basis of distinct chronological sequences (Lent, Easter, Advent, Christmas) adjusted to form a linear and coherent liturgical cycle.[287] The only witness to the Roman epistolary is the manuscript of Würtzburg,[288] whose importance for the evangeliary we have seen (see pp. 94–95).

Especially when it was exported from Rome to Gaul, where other systems of readings—represented in particular by the Lectionary of Luxeuil (Paris, B. N., lat. 9427)[289]—were in use, the Roman epistolary was submitted to remodeling and adaptations. As in the sacramentary and evangeliary, the changes affected principally the Sanctoral in order to bring it into accordance with the Eighth-Century Gelasian Sacramentary.[290] The principal manuscript witnesses are the Epistolary of Corbie (St. Petersburg, Publichnaya Bibl., cod. lat. Q.v.I, no. 16; about 770–780),[291] in which the pericopes are given in full; the *liber comitis* of the eighth or the ninth centuries from northern Italy (Paris, B. N., lat. 9451),[292] where all the readings from the epistles are combined with those from the Gospels, and sometimes with those from the Old Testament (in fact this is a true lectionary, see p. 100);[293] the *comes* of Murbach[294] (Besançon, B. M., ms. 184), from the end of the eighth century, in which the readings from the epistles are combined with those from the Gospels (fols. 57–73). For Romano-Frankish Gaul, let us mention also the "Alcuin Lectionary": in reality this is an epistolary containing 242 readings from the Old Testament, the epistles, and the Acts of the

---

287. For more details on the very complex mode of composition of the Roman epistolary, see G. Morin, "Le plus ancien *comes* ou lectionnaire de l'Eglise romaine," *Revue bénédictine* 27 (1910) 41–74, and especially A. Chavasse, "L'épistolier romain du codex de Würtzbourg: Son organisation," *Revue bénédictine* 62 (1981) 280–331.

288. Universitätsbibl., Cod. M.p.th.f. 62, beginning of eighth century (fols. 2v–10v). See Martimort, *Lectures liturgiques*, 31–32.

289. See Salmon, *Lectionnaire de Luxeuil.* The liturgies of northern Italy, southern Italy, and even those of the Spanish churches also possessed a lectionary which remained rather stable throughout the centuries despite the spreading of Roman usages. See Martimort, *Lectures liturgiques*, 47–51.

290. For details of the rearrangements, see Chavasse, "Evangéliaire," 250–255.

291. Martimort, *Lectures liturgiques*, 34–35.

292. R. Amiet, "Un *comes* carolingien inédit de la haute Italie," *Ephemerides liturgicae* 73 (1959) 335–367.

293. Martimort, *Lectures liturgiques*, 39.

294. Ibid., 32.

Apostles, arranged according to the liturgical year (Paris, B. N., lat. 9452; third quarter of ninth century, written in St. Amand and coming from Chartres cathedral).[295] Its originality is due to its supplement of sixty-five pericopes preceded by a preface probably penned by Helisachar (d. 836), the chancellor of Louis the Pious (reigned 813–840), and attributing this *comes* to Alcuin. This supplement, perhaps partly the work of Alcuin (as is suggested by the addition of both the vigil and feast of All Saints, as well as the vigil and feast of St. Martin) is added to a local Roman epistolary composed about 670–680, whose contents are identical to those of the Sacramentary of Padua (*Paduense*, about 660–670, see I of this part, the section on sacramentaries), but which has adapted the readings to the local Gallican feasts.

Besides the manuscripts cited above, there exists a large number of other witnesses from the ninth and tenth centuries, either complete or fragmentary, mere lists or epistolaries properly so called, about which information will be found elsewhere.[296] All are more or less representative of the Roman epistolary with some variants and do not bring supplementary elements to the understanding of the history of the epistolary as it has just been described.

7. THE LECTIONARIES

Before the lectionary properly so called took precedence over the evangeliary and epistolary (chiefly from the eleventh and twelfth centuries on), lists of readings from both the epistles and Gospels were added to Bibles or books of Gospels. The two oldest capitularies of this type however are small books inserted into artificial collections of the late Middle Ages. First, we have the sixteen sheets (fols. 1–16) of the codex kept in Würzburg (Universitätsbibl., M.p.th.f. 62; eighth century),[297] mentioned above, where epistles and gospels form two distinct lists. In the second document (Besançon, B. M., ms. 184; fols. 57–75, end of eighth or beginning of ninth century, Murbach),[298] the list of epistles and gospels form a homogeneous whole for every

295. Ibid., 36; A. Wilmart, "Le lectionnaire d'Alcuin," *Ephemerides liturgicae* 51 (1937) 136–197.

296. See Martimort, *Lectures liturgiques*, 34–36, who points out exceptions, such as two epistolary-graduals of the eleventh century (St. Gall, Stiftsbibl., cod. 374, and Bibl. Vat., Borghes. lat. 359) in which the two parts are written one after the other.

297. Ibid., 31–32.

298. Ibid., 32.

day of the year. The function of these small books is not easy to de-
lineate. Personally, I doubt that they were memory aids intended to
be consulted before the celebration in order to know the readings of
the day.[299] Rather, perhaps these *libelli* were a means for the transmission of the lists of pericopes, as was the case for other types of *libelli*.

The absence of complete manuscript witnesses as important as the
two manuscripts just cited does not in any way mean that lectionaries
containing all the Mass readings (Old Testament, Acts of the Apostles,
even Revelation, epistles, and Gospels) were not produced before the
end of the eighth century. Texts from the fifth and sixth centuries (see
pp. 87–88) attest to the existence of complete lectionaries at that period. A fair number of palimpsest fragments dating from between the
sixth and eighth centuries corroborates textual attestations.[300] The list
established by Klauser for the full lectionaries *(Voll-Lektionar)* shows a
concentration between the eleventh and fifteenth centuries of the
manuscripts used in Rome or in Romano-Frankish churches, with the
following distribution by century: eleventh—eighteen; twelfth—eighteen; thirteenth—fourteen; fourteenth—eighteen; fifteenth—twenty.[301]
The two oldest complete lectionaries are Paris, B. N., lat. 9451 (end of
eighth century, northern Italy,[302] see above), and Chartres, B. M., ms. 24
(destroyed in 1944), copied in Tours in the first half of the ninth century.[303] Let us also add that in the medieval library catalogues and inventories of church treasuries, the complete lectionaries are often
listed in greater detail than other liturgical books. It is not rare to read
references like *lectionarium cum evangeliis, lectionarium cum epistolae* or
to see in the same catalogue or inventory the evangeliary and epistolary clearly distinguished from the lectionary. Medieval librarians obviously knew the different types of books of readings and left us
precise indications on the contents of the lectionaries.[304]

Let us end this section on the books of Mass readings by specifying
that their typology extends much farther than the main configura-
tions we have examined here: it will be necessary to engage in more
detailed studies (modes of composition, history) which at this point

299. Ibid., 31; this hypothesis does not rest on any historical foundation.
300. Ibid., 37–39, where a non-exhaustive list is given.
301. Klauser, *Capitulare evangeliorum*, CXIV.
302. See Martimort, *Lectures liturgiques*, 39.
303. Ibid., 39–40.
304. For further details concerning these references, see Becker, *Catalogi;* Bischoff,
Schatzverzeichnisse.

are not available to historians of liturgical books. Among atypical documents, let us mention the evangeliaries with collects, necessary for the final part of the third nocturn of monastic vigils (see Part 3, on the Office). The readings joined or combined with a sacramentary or an antiphonal are part of the first missals in the strict sense and deserve, on that account, to be presented in the section dealing with them (IV of this part).

8. ILLUSTRATION OF THE BOOKS OF READINGS

Among the masterpieces of medieval illumination, the books for the Mass readings, particularly the book of gospel readings, occupy an important place because of both the decoration of the inside of the book and the careful execution of the binding. The privileged status of sacred Scripture in the liturgy explains in large part why these books were sumptuous in every period, despite Jerome's caution against overly luxurious Christian books. Let us recall that in the Middle Ages, the book of Gospels was carried in procession through the church to the altar, then to the ambo, where the deacon read from it.[305] Sometimes, medieval texts (library catalogues, inventories of church treasuries, customaries, and so on) were content with simply designating the books of readings by *liber aureus, textus aureus cum tabulis eburnea et gemmis, libri III auro et gemmis ornati* ["golden book," "golden text with ivory cover and precious stones," "three books adorned with gold and precious stones"],[306] terms emphasizing the lavishness of their inside appearance (gold letters on a purple background for instance) and their precious covers often richly ornamented with gems, ivory, and gold. The greatest number of the masterpieces of the medieval art of binding, at least during

305. See the many references in the *ordines romani,* Andrieu, *OR;* and also in the monastic customaries and, later on, the ordinaries. See also Jungmann, *MS,* 2:216–219, on the symbolic meaning of these processions.

306. Examples of this are found in the catalogue of the books of the Abbey of St. Riquier (851): *textus evangelii IV aureis litteris scriptus totus I* ["one copy of the text of the four Gospels entirely written in gold letters"], Becker, *Catalogi,* 28; also the list of the books of the Mainz cathedral (thirteenth century): *erant libri, qui pro ornatu super altare ponebantur, ut sunt evangeliorum, epistolare sive lectionarii, benedictionales, collectarii quidam vestiti ebore scuplto, alii argento, alii auro et gemmis* ["There were books which, because of their decoration, were placed on the altar, as are the evangeliaries, the epistolaries or lectionaries, the benedictionals, the collectars; some of those have covers ornamented with carved ivory, others with silver, still others with gold and precious stones"], Bischoff, *Schatzverzeichnisse,* p. 53, no. 48.

the High Middle Ages, was done for the gospels and other books of readings.[307] Episcopal capitularies of the ninth century direct priests to use liturgical books worthy of their function in worship services for the greatest glory of the word of God.

From antiquity on and during most of the Middle Ages, the Bible was the object of a rich decoration and gave rise to iconographic cycles of great amplitude.[308] From the end of antiquity, the iconographic traditions of the Bible progressively made their way into the different liturgical books. During the Carolingian period, the still unstable structure of these books is one of the causes for the lack of well-established iconographic cycles for each of the books. Only the sacramentary received at that time a new kind of illustration, different from that of the Bible (see I of this part, the section on sacramentaries). From the High Middle Ages until the twelfth century, the illustration of the books of readings was influenced by the paleo-Christian traditions, with which a few novel features were mixed.

The books of Gospels, with or without *capitulare*, then the evangeliaries are the two main books that were illustrated,[309] the paintings of the former supplying the latter with the major part of their iconographic subjects. The Carolingian books of Gospels often have for their sole decoration four full-page paintings (portraits of the evangelists, each at the beginning of his Gospel) and arches above the tables of Canons; more rarely, paintings inspired by paleo-Christian subjects, such as the fountain of life and the adoration of the Lamb.[310] In the Evangeliary of Godescalc (781–783; Paris, B. N., new acq. lat. 1203),

307. The catalogue compiled by Steenbock, *Kirchliche Prachteinband*, is quite revealing in this respect; on the liturgical and symbolic function of the decoration on precious bindings, see pp. 51–56.

308. Concerning the illustration of the Bible in the Middle Ages, see Cahn, *Bible romane*.

309. See the ground-breaking work of S. Beissel, *Geschichte der Evangelienbücher in der ersten Hälfe des Mittelalters* (Freiburg-im-Breisgau, 1906). For a recent update, see E. Palazzo, "L'illustration de l'évangéliaire au haut Moyen Age," *La Maison-Dieu* 176 (1988) 67–80.

310. As is seen in the Gospel Book of St. Médard of Soissons, Paris, B. N., lat. 8850 (first half of ninth century); F. Heber-Suffrin, "La Jérusalem céleste des Evangiles de St. Médard de Soissons, problèmes de perspective et d'iconographie à l'époque carolingienne," *Cahier du Centre de Recherche sur l'Antiquité tardive et le haut Moyen Age* 2 (Université de Paris X–Nanterre, 1977) 109–117. A good summary of the history of the gospel books and their illustration can be found in A. von Euw, *Das Buch der vier Evangelien: Kölns Karolingische Evangelienbücher*, Sonderheft des Kölner Museums–Bulletin 1 (1989).

named for the scribe who signed the colophon and written for Charlemagne in the court scriptorium, the paintings of the evangelists as well as those of the *Majestas Domini* and the fountain of life are all grouped together in the beginning of the manuscript because the Gospel by Gospel arrangement was no longer possible. They are directly inspired by the iconography of a book of Gospels from antiquity,[311] and would be reproduced shortly afterward, sometimes in larger programs, in Carolingian books of Gospels. The text of the Evangeliary of Godescalc is written in gold and silver letters on a purple background, which is fitting in view of the destination of the codex. In the dedicatory verse written at the end of the manuscript, Godescalc himself explains the reasons for this sumptuousness: purple symbolizes the heavenly kingdom which is opened by the red blood of Christ and gold, the splendor with which the words of God brilliantly shine.[312] This sort of praise is not restricted to the evangeliary; it is found also in psalters, like that of Dagulf (about 795) kept in Vienna (Österreich. Nationalbibl., cod. 1861). The decoration of the Godescalc manuscript shows that at least during a good part of the Middle Ages, the illustration of the evangeliary was not bound by a specific and clearly defined program, but came directly from that of the book of Gospels.

The Ottonian period marked a change in the illustration of the books of Mass readings, in particular the evangeliary. The end of the tenth and beginning of the eleventh centuries saw important typological transformations in the domain of liturgical books, notably those used for the readings. From then on, evangeliaries were mass-produced; and in certain scriptoria, like that of Reichenau, which worked for the Ottonian court, they were endowed with iconographic cycles adopted from the Carolingian sacramentaries. Only two designs from a fragment of a Carolingian evangeliary (Düsseldorf, Universitätsbibl. cod. B.113; Rheims[?], third quarter of ninth century)[313] suggest that as early as the ninth century, there existed evangeliaries adorned with iconographic cycles prefiguring those of the Ottonian manuscripts from the perspective of both the amplitude of the cycle and the treatment of

311. See F. Mütherich. "Manuscrits enluminés autour d'Hildegarde," *Actes du colloque "Autour d'Hildegarde": Cahier du Centre de Recherche sur l'Antiquité tardive et le haut Moyen Age* 5 (Université de Paris X–Nanterre, 1987) 49–62.

312. MGH, *Po.*, 1:94–95.

313. On this manuscript, see *Kostbarkeiten aus der Universitätsbibliothek Düsseldorf, Mittelalterliche Handschriften und Alte Drucke* (Wiesbaden, 1989) 24.

the images. The vast majority of the programs in the Ottonian evangeliaries are based on a Christological cycle which originated in biblical illustration drawn from the sacramentaries or, more rarely, from the books of Gospels.[314] The pericopes accompanied by a painting, either full-page or in the initial letter, are in general those of the big feasts of the liturgical year, as in the sacramentaries. The iconographic treatment is similar overall to that of the paintings devoted to the same subjects in the contemporary books of Gospels from Reichenau. However, some evangeliaries contain paintings foreign to the gospel cycles; let us cite the dedicatory miniature representing Henry II (reigned 1002–1024) and his wife Kunigunde on folio 2r of the evangeliary offered by the emperor to the new bishopric of Bamberg, which he had founded (Munich, Bayer. Staatsbibl., clm. 4452). Recent research has satisfactorily demonstrated the political import of this image since it was the emperor who had commissioned the manuscript.[315] Another novel aspect of the Ottonian evangeliaries is the important part given to images illustrating gospel parables.[316] In this regard, they are very close to the iconographic tradition of the Byzantine books of readings, thoroughly studied by K. Weitzmann.[317]

The illustration of the books of readings used in the Romanesque period, first of all evangeliaries, continued the Ottonian traditions, which explains why the most beautiful evangeliaries of this period originated in Germany. The innovations touch upon limited points and never result in a distinctive iconography. Even the character of the decor is identical to that of the Carolingian and, later, Ottonian periods (full-page illustrations, purely decorative or historiated initials, ornamental embellishments). This style denotes a taste for the archaic and seems to be a last surge of the iconographic tradition of

314. See the basic article of A. Weiss, "Die spätantike Lektionar-Illustration im Skriptorium der Reichenau," *Die Abtei Reichenau* (Sigmaringen, 1974) 311–362.

315. P. K. Klein, "Die Apokalypse Ottos III und das Perikopenbuch Heinrichs II," *Aachener Kunstblätter* 56–57 (1988–1989) 5–52.

316. As in Munich, Bayer. Staatsbibl., clm. 23338 (Reichenau, first half of eleventh century); see A. Korteweg, "Das Evangelistar Clm. 23338 und seine Stellung innerhalb der Reichenauer Schulhandschriften," *Studien zur mittelalterlichen Kunst 800–1250: Festschrift für Florentine Mütherich zum 70. Gerburtstag,* ed. K. Bierbrauer, P. K. Klein, and W. Sauerlander (Munich, 1985) 125–144.

317. Among the numerous studies devoted to this topic, let us mention, "The Narrative and Liturgical Gospel Illustrations," *New Testament Manuscript Studies,* ed. M. M. Parvis and A. P. Wikgren (Chicago, 1950) 151–174, 215–219, reprinted in *Studies in Classical and Byzantine Manuscript Illumination* (Chicago, 1971) 247–270.

the liturgical books from the High Middle Ages. To account for this state of affairs, one must remember the increasing attention the artists gave, from the twelfth century on, to the new categories of books in the liturgical domain, such as the missal and pontifical, and to manuscripts containing exegetical commentaries. After the twelfth century, evangeliaries and lectionaries would become less and less numerous.

A fair number of these Romanesque evangeliaries are of the festive type and comprise only the readings for the big feasts of the year. The manuscript of the Municipal Library of Laon (ms. 550; Alsace, end of twelfth century) has only twenty-three sheets; the text of its twenty-three pericopes all begin with a purely ornamental or historiated initial. This manuscript has portraits of the evangelists, figures of saints, and scenes from the life of Christ (presentation in the Temple and flagellation).[318] Let us also mention two true masterpieces of Romanesque illumination: the Evangeliary of Prüm (Paris, B. N., lat. 17325), whose date, 1110–1120, was recently determined by C. Nordenfalk; its iconographic cycle depends most of all on local traditions[319] interspersed with a few innovations having no direct connection with the text but referring to the history of the Abbey of Prüm;[320] and the Evangeliary of St. Erentrude (Munich, Bayer. Staatsbibl., clm. 15903) executed in the first half of the eleventh century in Salzburg, where the Ottonian tradition was also strongly implanted.[321]

Compared to the evangeliaries, the epistolaries never received any important decoration during the Middle Ages. This fact, peculiar to the West, contrasts with the iconographic tradition of the Byzantine epistolaries and books of the Acts of the Apostles, whose richness is often comparable to that of the Greek books of Gospels and evangeliaries.[322]

318. On this manuscript, see G. Cames, *La mémoire des siècles, 2.000 ans d'écrits en Alsace* (Strasbourg, 1988) 209–210.

319. Especially in the Troper of Prüm (Paris, B. N., lat. 9448), from the end of the tenth century, and another evangeliary written in the same abbey in the eleventh century (Manchester, John Rylands Library, ms. 7); see C. Nordenfalk, "A German Romanesque Lectionary in Paris: Date and Origin," *The Burlington Magazine* 130 (1988) 4–9, 318.

320. What is meant here is the painting of the washing of the feet, in which the sandals shown near Peter are an allusion to the relic the abbey possessed.

321. On this manuscript, see E. Klemm, *Die romanischen Handschriften der Bäyerischen Staatsbibliothek* 1 (Wiesbaden, 1980) no. 272, pp. 157–161.

322. See H. L. Kessler, "Paris grec 102: A Rare Illustration of the Apostles," *Dumbarton Oaks Papers* 27 (1973) 211–216. See also the manuscripts presented in *Liturgica Vaticana*, 108–157.

IV. Genesis and Development of the Missal

Thanks to the work of some great scholars of the twentieth century, we have gained a fairly good knowledge of the general conditions in which the genesis and development of the missal took place. The pioneering studies of A. Ebner,[323] A. Baumstark,[324] A. Wilmart,[325] A. Dold,[326] and V. Leroquais,[327] and more recently those of O. Nussbaum[328] and A. Häussling[329] lead to conclusions which have been confirmed and made more precise by analyses of particular points in the medieval manuscripts.

It is commonly accepted today that the rise of the missal cannot be explained solely by practical reasons such as the desire to make all texts (orations, readings, even rituals, blessings, and so on) available in one book. A certain evolution of the ecclesiology of the liturgy occurred after the Carolingian period, one consequence of which was the concentration of the liturgical action in the celebrant's hands, although the other actors in the celebration were not eliminated. Beginning with the eleventh century, the celebrant was under obligation to recite, at least in a low voice, the sung parts of the Mass, even though they were executed by the choir, and the various readings, even though they were proclaimed by the deacon and subdeacon.[330]

The manuscripts which have been preserved attest to this evolution and make it possible to establish a typology of the medieval

---

323. *Missale Romanum* (1896).

324. *Missale Romanum: Seine Entwicklung ihre wichtigsten Urkunden und Probleme* (Eindhoven-Nijmegen, 1929) especially 132–143.

325. "Les anciens missels de la France," *Ephemerides liturgicae* 46 (1932) 245–267.

326. *Vom Sakramentar, Comes und Capitulare zum Missale* (Beuron, 1943).

327. Leroquais, *Sacramentaires*.

328. *Kloster, Priestermönch und Privatmesse* (Bonn, 1961).

329. *Mönchskonvent und Eucharistiefeier*, LQF 58 (Münster, 1973).

330. Concerning this evolution, see Vogel, *Introduction*, 105–106.

missal.[331] Let us see the principal representative cases and their importance for the history of the Mass books.

A word of caution: the different types which will be described do not succeed one another according to chronological order. On the contrary, one observes as early as the ninth century the frequent coexistence of the different forms of the missal in the High Middle Ages. It is impossible to speak of a linear evolution that would lead from a "rudimentary" form of missal to an elaborate book. Nonetheless, the eleventh century marked a decisive turn in the history of the missal: at that time, the sacramentaries and the *libelli missarum* yielded to complete manuscripts which specialists call "plenary missals"—an obvious pleonasm.[332] As a consequence, from the first half of twelfth century on, there were fewer sacramentaries than missals, and their numbers would diminish further in the thirteenth and fourteenth centuries.[333]

In the ninth century, marginal notes appeared, as well as the first forms of the missal with juxtaposed parts and *libelli missarum*. In order to illustrate the first case, let us cite Rheims, B. M., ms. 213 (St. Amand, about 869);[334] a sacramentary from Tours dating from the second half of the ninth century (Paris, B. N., new acq. lat. 1589); and a sacramentary, probably from Amiens, going back to the ninth or tenth century (Paris, B. N., lat. 9432).[335] In these three documents, copyists have transcribed in the margin of each Mass formulary the incipits of the chants of the gradual. The insertion of indications for the readings corresponding to each Mass formulary in the margins of sacramentaries was not a practical solution because of the length of the pericopes, whereas the simple mention of the incipit of the chants was sufficient to bring to memory the piece to be sung.

The primitive forms of missals with juxtaposed parts (the parts follow one another) had a certain success during the High Middle Ages and even later in the eleventh and twelfth centuries, a time of full

331. For the manuscripts, see the nearly exhaustive list of Gamber, *CLLA*, 527–547, as well as the many fragments published by this author.

332. Concerning the medieval terminology of the missal and the ambiguity that occurs in the references indubitably designating sacramentaries, see I, the section on sacramentaries, in this part. Concerning the expression "plenary missal," see Vogel, *Introduction*, 133, n. 287.

333. Ibid., 134, n. 288.

334. See Deshusses, "Chronologie des sacramentaires."

335. Concerning these two manuscripts, see Huglo, *Livres de chant*, 121.

development for missals in which the different parts are combined. In a first phase, only the sacramentary and the Mass antiphonal are juxtaposed, as in Paris, B. N., lat. 2291; fols. 9–15 (Sacramentary of St. Amand, about 875–876)[336]—in this document, the orations of votive Masses (fols. 177v–188v) are accompanied by the readings from the epistles and Gospels. The same is true of the sacramentary-gradual of Corbie (Paris, B. N., lat. 12050; shortly after 853), where the gradual table occupies folios 3–16v.[337] In a later phase, in the eleventh and twelfth centuries, the Mass lectionary would be added to the sacramentary-gradual, thus forming a true missal with juxtaposed parts. The codex Gressly in Basel, an Alsatian missal from the end of the eleventh century, is a good sample of this: the antiphonal is on folios 1–51, the sacramentary on folios 56–150, and the lectionary on folios 150v–353v, the whole thing being followed by a series of *ordines* written on folios 354v–380v.[338] This type of missal would not long survive the arrival of the liturgical books called the "second generation" (missal in which parts are consolidated, pontifical, breviary, and so on). Typological evolution, together with the need to produce a book finally unified, favored the creation of a missal in which each piece is set in its right place, feast by feast.

Lastly, let us recall the essential role the *libelli missarum* played in the internal and external development of the missal.[339] Before reaching a complete and definitive form, the missal also went also through preliminary stages which can be considered embryonic forms: these are the *libelli missarum*. Composed in general of four or five fascicles, they contain all the texts of one or several feasts. The structure of the formularies is the following: the orations (drawn from the sacramentary); the readings (normally found in the lectionary and the evangeliary); and the incipits of the sung pieces (contained in the Mass antiphonal), sometimes with musical notation. As all the elements

336. Deshusses, "Chronologie des sacramentaires."

337. See Hesbert, *AMS*, XXIff.

338. The study of this manuscript, accompanied by its critical edition, is due to be published in the near future in the series Spicilegium friburgense by A. Hänggi and G. Ladner; see E. Palazzo, "L'illustration du codex Gressly: Missel bâlois du XIᵉ siècle," *Histoire de l'art* 11 (1990) 15–22.

339. See Palazzo, "Rôle des *libelli*," especially 24–27. See also the remarks of N. K. Rasmussen, "Célébration épiscopale et célébration presbytérale: un essai de typologie," *Segni e riti nella Chiesa altomedievale occidentale, 11–17 aprile 1985*, 2 vols, Settimane di studio del Centro italiano di studi sull'alto medioevo 33 (Spoleto, 1987) 2:581–607.

necessary to the eucharistic celebration were gathered into one book, the priest was able from then on to celebrate by himself if he so desired. The *libelli missarum*, coming especially from monasteries, sometimes served for quite specific liturgical actions, like private Masses;[340] they also could have been the means of diffusing a new Mass.[341] In monasteries, the profusion of votive Masses, often private, is explained principally by a liturgical use which favored personal devotion over the collective and ecclesial celebration.[342] Aided by a modest *libellus missarum*, the priest-monk said his Mass all by himself either for his own salvation or for that of sinners, whether alive or dead, or for the poor or for the gift of rain or for the deceased brethren.[343] Thanks to these *libelli* used for private Masses one glimpses a whole phase in the evolution of the status of both the monastic and monastic spirituality in medieval society.

340. See A. Häussling, *Mönchskonvent und Eucharistiefeier,* LQF 58 (1973); N. K. Rasmussen and E. Palazzo, "Messes privées, livre liturgique et architecture: A propos du ms. Paris, Arsenal 610, et de l'église abbatiale de Reichenau-Mittelzell," *Revue des Sciences philosophiques et théologiques* 72 (1988) 77–87.

341. This latter case is attested by the first fascicle of Rouen, B. M., ms. A 566 (275), which contains votive Masses for the Virgin and All Saints (ninth century). In a later phase, this *libellus* was used in the eleventh century for the composition of a more complete missal whose contents were exactly those of the Carolingian document; see E. Palazzo, "Un *libellus missae* du *scriptorium* de Saint-Amand pour Saint-Denis: Son intérêt pour la typologie des manuscrits liturgiques," *Revue bénédictine* 99 (1989) 286–292.

342. See C. Vogel, "Deux conséquences de l'eschatologie grégorienne, la multiplication des messes privées et des moines-prêtres," *Grégoire le Grand,* 267–273.

343. C. Vogel, "Une mutation cultuelle inexpliquée, le passage de l'Eucharistie communautaire à la messe privée," *Revue des Sciences religieuses* 54 (1980) 231–250; A. Angenendt, "*Missa specialis:* Zugleich ein Beitrag zur Entstehung der Privatmessen," *Frühmittelalterliche Studien* 17 (1982) 153–221.

Part Three

The Books of the Office

I. History and Function of the Office in the West

1. RECALLING SOME HISTORICAL FACTS

The history of the Office, today more often called the *Liturgy of the Hours*, has for a long time awakened the researchers' interest. Recently, excellent surveys have been published; as a consequence, I shall limit myself here to recalling the main phases of the development of the Prayer of the Hours in the West, without neglecting the important part the East took in the elaboration of this liturgy. I shall try to introduce readers to the general structure of the Divine Office by highlighting the different ritual acts that compose it (psalmody, chant, prayer, reading, and so on) but without dealing with the particularities proper to either the many Western traditions (Iberian, Ambrosian, and so on) or the Eastern traditions during the Middle Ages. Before approaching the history of the different books of the Office, we shall present some of the processes at work in the celebration of the Hours and give precise definitions of the principal terms belonging to the vocabulary in use. As in the other parts of this manual, the Roman rite will receive most of the attention because, very early, its usages in the Office came to dominate almost every region in the West.[1]

Origins of the Prayer of the Hours

Unceasing prayer on a daily basis, such is the spiritual goal of the *Liturgy of the Hours*, a goal suggested by the New Testament. The New

---

1. Concerning the reasons for this choice, see the Introduction. For an overall history of the Office, one must consult above all Taft, *Liturgy of the Hours*. This book is a rich mine because of its historical and scientific approach; it treats of all rites, Western and Eastern. See also *CP*, 4:153–275; the bibliography given by R. Pfaff, *Medieval Latin Liturgy*, section D; along with the contribution of Davril, incorporating the notes he took at conferences on the *Liturgy of the Hours*, during sessions in Limon (July 1985), *Le lien* 88 and 89, 60 pages; and Hughes, *Mass and Office*.

Testament texts concerning prayer are numerous and can be classified under the following categories: (1) references to Jesus (and others) being at prayer, (2) exhortations or invitations to prayer, (3) instructions on the manner of praying, (4) texts of hymns and prayers.[2] From its beginnings, Christian prayer inherited customs from ancient Judaism, such as regular prayer, strongly domestic in character and said at least twice a day at fixed hours in the morning and evening.[3] This contribution of Judaism is only one factor in the origin of the *Liturgy of the Hours*, which is also rooted in the message of Christ, transmitted to us in the New Testament. The hymn of praise to the Father and Christ must be renewed day after day morning and evening, and even during the night. Going back to the first century, the *Didache*, Antiochene[4] in origin, exhorts Christians to pray three times a day, which suggests already a regular and daily schedule of prayer. Moreover, this text attests to the use of the Our Father (ch. 8.1-3).

For the first three centuries, the documents do not allow us to ascertain whether the Prayer of the Hours was structured according to one single scheme and timetable.[5] However, a certain number of testimonies coming from prestigious authors demonstrate the progressive stabilization of the various elements of the Divine Office. In Egypt, in the beginning of the third century, Clement of Alexandria (c.150–c.215) insists on the fixed times of the day devoted to prayer: at the third, sixth, and ninth hours; it is also from him that for the first time, we hear of turning to the east when praying.[6] In the first half of the third century, Origen (c.185–c.254) repeats Clement and introduces the practice of regularly saying certain psalms for a particular Hour, for instance, Psalm 140 for the evening prayer. Tertullian (c.160–c.225) is the first to describe the pattern of daily prayer, a pattern which will become the rule by the end of the fourth century.[7] In the middle of the third century, St. Cyprian (d. 258), bishop of Carth-

2. See Taft, *Liturgy of the Hours*, 4–5; *CP*, 4:157–162.

3. On the Jewish foundation of the Christian Liturgy of the Hours, see Taft, *Liturgy of the Hours*, 5–11; A.-G. Martimort, "L'histoire de l'office et son interprétation," *Seminarium* 1 (1972) 65–85, and chiefly 67–69.

4. J.-P. Audet, *La Didachè: Instruction des apôtres* (Paris, 1958) 219; W. Rordorf and A. Tuilier, eds., *La doctrine des douze apôtres (Didachè)* SC 248 (1978) 172–175.

5. Taft, *Liturgy of the Hours*, 13–29; *CP*, 4:162–170. See also A. Hamman, *La prière*, vol. 2: *Les trois premiers siècles* (Paris, 1963).

6. Taft, *Liturgy of the Hours*, 14–16.

7. Chapter 25 of his treatise *On Prayer*, written in 198 and 204; see Taft, ibid., 16–18.

age, confirms for the church of North Africa Tertullian's testimony on the structure of prayer.[8] Finally, the *Apostolic Tradition*,[9] the liturgical document (which is also a collection of canons) of greatest importance from the third century and one of the earliest, says in chapter 35, which concerns morning prayer at home, "The faithful, as soon as they have awakened and gotten up, and before they turn to their work, shall pray to God and then hurry to their work."

The documentation from the third century shows that what would become the complete series of the Hours in the fourth century was on its way; this series will then be: when rising, at the third, sixth, and ninth hours, in the evening, and during the night. The contents of these prayers were probably centered on sacred Scripture, catechesis, and hymns. It is also at this period that the deep meaning of daily prayer was underlined, notably the remembrance of the life and death of Jesus, symbolized by the rising and setting of the sun. The evening lamp, which already had an eschatological connotation, was Christ, the light of the world. However, let us remember that this was not yet liturgy properly so called but, more simply, regular hours at which Christians were exhorted to pray, either collectively or in private.

Origins of the Office in the West (Fourth to Sixth Centuries)

From the fourth century on, but especially in the fifth, the peace of the Church and the constant spread of Christianity among various peoples, favored the development of a more intense liturgical life with carefully organized prayer meetings, that is, the Office. In the West, two distinct forms of prayer in common arose: that of the urban Christian community (cathedral or parish Office) and that of the monastic community (monastic Office).[10]

Due to a lack of any official liturgical document, the cathedral Office is known to us only through the testimonies the Church Fathers have left us in their homilies, hagiographic stories, and also the decisions

8. P. Salmon, "Les origines de la prière des Heures d'après le témoignage de Tertullien et de saint Cyprien," *Mélanges offerts à Mademoiselle Christine Mohrmann* (Utrecht, 1963) 202–210.

9. Concerning the date and the disputed character of this document, see especially M. Metzger, "Nouvelles perspectives pour la prétendue Tradition apostolique," *Ecclesia Orans* 5 (1988) 241–259; B. Botte, *La Tradition apostolique de saint Hippolyte: Essai de reconstitution*, LQF 39 (Münster, 1963).

10. Taft, *Liturgy of the Hours*, 93–213, has a complete panorama; *CP*, 4:170–175, 233–255.

made by councils, especially at the time of Caesarius, Archbishop of Arles (502–542), in the beginning of the sixth century. The Office essentially comprised a morning praise and an evening chant which develop the symbolism of, respectively, the rising sun and, in the evening, the light of the world, Christ. Already, the choice of psalms was determined by the hour of day; and the Office comprised prayers, hymns, responsories, and so on, according to a plan more and more clearly defined. Sunday vigils, featuring psalmody—of a particular amplitude at Easter—were added to the cathedral Office.

The monastic Office is better known because of the many traditions that arose in the period extending from the fourth to sixth centuries and through several fixed schemes for daily prayer, the *cursus,* resulting from the need and obligation for the monk to practice the *laus continua* ["continual praise"].

In the numerous monastic *cursus* which were established at this time in the West and the East, are several common points on the manner of celebrating the Office: the structure of the Hours, which acquires a quasi-definitive form (see pp. 124–125); the development of psalmody; the increasing use of antiphons, invitatory or responsorial psalms, various sorts of readings, hymns. Most monastic *cursus* had their origin in the practical application of the rules laid down by the reformers of monastic life, without the Church officially stepping in to mandate this type of celebration. In the first place, let us cite the Rule of St. Benedict (first half of the sixth century) whose role is most important for the development of the Office, Roman as well as monastic, in the West. But we must also mention the Rule of St. Augustine (end of the fourth century); the Gallican *cursus,* with the Rules of Aurelian of Arles and the monastery of Lerins (fifth century); the Rule of the Master (sixth century), Italian in origin, whose chapters 33 to 43 are devoted to the Office; the Rule of St. Columban (about 615), whose chapter 7 is at the source of the Irish monastic *cursus;* and lastly the Iberian tradition, resting mainly on the Rule for Monks by Isidore of Seville (between 590 and 600) and the rules written by St. Fructuosus of Braga (d. about 665).[11]

11. On all these rules and what they contain that is relevant to the history of the Office in the West and the East, see Taft, *Liturgy of the Hours,* 93–140; see also O. Heiming, "Zum monastischen Offizium von Kassianus bis Kolumbanus," *Archiv für Liturgiewissenschaft* 7 (1961) 89–156; A. De Vogüe, "Le sens de l'office divin d'après la Règle de saint Benoît" *Revue d'Ascétique et de Mystique* 42–43 (1966–1967), among other writings by this author.

The Roman Office in the Middle Ages (Sixth to Fifteenth Centuries)

Prepared by the different monastic traditions enumerated above, the Roman Office acquired, from the sixth century on, the form it kept until the twentieth century, a form based on two *cursus* having a monastic structure: the Roman Office and the Benedictine Office. Before St. Benedict, Rome possessed, perhaps as early as the fourth century, a monastic *cursus* (coexisting with the cathedral Office), that of the monasteries which served the great urban basilicas and the sanctuaries of the martyrs.[12] In the sixth century, Benedict utilized the Roman monastic Office to establish the *cursus* found in his Rule. Synthesizing what was already in use in Rome on the one hand and his own views concerning the Office on the other, Benedict was the creator of the Benedictine Office as it is known to us from documents of the eighth and ninth centuries. Today, all authors agree that the Benedictine Office derives from the Roman monastic Office, even though in the course of the centuries and especially during the High Middle Ages, the elements of the Prayer of the Hours, as defined by Benedict, have enriched and even "corrected" the structure of the Roman monastic office, thus substantially lightening the liturgical scheme. However, in Rome itself, the Benedictine Office never supplanted the local usage, whereas it met with enormous success in most Western monasteries.[13]

From the time of Benedict to the end of the Middle Ages, and even until Pius X and then Vatican II, the structure of the Roman Office did not undergo any fundamental changes, but only partial modifications in the allotment of psalms, the addition of proper offices to the Sanctoral at the expense of the Temporal, the rise and then multiplication of votive offices, the Office of the Dead, and the office of the chapter after Prime.[14] In the eighth century, the first efforts of the Carolingian rulers, particularly Pepin the Short, and certain dignitaries of the Church, favored the establishment of the Roman *cursus* beyond the Alps; this resulted in the coexistence of two parallel *cursus*, the Roman and the Benedictine. Twice, at the time of Chrodegang, bishop of Metz (742–766), who was a great admirer of the Roman liturgy,[15] then at

12. See Taft, *Liturgy of the Hours*, 131–134; *CP*, 4:249–250.

13. Taft, ibid., 134–140.

14. *CP*, 4:251; Salmon, *Office divin*; V. Raffia. "L'officio divino del tempi dei carolingi e il Breviario di Innocenzo III confrontati con la liturgia delle ore di Paolo VI," *Ephemerides liturgicae* 85 (1971) 206–259.

15. See Part 2, I, the section on sacramentaries.

the Council of Aachen in 816–817, which ratified several of the initiatives of Pepin the Short and Charlemagne, the Roman Office benefited from the reform of the clergy—under the form of the institution of Canons—so that it easily gained full acceptance in the cathedral chapters. Except for the Iberian peninsula, the Roman rite was solidly implanted in the West from the Carolingian period on. But only at the end of the eleventh century, under the pontificate of Gregory VII (1073–1085), would it be imposed by the Roman Curia.

During the whole of the Middle Ages, both *cursus* (Roman and Benedictine) were in use, often with adaptations due to the insertion of new liturgical compositions, sung pieces in particular; there were also instances of a mixed *cursus* of the Roman and Benedictine Offices. Indeed, the important differences between the two *cursus* occasionally obliged monks to bring the two into agreement. One of the important differences concerns the number of responsories at the night office (twelve in the Benedictine Office, nine in the Roman) which communities had to increase or diminish as the case might be, thus setting down their own lists of responsories; today, these lists are most useful in determining what the liturgical usages were.

In the second half of the Middle Ages, the history of the Office is characterized by a growing inflation; this caused uneasiness in certain communities where it was felt that the length of each hour had become excessive in relation to the other demands of the monks' lives. In addition, the reform of the Roman liturgy by the Curia in the thirteenth century contributed to establish the Roman Office as the model for the whole Church through the composition of new books (the breviary in particular).[16] Only in the second half of the thirteenth century was the Office of the Roman Curia—revised by the Master General of the Franciscan order, Haymo of Faversham (d. 1244)—to really take over, thanks to the action of the Friars Minor, who had adopted it for their order.[17] Afterward, it was not before the fifteenth century and the Reformation that many successive rearrangements took place in the Roman breviary, which had become the office book par excellence.

Finally, let us recall that one of the striking facts in the history of the Office in the Middle Ages is the progressive development, starting in the middle of the eighth century, of the private recitation of the

16. See Salmon, *Office divin*, 86–88 and especially 124–151.
17. Ibid., 152–170; G. Abate, "Il primitivo breviario francescano (1224–1227)," *Miscellanea francescana* 60 (1960) 47–240; the fundamental study of Van Dijk and Walker, *Origins*.

Office. In the Rule of Benedict (ch. 50) and that of Chrodegang (ch. 4), it is prescribed that anyone not present in church for the celebration of the Hours in common, must recite them in private. This practice became common among the clergy about the tenth century and became even more prevalent in the thirteenth century with the Mendicant Orders adopting it because of their pastoral activities, which were often itinerant.

The innumerable books of Hours in the fifteenth century, either modestly decorated or richly illustrated, demonstrate a definite enthusiasm on the part of the wealthier classes for the Office, recited privately or perhaps more often in a collective setting such as confraternities; the accent was placed particularly on the offices of the Virgin and the dead as well as on the penitential psalms. The brilliance of the colors and the freshness of the pages which characterize the most beautiful examples that have endured to our time reveal that the liturgical book had become at the dawn of modern times and in the hands of lay people an object denoting social prestige.[18]

2. RITES, SPIRITUALITY, AND STRUCTURE OF THE OFFICE

Like the Eucharist, the Liturgy of the Hours comprises several ritual acts belonging to the categories of prayer, singing, and reading. One of the original traits of the Divine Office is the connection, often closer than that of the eucharistic celebration, between the different parts of the rite. Hence the necessity of a good synchronization between the officiants, more necessary than elsewhere if the ritual performance is to be worthily conducted. A certain number of persons play their own clearly defined roles along with an assembly, composed of monastics or canons, whose part is as essential as those entrusted to individuals. The monastic customaries and ordinaries supply the richest documentation on the way the Office was conducted in the Middle Ages, whether in monasteries or cathedrals.

Depending on the time of day, the celebration of the Office is more or less elaborate and its contents more or less substantial. This variability from one Hour to the other explains why it is difficult to describe in too detailed a fashion the general structure of the Office, even without taking into account the fact that most orders and monastic

---

18. See Leroquais, *Livres d'Heures*; C. Rabel, "Le ore del Laico," *Storia* 5/42 (1990) 35–40; J. M. Plotzek, *Andachtsbücher des Mittelalters aus Privatbesitz* (Cologne, 1987); R. S. Wieck, et al., *The Book of Hours in Medieval Art and Life* (London, 1988).

communities had their own particular usages. Finally, each Hour is imbued with its specific spiritual meaning so that the choice of pieces and the way of rendering them vary from Hour to Hour.

What follows is simply a presentation of the principal ritual characteristics of the Office (the invariable elements), its actors, its structure (Roman and Benedictine), and lastly the essential aspects of the spirituality of the Hours.[19]

The Rites and Officiants

The synaxis (the gathered assembly) is presided over by the bishop (or a canon) in the cathedral Office and by the abbot or abbess in the monastic Office. The presider's part is principally the recitation of the prayers and the reading of the Gospel, when this is called for. In certain circumstances, as in the Office of the chapter after Prime, the abbot addresses matters concerning the life of the monastery, for example, the assignment of penances for faults (culpae) committed by the monks. As a rule, any monk in the community can be the reader at the Office. Then there is the whole of the community, generally divided into two choirs for the requirements of the psalmody, under the guidance of one or two soloists.

In all liturgical families, the Liturgy of the Hours is prayer, and principally prayer with the psalms, or psalmody (from the Latin psalmus).[20] Already in the ancient monastic rules, psalmody plays a preeminent role in the monk's prayer.[21] In the Middle Ages, the recitation of psalms held an essential place in the Office and took on more and more complex forms.[22] By adopting the principle of lectio continua

19. For a more thorough documentation on all these topics, see Taft, Liturgy of the Hours; CP, 4; Salmon, Office divin.

20. See Taft, Liturgy of the Hours; CP, 4:190–206; A.-G. Martimort, Mirabile laudis canticum, mélanges liturgiques, études historiques, la reforme conciliaire, portraits de liturgistes, Bibliotheca "Ephemerides liturgicae," subsidia 60 (Rome, 1991) 15–29 ("La prière des psaumes dans la liturgie des Heures") and 75–97 ("Fonction de la psalmodie dans la liturgie de la Parole").

21. See the unpublished thesis of Th. Elich, Le contexte oral de la liturgie médiévale et le rôle du texte écrit, 3 vols. (Paris: Paris IV–Sorbonne and Institut catholique de Paris, 1988) 145–234; A. De Vogüe, "Psalmodier n'est pas prier," Ecclesia Orans 6 (1989) 7–32, where the author develops the idea, held in antiquity, that psalmody was rather a preparation to prayer, the latter taking place in the silent period following each psalm.

22. See J. Dyer, "Monastic Psalmody of the Middle Ages," Revue bénédictine 99 (1989) 41–74.

prescribed in Benedict's Rule or by choosing psalms according to the available time, one ends up with several forms of psalmody. Here are the principal ones: direct psalmody in which one or several soloists sing the psalm *in directum* [straight through, without antiphons or refrains] on one melody and without interruption; responsorial psalmody, in which one or several soloists execute the psalm verses, but at the end of each verse, the community takes up a brief responsory, a sort of refrain ranging from the simple word "alleluia" to part of a psalm verse or a whole verse;[23] alternating psalmody, in which two choirs alternate the singing of the whole psalm without interruption, verse by verse or strophe by strophe. The chanting of the psalms at the Office is enriched by antiphons (a kind of refrain generally sung at the beginning and end of the psalm, or even between strophes; hymns; tropes, always executed by the soloist or soloists and the choir.[24]

The readings at the Office (also called lessons, from *lectiones*) are of three kinds: biblical, patristic, and hagiographic.[25] The biblical reading (Old and New Testaments) is the oldest and most important; as a general rule, the proclamation of the Gospel is the abbot's or abbess's privilege. The number and choice of readings vary from one tradition to the next and according to the Hours. The reading of the Church Fathers (homilies, sermons) and the hagiographic writings (legends about the saints, passions of the martyrs) also appeared very early in the history of the Office, in Africa and the East, and greatly developed during the Middle Ages. Like the sung pieces, the readings at each Office can be divided into several chapters, passages (lessons) of variable length and number, according to the Hours.[26]

Finally, the celebration of the Hours, like that of the Mass, makes room for the recitation of prayers of intercession and thanksgiving. In

23. This mode of psalmody became the most frequent throughout the Latin Church as early as the sixth century.

24. See Huglo, *Livres de chant*, 19–29, and also the definitions given below.

25. On the history of the readings during the Office, see *CP*, 4:220–227; Martimort, *Lectures liturgiques*, 69–72; P.-M. Gy, "La Bible dans la liturgie au Moyen Age," *Le Moyen Age et la Bible*, ed. P. Riché and G. Lorichon (Paris, 1984) 537–552, especially 543–552; and more generally, G. Lorichon, "Gli usi della Bibbia," *Lo spazio letterario del Medioevo*, vol 1: *Il Medioevo latino*, pt. 1: *La produzione del testo* (Rome, 1993) 523–562.

26. A recent study by Davril has demonstrated that several factors contributed to the variability and length of the Office lessons in the Middle Ages (the churches, the hierarchy of feasts, and so on), "La longueur des leçons dans l'office nocturne: Etude comparative," *Rituels: Mélanges offerts au P. Gy, OP* (Paris, 1990) 183–197.

the earliest monastic rules, the custom of concluding certain Offices with prayers of intercession (especially Lauds and Vespers) is well attested.[27] In most traditions, it became customary to introduce the recitation of the *Pater* (Our Father) at least three times a day at the beginning or end of the celebration. Such recitation could be accompanied by that of an oration reserved to priests, a collect; this was said also, without the Our Father, at certain Hours, always as a conclusion to the Office. The collect said at Mass is also often used as the prayer said by the presider at the Office. In rare occasions, a blessing was foreseen, as Benedict's Rule prescribes at the end of Compline.

Structure and Spirituality of the Hours

For a long time, liturgists have been aware of the specificity of each Hour, of its own character, of its spirituality, and they have established a hierarchy of the Hours.[28] The more or less substantial contents of each office is in large part explained by this hierarchy which was strongly affirmed during the Middle Ages.

All traditions begin the first Hour with an introduction, the invitatory, a sort of solemn exhortation to divine praise. This office is made up of several psalms with antiphons, variable from one rite to another and according to the liturgical time.[29] The morning and evening praises, corresponding to the natural rhythms of daily life, gave rise to the offices of Lauds (*officium matutinale* ["morning office"]) and Vespers.[30] Christians begin and end the day by praising God. The choice of readings (if there are any) and in particular of psalms is determined by the themes of setting and rising, references to the death and resurrection of Christ.[31]

Between Lauds and Vespers, the three intermediary Hours of Terce, Sext, and None[32] take place. Punctuating the monastic day by prayer, these three Hours alternate with the demands of work and community life, as well as the eucharistic celebration. They are the deepest expression of the unceasing prayer of Christians; their structure, the same for the three Hours, remained unchanged during the Middle

27. See *CP*, 4:227–229.

28. See Taft, *Liturgy of the Hours*, 141–163.

29. J. Pascher, "Das *Invitatorium*," *Liturgisches Jahrbuch* 10 (1960) 149–158.

30. V. Raffia, "Lodi e Vespro, cardine della preghiera oraria ecclesiale," *Rivista liturgica* 55 (1968) 488–511.

31. See *CP*, 4:258–266.

32. Ibid., 270–271.

Ages. Compline is the last office of the day, preceding the night rest.[33] Its elements, notably its penitential aspect, are particularly chosen because of the approaching night and the spiritual preparation it requires.

The night office comprises Vigils (first office of the day to come and not the last of the preceding day), whose composition varies, according to the day, from one nocturn to three (on Sunday). The essential goal of Vigils is the fostering of watchfulness and the stimulation of the expectation of the Lord, who will come back at daybreak.[34] The Easter Vigil, then secondarily various prayer meetings at night are probably at the root of the progressive evolution of the night office (hence its name of Vigils, sometimes called Matins), first for the big feasts of the Temporal and later on for the celebrations of certain feasts of saints, especially at their burial places.[35] The night office invariably opens with a verse repeated three times and a hymn; the length of each nocturn is variable, and the third on Sunday is the most developed.

The last Hour to be established in the *cursus,* Prime (office of the first hour of day) probably goes back to the fifth century and was perhaps instituted by John Cassian (c.360–435). It is celebrated in the choir as are the other Hours, but it is very short and has long been perceived as duplicating the morning office. In the eighth century (as attested by the Rule of Chrodegang destined for the cathedral of Metz) and perhaps earlier, it was followed by a sort of "supplement," the office in chapter.[36] The office of Prime in chapter is seen as half-liturgical, half-administrative since it was during this assembly that matters concerning the life of the monastery were addressed.[37] The office of Prime in chapter was not eliminated from the Roman Office until Vatican II.[38]

33. Ibid., 271–272.

34. Ibid., 266–270.

35. On the disputed origins—no doubt multiform—of Vigils, as well as their connections with Lauds and Prime, see Taft, *Liturgy of the Hours,* 191–213.

36. See J. Froger, *Les origines de prime,* Bibliotheca Ephemerides liturgicae 19 (Rome, 1946). See also the update on the state of these questions and the corrections proposed by Taft, *Liturgy of the Hours,* 207–208.

37. See M. Huglo, "L'office de prime au chapitre," *L'Eglise et la mémoire des morts dans la France médiévale, communications présentées à la table ronde du CNRS, le 14 juin 1982,* ed. J.-L. Lemaître, Etudes augustiniennes (Paris, 1986) 11–18. On the books used for Prime, see section V of this part.

38. See *CP,* 4:270.

Simplified Structure of the Content of the Hours of the Roman Monastic Office (Benedictine Form) (after Taft, Liturgy of the Hours, *pp. 134–138)*

VIGILS:
   Opening verse, said three times
   Psalms 3 and 94
   Hymn
   —First nocturn:
      6 psalms with refrain
      Versicle
      Blessing by the abbot or abbess
      3 lessons and responsories in winter; 1 in summer; 4 on Sundays
   —Second nocturn:
      6 psalms with alleluia
      Brief biblical reading to be recited by heart
      Versicle
      Litany
   —Third nocturn (on Sunday):
      3 canticles with alleluia
      Versicle
      Blessing by the abbot
      4 lessons (New Testament) and responsories
      Te Deum
      Gospel
      Te decet laus ["it is fitting to praise you"]
      Blessing

LAUDS:
   Psalm 66
   Psalm 50 with refrain
   2 variable psalms
   Canticle
   Psalms 146 to 150
   Reading from the epistles (Revelation on Sunday)
   Responsory
   Hymn
   Versicle
   Canticle from the Gospel
   Litany
   Our Father

Intermediate Hours (Prime, Terce, Sext, and None):
  Opening verse
  Hymn
  3 variable psalms, with or without refrain
  Reading (brief lesson)
  Versicle
  Litany
  Dismissal (prayer)

Vespers:
  Opening verse
  4 variable psalms
  Reading
  Responsory
  Hymn
  Versicle
  Canticle from the Gospel
  Litany
  Our Father
  Dismissal

Compline:
  Opening verse
  Psalms 4, 90, and 133, without refrain
  Hymn
  Reading (brief lesson)
  Versicle
  Litany
  Blessing
  Dismissal

Definitions of the Principal Elements of the Office
  —*Antiphon:* from the Latin *antiphona* (abbreviated *Ant.* or *A.* in the manuscripts) designates a chanted piece, brief as a rule. Its function is to frame the singing of each psalm and to indicate what psalm tone is to be used. Originally, it was composed of one or two Scripture verses, in general drawn from the psalm it frames; in this case, it is called a psalmic antiphon. Starting with the fifth century, longer, non-biblical antiphons were created; some of them were independent pieces, for instance, antiphons for processions, Marian antiphons, and so on.

The function of the antiphon is musical, lyrical, and spiritual since it highlights the meaning of the psalm. On the liturgical plane, by connecting the psalms one with the other, it insures the cohesion of an office in the same way it unites the community that sings it through antiphonal psalmody.

—*Psalms:* see the next section.

—*Responsory:* from the Latin *responsorium* (generally abbreviated ℟ in manuscripts), designates what follows a reading whether at Mass or during the Office. Originally, the responsory derived from the psalmody since it was a psalm reduced to one or two verses, and it is characterized by the repetition of a limited number of psalm verses. Later on, when the reading was excerpted from other books of the Old Testament, the responsory also was taken from the same text. In the Middle Ages, a given liturgical time, a given feast, had a common treasury of responsories from which each church drew to organize its own series. The study of responsories is one of the means of determining the liturgical use of a manuscript.

—*Versicle:* from the Latin *versus* (abbreviated ℣ in the manuscripts), designates a short sentence drawn from the Psalms or other parts of Scripture. There are versicles of introduction ("O God, come to my aid"), of conclusion ("Let us bless the Lord"), of transition, leading from the recitation of psalms to listening to the word of God or else from the reading to the oration.

—*Hymn:* from the Latin *hymnus,* designates lyrical chant in metric or rhythmic verses meant to enrich the spiritual power of the Office. It expresses in poetical terms the mystery of the day while being at the same time a solemn profession of faith. It is placed either in the beginning of the office or after the reading; in the latter case, it fosters reflection on God's word. Some hymns were composed by great figures of Latin Christianity, such as St. Hilary of Poitiers and St. Ambrose. They were collected into hymnals to facilitate their diffusion.

—*Lesson:* from the Latin *lectio,* designates any reading done during the Office. A brief reading from Scripture is called *capitulum* ["chapter"] in Latin (see Martimort, *Lectures liturgiques,* 74–76). A reading from the Fathers of the Church is called a *homily* or *sermon* (gathered in the homiliary), while the hagiographic readings are termed *legends* or *passions* (gathered in the legendaries or passionals). The number and selection of lessons characterize the liturgical usages of a given tradition (monastic, Roman, and so on), a given Church, even a given diocese.

—*Biblical canticle:* designates a rhythmed poem coming in general from books of the Old Testament other than the Psalter. Some are adapted from Gospel passages, for example, Luke 1:46-55. The number and distribution of the biblical canticles are characteristic of the different liturgical traditions.

—*Trope:* see Part 2, II, 6, the section dealing with the chant books used at Mass.

—*Collect, blessing,* and *litany:* see Part 2, I, the section on sacramentaries.

II. Chant at the Office

1. THE PSALTER

The oldest liturgical book is the Psalter, which was probably composed between the tenth and third centuries B.C.E. This collection of lyrical poems, numbering 150,[39] was written in Hebrew and later on translated into Latin from the Greek version of the Septuagint. Particularly suitable for spiritual meditation, this biblical book was used very early in the liturgy, separated from the rest of the Bible and entrusted to the cantor directing the monks' choir.[40] The use of the Psalter at the Office was mandated early on in the different rules, notably Benedict's.[41] The ancient monastic rules allow us to discern the multiple functions of the Psalter, used notably to teach reading.[42] In the beginning, each *cursus* of the Liturgy of the Hours had its own particular distribution of the psalms.[43] Clearly formulated for the first time in Benedict's Rule but in all likelihood already in use in the Roman Office, the *lectio continua* of the Psalter dominated the Office in the Middle Ages according to two weekly arrangements: the Roman *cursus* and the Benedictine *cursus*.[44] The principal difference between

39. On the problem of numbering the psalms, see *Le psautier oecuménique,* a liturgical text (Paris, 1987) 8.

40. On the history of the psalms and the psalter in general, see *CP,* 4:190–203 (with a bibliography); Gy, "Bible dans la liturgie," 537–552, especially 544–550; Leroquais, *Psautiers;* and *Liturgica Vaticana,* 52–54.

41. See Elich, *Contexte oral;* N. Lohfink, "Psalmengebet und Psalterredaktion," *Archiv für Liturgiewissenschaft* 34 (1992) 1–22.

42. See P. Riché, "Le psautier, livre de lecture élémentaire d'après les vies des saints mérovingiens," *Etudes mérovingiennes: Actes des Journées de Poitiers, 1er–3 mai 1952* (Paris, 1953) 253–256.

43. See Taft, *Liturgy of the Hours,* 94–96.

44. Tables of the distribution of psalms in the Roman and Benedictine Offices can be found in Gy, "Bible dans la liturgie," 546–559, and Taft, *Liturgy of the Hours,* 136–137.

the two *cursus* is the number of responsories at Vigils on feast days, nine for the Roman, twelve for the Benedictine.

The Manuscripts

The psalters which have been preserved present a great variety enabling us to reconstruct the history of this liturgical book. In the fifth and sixth centuries, and indeed throughout the Middle Ages, the psalter used at the Office never stopped evolving and being perfected.[45] At that time, some writers, like Jerome (c.347–420) and Cassiodorus (490–c.585), set forth rules for the intelligible reading of the sacred texts, including the Psalter. Most important among these rules was the method of *cola et commata* ["colons and commas"], based on the distinctions to be made within one sentence, and strongly commended by Cassiodorus for a sound recitation of the Psalter. This system consists in dots placed at different heights between words and sentences.[46] The oldest sources of the liturgical psalter that have come down to us show that the text was copied *per cola et commata*.[47] Since the psalms are the pieces around which the other elements of the Office are organized, it was natural for the Psalter, as a book, to become the nucleus to which other collections were attached. This procedure quickly gave rise to several types of composite psalters. Furthermore, from the High Middle Ages on, the biblical Psalter and the liturgical psalter must be distinguished. Whereas the former keeps its biblical structure with its division into five books (pss. 1 to 40, 41 to 71, 72 to 88, 89 to 105, 106 to 150) and does not have any additional items, the liturgical psalter specifies the seven subdivisions corresponding to the days of the week (following either the Roman or monastic arrangement); this is the *psalterium per ferias* or *psalterium feriale*. From the Carolingian period on, other series of pieces came to swell the contents of the liturgical psalter: invitatories, hymns, antiphons, orations, brief lessons, thus establishing a true typology of this book.[48] In the liturgical psalter properly so called, each psalm is assigned to its place in the

---

45. Concerning this evolution, see Leroquais, *Psautiers*, XLIVff.; Salmon, *Office divin*, 46–50.

46. See A.-V. Gilles, "La ponctuation dans les manuscrits liturgiques au Moyen Age," *Grafia e interpunzione del latino nel Medioevo*, International seminar, Rome, 27–29 September 1984 (Rome, 1988) 114–133, especially 116–118.

47. Ibid., 117, and Gamber, *CLLA*, notably nos. 1601, 1603, and 1605, for the oldest sources.

48. See Leroquais, *Psautiers*, LIff., and Gamber, *CLLA*, 576–587.

Office; the book always ends with a series of canticles, which reflect the different traditions, along with the Te Deum, the Gloria Patri, and a litany. Among the main types, let us cite the collectar-psalter, in which each psalm is followed by a collect (called psalmic), and the hymnal-psalter, which besides the psalms contains all the hymns for the entire week. In rare instances, the psalter is combined with the antiphonal (antiphons and responsories).[49] A list—not exhaustive—of the oldest liturgical psalters has been compiled by K. Gamber,[50] featuring among others two manuscripts from northern France. The first one, Paris, B. N., lat. 13159 (for St. Riquier, end of seventh century) contains the Gallican psalter, canticles, Carolingian litanies, psalmic collects.[51] The second, Amiens, B. M., ms. 18 (Corbie, beginning of ninth century) contains the Gallican psalter, canticles, directions for liturgical practice, litanies.[52] The convenience of this composite liturgical book is obvious: during the celebration of the Office, each participant was provided with the basic book for the celebration of the *Liturgy of the Hours,* enlarged by a variable number of pieces (hymns, canticles, litanies, and so on) which he or she could execute or simply follow in the book. This first grouping of different elements of the Office would be completed in the eleventh century with the advent of the breviary. The active participation—sometimes only partial—of the whole assembly greatly contributed to the creation of this type of composite book, whose contents were by definition intended for different categories of users.

In the second half of the Middle Ages, from the twelfth century on, one witnesses an ever-growing specialization of the various types of liturgical psalters.[53] Thus books were compiled which contained all the pieces necessary for the night offices (the nocturnal), for the morning

49. See Huglo, *Livres de chant,* 116–117. To designate the psalter in the early library catalogues and inventories of church treasuries, the people of the Middle Ages used terms enabling historians to recognize the various composite psalters (*psalteriun cum ymnario, psalterium glosatum, duo psalteria in choro cum gradali et ymnario,* and so on ["a psalter with hymnal," "a psalter with glosses," "two psalters for choir with gradual and hymnal"]); see the numerous references in Becker, *Catalogi,* and Bischoff, *Schatzverzeichnisse.*

50. Gamber, *CLLA,* 576–587.

51. See ibid., no. 1619.

52. *La Neustrie: Les pays au nord de la Loire, de Dagobert à Charles le Chauve (VIIᵉ–IXᵉ siècle,* ed. P. Perin and L.-C. Feffer (Rouen, 1985) 267.

53. See Salmon, *Office divin,* 48–49.

Hours (the matutinal), for the day Hours (the diurnal).[54] The ancient catalogues of medieval libraries offer references corresponding to these books (*nocturnalis liber, diurnale, matutinale,* or *liber matutinalis*) as early as the eleventh century.[55] However, these psalter-based books are not the origin of the breviary, which rather evolved from the collectar, as will be seen below.

In the same spirit and in a way parallel to the multiplication of the forms taken by the liturgical psalter and certain books specific to certain Hours, one witnesses during the Middle Ages the appearance of responsorials (*responsoriale*) which are collections of the responsories generally contained in the antiphonals. Among responsories, one can distinguish those intended for the night office and those, shorter, following the readings.[56] There were also vesperals (*vesperale*), containing everything necessary for the celebration of Vespers, in particular those of the big feasts and Sundays, and books of invitatories, that is, collections of invitatories with their different melodies.[57]

Decoration of the Psalter

The history of the illustration of the Psalter during the antiquity and the Middle Ages is probably one of the most beautiful chapters of the history of art in the West.[58] In the East as well as in the West, the illustrated psalters offer full-page paintings, sometimes also historiated or purely decorative initials and marginal illustrations.

The full-page paintings grant a place of honor to the supposed author of the Psalter, David, whose figure is often placed at the beginning of the book, facing the incipit of the text, or inserted in the large initial B of the first psalm (*Beatus vir* ["Happy are those"]).[59] St. Jerome

54. Concerning these different types of books, see Fiala and Irtenkauf, *Liturgische Nomenklatur,* 120; Baroffio, "Manoscritti liturgici," 160–165; J. Dubois and J.-L. Lemaître, *Sources et méthodes de l'hagiographie médiévale* (Paris, 1993) 89–98.

55. See Becker, *Catalogi,* and Bischoff, *Schatzverzeichnisse.* On the principal manuscripts attesting to these books, see Leroquais, *Psautiers.*

56. See Fiala and Irtenkauf, *Liturgische Nomenklatur,* 123; Baroffio, "Manoscritti liturgici," 163.

57. See Baroffio, "Manoscritti liturgici," 163–164. On the manuscript witnesses of responsorials and vesperals, see Leroquais, *Psautiers.*

58. See the recent report, with a bibliography, in *Liturgica Vaticana,* 52–54. See also O. Pacht, *Buchmalerei des Mittelalters* (Munich, 1984) 167ff.

59. See, for instance, the initial on fol. 1v of the Psalter of Corbie, Amiens, B. M., ms. 18 (beginning of ninth century); see *Neustrie,* 266–267. In certain illustrated

is represented in his capacity as translator in the Psalter of Charles the Bald (Paris, B. N., lat. 1152; fol. 4, second half of ninth century).[60]

The great originality of illustration in the Psalter in the Middle Ages resides in the literal translation into images of the psalm texts. In certain cases, the image develops a true exegesis of the psalms.[61] The Psalter of Stuttgart (Würtembergische Landsbibliothek, cod. Bibl. fol. 23), composed at Saint-Germain-des-Prés in the first half of the ninth century,[62] and the Psalter of Utrecht (Universiteitsbibl., cod. 32) originating in Hautvillers (near Reims), also from the first half of the ninth century,[63] are the two best examples of this sort of illustration from the High Middle Ages. Studies, especially those centered on the Psalter of Utrecht, have shown that most scenes had their source in antiquity. In the second half of the Middle Ages, the psalters with glosses would give a fresh impetus to the literal and exegetic illustration of the Psalter, as, for instance, Paris, B. N., lat. 8846 (Canterbury, last quarter of twelfth century, and Catalonia, fourteenth century).[64] In still other initials, scenes from the Old and New Testaments are represented, associating passages from the Psalter with events in the life of Christ.

V. Leroquais has felicitously distinguished five principal systems of illustration of the Psalter during the Middle Ages:[65] (1) illustration of every psalm with, in general, one image per psalm; (2) illustration based of the division of the Psalter into three groups of fifty, with

---

psalters of the High Middle Ages, one finds cycles, with a small number of images, illustrating the life of David.

60. J. Hubert, J. Porcher, W. F. Volbach, *L'Empire carolingien* (Paris, 1968) fig. 136.

61. See the important article of F. Mütherich, "Die verschiedenen Bedeutungsschichten in der Frühmittelalterlichen Psalterillustration," *Frühmitterlalterliche Studien* 6 (1972) 232–244.

62. *Der Stuttgarter Bilderpsalter* (Stuttgart, 1968).

63. See E. T. De Wald, *The Illustrations of the Utrecht Psalters* (Princeton, 1932), and S. Dufrenne, *Les illustrations du psautier d'Utrecht: Problèmes de sources et de l'apport carolingien* (Strasbourg, 1978).

64. On this psalter with glosses, which presents in three columns a threefold version of the text (Hebrew, Roman, and Gallican), and its illustrations, see F. Avril and P. Stirnemann, *Manuscrits enluminés d'origine insulaire (VIIᵉ–XXᵉ siècle)*, Bibliothèque National, CRME (Paris, 1987), no. 76, pp. 45–48, and P. Stirnemann, "Paris, BN, ms. lat. 8846 and the Eadwine Psalter," *The Eadwine Psalter: Text, Image and Monastic Culture of the Twelfth–Century Canterbury*, ed. M. Gibson, T. A. Heslop, and R. W. Pfaff (London, 1992) 186–192.

65. See Leroquais, *Psautiers*, XCff.

only the first psalm of each group being illustrated (pss. 1, 51, and 101); (3) the same principle applied when the Psalter is divided into five books as in the Bible (pss. 1, 41, 72, 89, 106); (4) illustration of the first psalm of each feria, when the psalter is a liturgical one with its seven divisions; (5) illustration combining systems 2 and 4. During the Middle Ages, certain regions of the West developed their own particular iconography. Thus, a few Anglo-Saxon psalters of the High Middle Ages are characterized by a mode of illustration proper to the insular tradition, featuring symbolic images corresponding to the way Irish and English spiritualities of the eighth and ninth centuries perceived the Psalter. The dominant theme is the battle between good and evil, especially the combat between David-Christ and Satan.[66]

Lastly, let us cite psalters that are small, sometimes minuscule in size and were perhaps used as amulets. The majority of these were commissioned by highly placed civil or ecclesiastical personages and attest to practices of private devotion which flourished in the second half of the Middle Ages.[67] The illustration of this kind of psalter was ordinarily limited to ornamental decoration with, at times, the portrait of David. Aristocratic psalters of the twelfth to fourteenth centuries—the Psalter of Ingeborg for instance—are the heirs of the Carolingian prayer books used by lay people and are the forerunners of the richly illustrated books of Hours of the end of the Middle Ages, which were produced for the devotional needs of well-to-do members of society.

2. THE ANTIPHONAL OF THE OFFICE

The monumental publication of the six volumes of the *Corpus Anti-phonalium Officii (CAO)* by R. J. Hesbert has entirely renewed our knowledge of the history of the antiphonal of the Office in the Middle

---

66. On all these points, see the innovative work of K. M. Openshaw, "The Symbolic Illustrations of the Psalter: An Insular Tradition," *Arte Medievale* 6 (1992) 41–60, and "The Battle between Christ and Satan in the Tiberius Psalter," *Journal of the Warburg and Courtauld Institutes* 52 (1989) 14–33.

67. A good example of this sort of small illustrated psalter is the manuscript kept in St. Peter's Abbey in Salzburg (Stifsbibl. St. Peter, cod. A I o), 4 cm. high, probably written in a scriptorium of northern France in the third quarter of the ninth century, later on transferred to Salzburg, perhaps during the Carolingian period; see F. Mütherich, "Der Psalter von St. Peter in Salzburg," *Scire litteras: Forschungen zum mittelalterlichen Geistleben*, Akademie der Wissenschaften, Philosophisch-Historische Klasse, Abhandlungen, Neue Folge, Heft 99 (Munich, 1988) 291–297.

Ages, a field singularly neglected in the research of medieval liturgical sources.[68] Hesbert undertook to explore the history of the Divine Office of the Latin Church; to this end, he had to study the history of one of the principal office books, the antiphonal, availing himself of the impressive manuscript tradition.

As is the fate of any work of this magnitude, Hesbert's *CAO* received both praise and criticism; some of the latter address basic questions concerning his method, some bear on certain of his conclusions.[69] To exculpate Hesbert, one must say that the task was particularly difficult, given the great complexity of the repertories of the Office in the Middle Ages.

Content of the Antiphonal

There are two principal categories of Office antiphonals: the secular (the Roman Office) and the monastic (Office inherited from Benedict's Rule). The difference resides in the number of pieces at the night office (Vigils), the Little Hours (Prime, Terce, Sext, and None), and Vespers: for the secular, nine antiphons and nocturn responsories at Vigils, one brief responsory at the Little Hours, and five psalms at Vespers; for the monastic, twelve antiphons at Vigils, no brief responsory at the Little Hours, and four psalms at Vespers.

One of Hesbert's most important conclusions was the definitive proof that the monastic tradition of the Office derives entirely from that of the secular clergy.

---

68. *Rerum Ecclesiasticarum Documenta, Series maior, fontes VII, VIII, IX, X, XI, XII:* vol. 1: manuscripts of the Roman *cursus,* vol. 2: manuscripts of the monastic *cursus,* vol. 3: *Invitatoria et antiphonae: Editio critica,* vol. 4: *Resposoria, versus, hymni et varia: Editio critica;* vol. 5: *Fontes earumque prima ordinatio* (list of 800 manuscripts; classification of their responsories at Vigils for Advent); vol 6: *Secunda et tertia ordinationes* (second classification, based on the versicles of the Advent responsories; third classification, based on textual variants) (Rome, 1963–1979).

69. For a critical discussion of Hesbert's conclusions and of the objections they have sometimes met with, see the reports mentioned by Huglo, "L'antiphonaire, archétype ou répertoire originel?" *Grégoire le Grand: Chantilly, Centre culturel Les Fontaines, 15–19 septembre 1982: Actes,* CNRS: International Colloquies (Paris, 1986) 667. See also Gy's note, "Le *Corpus Antiphonalium Officii* et les antiphonaires carolingiens," *Grégoire le Grand,* 645–648; J. Froger, "La méthode de dom Hesbert dans le vol. V du *Corpus Antiphonalium Officii,*" *Etudes grégoriennes* 18 (1979) 97–143. For the study of a particular case, reviewing Hesbert's conclusions, see K. Ottosen, *The Responsories and Versicles of the Latin Office of the Dead* (Århus, 1993).

As early as the ninth century, the office antiphonal[70] contained all the sung pieces grouped into formularies (antiphons and responsories),[71] classified according to the Hours and in the order of the liturgical year.[72] The Temporal and Sanctoral are generally combined; the Common of Saints is found at the end of the book, where one may also encounter a section in which the pieces are arranged according to the eight tones of Gregorian chant. For the antiphons and responsories, the (almost) general rule was to write only the opening words (the incipit) of each piece, since the monastics knew by heart the major part, if not the whole, of the repertory.[73] Along the same lines, it was only in the tenth and eleventh centuries that the scribes almost systematically added to the texts a neumatic notation.[74] The earliest sources we possess of the Office antiphonal transmit a repertory without notation, for example, Paris, B. N., lat. 17436 (second half of ninth century, see pp. 137–138).

In the manuscripts, the different pieces and Hours of the day are generally indicated in abbreviated forms: *A.* or *Ant.* for *Antiphona; R.* or *Resp.* for *Responsorium; Ps.* for *Psalmus; V.* or *Vs.* for *Versus; Cant.* for *Canticum; Ad Vesp.* for *Ad vesperas; Inv.* for *Invitatorium; In I (II, III) noct.* for *In primo (secundo, tertio) nocturno; Mat. laud.* for *Ad matutinas (laudes); Ad hor.* for *Ad horas; Ad I, Ad III, Ad VI, Ad IX* for *Ad primam, Ad tertiam, Ad sextam, Ad nonam; In ev.* for the canticle from the Gospel (Magnificat, Benedictus); *Ad compl.* for *Ad completorium.*

The Manuscript Tradition

From the centuries prior to the year 1000, we possess only a limited number of Office antiphonals, all in various degrees of incompleteness. Therefore, it is not easy to reconstruct the history of this liturgical

70. Not to be confused with the Mass antiphonal, also called gradual; see Part 2, II, the section on the chant books for the Mass.

71. Concerning antiphons and responsories, see pp. 125–126, as well as *CP,* 4:217–219, and Huglo, *Livres de chant,* 23–27.

72. For a brief presentation of the contents of the Office antiphonal, see Huglo, *Livres de chant,* 81–82. See also the notices of Fiala and Irtenkauf, *Liturgische Nomenklatur,* 121–122; Baroffio, "Manoscritti liturgici," 163–164; and Thiel, "Liturgische Bücher," 3280.

73. Let us remind the reader of the primordial role played by oral channels in the transmission of liturgical chant in the Middle Ages. See Part 2, on the Mass books.

74. See Huglo, *Livres de chant,* 82ff.

book. In order to remedy this lack, we first have recourse to other forms the antiphonal took during the High Middle Ages (tables of incipits, composite antiphonals, and so on) and then to the complete antiphonals of the eleventh and twelfth centuries, at a time the antiphonal had not yet been incorporated into the breviary.[75]

Before the year 1000, the list of antiphonals in the strict sense comprises only six manuscripts:[76]

—Lucca, Bibl. Cap., cod. 490, perhaps produced in Lucca itself as early as the eighth century: it is a fragment, containing only pieces for Advent;[77]

—Paris, B. N., lat. 17436, the Antiphonal of Compiègne, dating from the second half of the ninth century: it juxtaposes both the office repertory (fol. 21v) and the Mass repertory (fols. 1v–30v);[78]

—Albi, B. M., ms. 44, from the first half of the tenth century (unpublished);

—Antiphonal of Mont-Renaud, dating from the tenth century (Corbie?), Noyon;[79]

—St. Gall, Stiftsbibl., cod. 390/391, from the tenth or eleventh century, St. Gall, Antiphonal of Hartker of St. Gall;[80]

—Berlin, Staatsbibl., ms. Mus. 40047, going back to about the year 1000, Quedlinburg.[81]

These manuscripts present an already developed structure that suggests the existence of first "attempts" at compiling antiphonals before the ninth century.[82] For instance, in the codex of Compiègne, the liturgical year is divided into two parts: from Advent to Pentecost, with all the offices of the Temporal and Sanctoral, and from Pentecost

75. On all of the manuscript witnesses, see Hesbert, *CAO*.

76. See Gy, "*Corpus Antiphonalium Officii*," 150, and "L'antiphonaire de l'office," *Bulletin du Comité des Etudes* 32 (1961) 21–28.

77. See Gamber, *CLLA*, no. 1302; Froger, "Les fragments de Lucques (fin du VIIIᵉ siècle)," *Etudes grégoriennes* 18 (1979) 148–153.

78. See Froger, "Le lieu de destination et de provenance du *Compendiensis*," *Ut mens concordet voci: Festschrift E. Cardine zum 75. Geburtstag* (St. Ottilien, 1980) 338–353.

79. See *Le manuscrit du Mont-Renaud*, Paléographie musicale 16 (Solesmes, 1980); Gamber, *CLLA*, no. 1307.

80. Gamber, *CLLA*, no, 1308; *CAO*, vol. 2.

81. See H. Möller, *Das Quedlinburger Antiphonar (Berlin, Staatsbiblothek Preussicher Kulturbesitz, Mus. ms. 40047)*, 3 vols. (Tutzing, 1990).

82. The fact that a certain number of fragments of palimpsests of the eighth and ninth centuries exist supports the hypothesis of "first attempts" at antiphonals,

to Advent, with, in succession, the Sanctoral, the various commons, and finally the responsories and antiphons for the Temporal. The invitatory antiphons, the canticles Benedictus and Magnificat, the Sunday antiphons drawn from the Gospels, and the short responsories are given in an appendix.[83] As we shall see shortly, these manuscripts demonstrate to what degree the Carolingian reform had advanced, not only for the Mass but also for the Liturgy of the Hours. The importance of these six manuscripts is great for the study of the repertory of the Office since they were used in various degrees by Hesbert in his monumental publication *(CAO)*. Thus the author was able to address, more or less successfully depending on the cases, the three basic principles for the critical edition of any liturgical book: its general organization, the composition of its formularies, and the textual analysis of each individual piece. On the basis of this work, it is henceforth possible to place within the liturgical tradition of the antiphonal any manuscript of the Office by classifying it under one of the groups defined by Hesbert; these groups result from the study of the order of responsories, the choice of versicles, and the variants in the pieces.

Besides these completely structured antiphonals, there existed other forms of this book in the eighth and ninth centuries. Let us cite in particular the antiphonal table (with incipits) incorporated into other liturgical books, such as the collectar used by the presider at the choral Office.[84] Let us recall also the manuscripts—forerunners of the breviary[85]—in which the antiphonal was juxtaposed to other parts of the Office; the manuscript tradition suggests that this juxtaposition, occurring from the eleventh century on, originated in Alsace, in Switzerland (St. Gall),[86] and perhaps also at Monte Cassino.[87]

---

even of *libelli* with parts of the Office, before the Carolingian reform; on this topic, see the hypotheses of Salmon, *Office divin*, 28ff., and Möller, "Research on the Antiphonar: Problems and Perspective," *Journal of the Plainsong and Mediaeval Music Society* 10 (1987) 1–14; on all these points, see Gamber, *CLLA*, 495–500.

83. On the central role of the organization of the pieces of the Office in the formation of a liturgical book, the antiphonal, see Salmon, *Office divin*, 37–43.

84. See the section on the collectar (III below).

85. On these early forms of the breviary, more usually called *Liber officialis*, see the section on the breviary (VI below).

86. See Gy, "Les premiers bréviaires de Saint-Gall (deuxième quart du XIᵉ siècle)," *Liturgie, Gestalt und Vollzug: Festschrift für J. Pascher* (Munich, 1963) 104–113.

87. Huglo, *Livres de chant*, 117–118.

Historical Importance of the Antiphonal of the Office

Experts agree today that the Office antiphonal was progressively formed from an original repertory and not from an archetype whose composition was ascribed to Gregory the Great.[88] However, as was the case for the Mass antiphonal (the gradual), the attribution to Gregory was not without foundation. In his *Vita sancti Gregorii (Life of St. Gregory)*, John the Deacon (825–880) declares him to be the author of the Roman antiphonal in connection with the creation of the *schola cantorum*.[89] This statement was sufficient for the Carolingian tradition to perpetuate this idea, strengthened by the liturgical reform developing in the eighth and ninth centuries at the instigation first of Pepin the Short and especially Charlemagne afterward.[90] Without denying that Gregory the Great might have been the author of certain pieces, it is impossible to hold that he compiled a whole antiphonal any more than he composed a complete sacramentary.[91] One can reasonably suppose that in the eighth and ninth centuries, and perhaps even before, the Office antiphonal acquired successive components, Roman in origin and combined more or less felicitously with Gallican repertories. In contrast to the Gregorian Sacramentary and the Mass antiphonal (the gradual), the Office antiphonal never attained, at least under Charlemagne, the status of an official liturgical book. In all likelihood, this was largely due to the impossibility of unifying the whole empire through the liturgy on the basis of the Office repertory, given its extreme diversity, whereas the Mass books, with their greater uniformity, offer a basis much more appropriate to unification. Huglo has justly noted that the divergences in the arrangement of antiphons and responsories, despite a fairly homogeneous global structure, give a strong specific character to the antiphonals (or the repertories), thus demonstrating the differences between churches; this shows that the driving force in these compilations was attachment to local practices rather than a desire for unity.[92] In 817, the Council of Aachen imposed a choice between the Benedictine Rule (twelve responsories at the night office) and the canonical Office,

---

88. See the state of the question and the details given by Huglo, "Antiphonaire, archétype," and also by Huglo, "L'édition critique de l'antiphonaire grégorien," *Scriptorium* 39 (1985) 130–138.

89. *PL* 75, col. 90c.

90. On the Carolingian liturgical reform, see Part 2, on the Mass books.

91. On all these problems, see Part 2, I, the section on the sacramentary.

92. Huglo, *Livres de chant*, 86ff.

(Roman or secular, with nine responsories), necessitating for the latter progressive adaptations in the course of the ninth century.

However, after Charlemagne's death in 814, the Office antiphonal was locally subjected to reworking at the hands of famed liturgists and theologians of the empire who, having observed the impossibility of constituting one single repertory, composed their own antiphonals, all based on the elements Rome had contributed.[93]

First of all, Helisachar (d. 836), the chancellor of Louis the Pious (reigned 813–840) and then from 822 on the abbot of St. Riquier,[94] took upon himself to modify the verses whose correspondence with the responsories did not favor, in his opinion, the spiritual understanding of the texts. This undertaking is at the root of the split between the eastern group, which maintained the primitive verses, and the western group, where the marks of Helisachar's changes are the most obvious. Afterward, Amalarius (c.780–c.850), concerned about the important variants in the order of the pieces, the responsories in particular, proposed an arrangement for his church (the diocese of Trier) on the basis of the Metz Antiphonal, which was imbued with Roman influences. The hybrid character of Amalarius' antiphonal resulted from the lack of a fixed tradition in Rome, which Amalarius recognized, not without sadness:[95] *Ex utrisque (romanis et mettensibus) collegi ea quae recta mihi videbantur, et rationabili cursui congruere, atque ea redacta in unum corpus posui sub uno textu in fine antiphonarii nostri* ["I have collected from the two traditions (that of Rome and that of Metz) what seemed to me right and in agreement with a reasonable cursus; then, written into one whole with one single text, I placed them at the end of our antiphonal"] (*PL* 105, col. 1314). This anti-

93. Huglo, "Les remaniements de l'antiphonaire au IXe siècle: Hélisachar, Agobard, Amalaire," *Atti del XVIII Convegno di studi sul tema Culto cristiano e Politica imperiale carolingia, Todi, 9–12 ottobre 1977* (Todi, 1979) 89–120; Huglo, *Livres de chant*, 85–94, where the author underlines the consequences of the reworking of the Carolingian liturgists' antiphonal, which lasted well into the fourteenth century.

94. On the disputed attribution of the supplement to the Gregorian sacramentary to Helisachar, see Part 2, I, 3, the section on the history of the sacramentary; on Helisachar's work and his contribution to the Carolingian liturgy, see Huglo, "Trois livres manuscrits présentés par Hélisachar," *Revue bénédictine* 99 (1989) 272–285.

95. *Liber de ordine antiphonarii, PL* 105, cols. 1243–1316; J. M. Hanssens, ed., *Amalarii episcopi opera liturgica omnia*, vol. 1: *Liber de ordine antiphonarii*, Studi e testi 138 (Vatican City, 1948) 5–224; R. J. Hesbert, "L'antiphonaire d'Amalaire," *Ephemerides liturgicae* 94 (1980) 176–194.

phonal remained without descendants. Finally, in Lyons, where the Gregorian antiphonal had been introduced by Leidrad (d. 813),[96] Florus (d. c.860) and Agobard (769–840) corrected the antiphonal by substituting responsories drawn from Scripture for non-biblical responsories. By affirming as a principle that only biblical readings should be used in the liturgy, Agobard, whose corrections met with great success, prevented the subsequent creation of non-biblical pieces, such as tropes, in the region of Lyons and in the religious communities influenced by his antiphonal.[97]

After this period of remodeling, each monastery or group of monasteries elaborated its own *cursus* with its own variants; however, one cannot speak of antiphonals properly so called.[98]

3. THE HYMNAL
History, Forms, and Functions of Hymns

As early as the sixth century, the ancient monastic rules, in particular those of Benedict and Caesarius of Arles, mention the liturgical role of hymns and suggest that there existed repertories proper to the different Hours.[99] The fact that the singing of hymns is rooted in the monastic rules is the more important since until the end of the eleventh century, hymns were exclusively used by monasteries before being adopted by communities of canons and any cleric celebrating the Divine Office.[100] Adding an extra dimension to the poetic character of the *laus perpetua* at the Office, hymns introduce a lyrical element into the liturgy that fosters the mystery-oriented and spiritual

96. See MGH, *Ep.* 4, Aevi Karolini, pt. 2, p. 542.

97. See P.–M. Gy's remarks, "Les tropes dans l'histoire de la liturgie et de la théologie," *Research on Tropes* (Stockholm, 1983) 7–16, especially 8–9.

98. On this evolution of the adaptation of the reworked antiphonal among the Cluniacs, Cistercians, Carthusians, and the mendicant orders (Franciscans and Dominicans), see Huglo, *Livres de chant*, 89–94.

99. On the hymns as literary and poetical compositions, see *CP*, 4:213–216; J. Szöverffy, *Die Annalen der lateinischen Hymnendichtung: Ein Handbuch*, vol. 1: *Die lateinischen Hymnen bis zum Ende des 11. Jahrhunderts*, vol. 2: *Die lateinischen Hymnen vom Ende des 11. Jahrhunderts bis zum Ausgang des Mittelalters* (Berlin, 1984); J. Szöverffy, *Latin Hymns*, Typologie des sources du Moyen Age occidental, fasc. 55 (Turnhout, 1989), with a bibliography.

100. On the role and respective place of hymns in the different Latin traditions of the *Liturgy of the Hours,* see A.-G. Martimort, "La place des hymnes à l'office dans les liturgies d'Occident," *Studi ambrosiani in onore di mons. Pietro Borella*, ed. C. Alzati and A. Majo, Archivio Ambrosiano 43 (Milan, 1982) 138–153.

reflection proper to prayer.[101] Connection with the psalms, pervasive reference to the hour of day, as well as omnipresent Trinitarian praise characterize the profound essence of the hymns.

The Hymn Repertories

The question of the origins of a liturgical hymnal, and therefore of an appropriate book, has been debated all through this century in order to arrive at trustworthy elements of a solution.[102]

Although it is not possible to go back to the Benedictine hymnal, we have from the period preceding the middle of the eighth century, fragments of repertories, from which we must exclude the Ambrosian hymns, which were not circulated in book form in the Middle Ages.[103] At the end of the eighth and beginning of the ninth centuries, the first Frankish monastic hymnal was completed, soon to be supplanted by the "official" hymnal of Benedict of Aniane; this hymnal, perhaps the work of Alcuin at Tours, shows the influence of Ambrose. Several outstanding hymns were composed during the Carolingian period[104] and enriched the repertory which became more and more carefully related to the Hours and the days of the liturgical year. Some hymns were even an opportunity for their authors to state their positions in contemporary theological debates.[105] From the Carolingian period to our own day, the repertories of the hymnal do not cease to increase since each new feast or office entails the creation of proper hymns.[106]

101. See J. Fontaine, *Naissance de la poésie dans l'Occident chrétien: Esquisse d'une histoire de la poésie latine chrétienne du IIIe au VIe siècle* (Paris, 1981); J. Perret, "Aux origines de l'hymnodie latine: L'apport de la civilisation romaine," *La Maison-Dieu* 173 (1988) 41–60.

102. On this topic, see P.-M. Gy, "Le trésor des hymnes," *La Maison-Dieu* 173 (1988) 19–40, especially 23–29.

103. On the importance and influence in the Middle Ages of hymns composed by St. Ambrose, see *Hymnes/Ambroise de Milan*, ed. J. Fontaine, text established, translated, and annotated by J.-L. Charlet et al. (Paris, 1992).

104. See Gy, "Trésor des hymnes," 25–29.

105. This hypothesis was recently advanced for the hymn *Veni creator spiritus*, which was perhaps composed by Rabanus Maurus (d. 856) and bears marks of the debate on the *Filioque*; see H. Lausberg, *Der Hymnus "Veni creator spiritus"* (Opladen, 1979).

106. On the post-medieval evolution of hymns, as much on the literary and liturgical planes as on the spiritual, see Gy, "Trésor des hymnes," 29–34.

The Manuscript Tradition

The oldest hymnals known to us appeared under the form of composite books. Many are hymnal-psalters or are twinned with other pieces of the Office (collects, canticles, readings).[107] In the non-liturgical psalters, the hymn part is generally last in the manuscript. In liturgical psalters, the hymns are placed within the Hours and feasts;[108] the oldest witnesses go back to the eighth century, like Vat. Regin. lat. 11 (middle of eighth century) written in northern France, perhaps in the region of Paris.[109]

In the ninth century, the first independent hymnals made their appearance.[110] A few mentions in library catalogues confirm the existence of this book: *Librum ymnorum optimum* ["an excellent book of hymns"] (St. Gall, second half of ninth century);[111] *Himnorum libelli, volumina tria* ["three volumes of small books of hymns"] (Cremona, in 984);[112] *Ymnaria duo in choro semper habenda* ["two hymnals which must always be available in choir"] (Monte Cassino, in 1023).[113] The mentions of the hymnal as an autonomous book also grow more numerous in monastic customaries from the tenth and eleventh centuries. Most often, these manuscripts record the repertory of a particular a tradition in which the pieces are arranged according to the liturgical year but without musical notation. Let us also keep in mind the great diversity of hymnals, confirmed by the manuscripts, that endured throughout the Middle Ages because there was not one single repertory imposed in the beginning over all the liturgical traditions of the West. From one manuscript to the next, it is not rare to be faced with an Ambrosian, a Gallican, or any other repertory. This diversity is reinforced by the extreme variety of the melodies existing for the same hymn.[114]

107. See the non-exhaustive list of the manuscript witnesses in Gamber, *CLLA*, 602–605. For a brief presentation of the hymnal, see also Fiala and Irtenkauf, *Liturgische Nomenklatur*, 123; Baroffio, "Manoscritti liturgici," 163; B. Stäblein, "Hymnar," *Die Musik in Geschichte und Gegenwart, allgemeine Enzyklopadie der Musik*, ed. F. Blume, vol. 6 (Kassel, 1957) cols. 986–987.

108. For the hymnal–psalters, see the list of sources in Gamber, *CLLA*, nos. 1601–1624, pp. 576–587.

109. See ibid., no. 1617, p. 583.

110. See the remarks of Huglo, *Livres de chant*, 108–110.

111. See Becker, *Catalogi*, 55.

112. Ibid., 81.

113. Ibid., 133. See also the mentions in church treasuries, Bischoff, *Schatzverzeichnisse*, no. 60, 1.11; no. 121, 1.1.

114. See Huglo, *Livres de chant*, 109.

The hymnal as such did not survive the fusion of all the different books of the Office into the breviary, a process occurring in the eleventh century for the most primitive forms, but especially from the twelfth and thirteenth centuries on.

III. Prayer at the Office: The Collectar

Nature and Content of the Book

"It is the celebrant's book at the Office, containing the readings and collects. Today only a few exist in one or the other religious order, to the point that many a liturgist does not even know the word "collectar." The function of this book was parallel to that of the sacramentary: it provided the celebrant with the texts that were his to proclaim; readings or chants not pertaining properly to the celebrant were found in other books." Such is the definition given by Gy in his study on the collectar and its connection with the ritual and the processional.[115]

From an in-depth analysis of the oldest manuscript sources, Gy in the first place, then Salmon, have demonstrated that the collectar played a central role, along with the psalter, in the process of the formation of one single book for the Office, the other books having progressively gathered around this twofold nucleus in order to constitute the breviary.[116] Before the appearance of the collectar, the sacramentary was used at the Office for the recitation of the orations; in general the collect of the Mass of the day was used. In certain regions, this usage probably persisted even after the ninth century, when the first collectars were produced. Several sacramentaries of the eighth and ninth centuries, whether of the Gelasian or Gregorian type, contain collects *ad matutinas* ["at Lauds"] and *ad vesperum* ["at Vespers"]; this perhaps corresponds to the original structure of the Roman Office,

---

115. Gy, "Collectaire." This text is repeated in an updated form in P.-M. Gy, *La liturgie dans l'histoire* (Paris, 1990) 91–126. On the history of the collectar, see also A. Corréa, *The Durham Collectar,* Henry Bradshaw Society 107 (London, 1992). On the ritual and processional, see the corresponding sections in this manual, Part 4, II and III.

116. Gy, "Collectaire," 442–451; Salmon, *Office divin,* 23–26, 44–45, 50–60.

which was limited to two Hours.[117] These collects are often grouped together, forming one section of the sacramentary, or else they follow the Mass formularies on certain days, Easter in particular. The Leonine Sacramentary also gives, between formularies XXXI and XXXII, a series of four orations for Lauds and Vespers.[118] These collects and the multiple *aliae orationes* ["other orations"] of the sacramentaries are the storehouse from which the independent collectar drew its material.

In its purest form, during the ninth century, the collectar contained only collects[119] for the different Hours, in general borrowed from the Mass of the day. In addition, it has collects specific for Lauds and Vespers, according to the order of the liturgical feasts, with Temporal and Sanctoral combined; very soon, *capitula* (short readings from sacred Scripture) and an assortment of other *preces* (orations) were added to the collectar. From the tenth century on, it was enlarged by the addition of other pieces,[120] and took various forms belonging to strongly characterized types in which the books were either juxtaposed or combined. Thus, one meets with hymnal-(collectar)-psalters, antiphonal-collectars, benedictional-collectars in which the blessings are distributed throughout the liturgical year at their proper places. The evangeliary with collects[121] contained the gospel pericopes with the corresponding orations; this book was for the presider, who was to read these pieces at the night office. In the eleventh and twelfth centuries, especially in monasteries, a ritual was joined with the collectar.[122] Overall, the books we have mentioned were most of the time complete books to be used throughout the entire liturgical year and, more rarely, festive composite collectars intended for abbots, abbesses, and bishops who officiated only on big feasts.

In contrast to the sacramentary, whose contents were assigned very early to the different days of the year (Temporal and Sanctoral), the

---

117. Gy, "Collectaire," 442; A. Chavasse, *Le sacramentaire gélasien* (Tournai, 1958) 453–455.

118. See L. C. Mohlberg, *Sacramentarium Veronense* (Rome, 1956) 75–76.

119. On the origin of the word "collect," see Part 1, I, the section on sacramentaries, and Corréa, *Durham Collectar*, 5–21.

120. Those which Salmon calls the "enriched collectars" in contrast to the "simple collectars" (of the ninth century), *Office divin*, 50–60.

121. We are far from having shed all possible light on this particular category of books; see Gy, "Collectaire," 451, and P.-M. Gy, "Bulletin de Liturgie," *Revue des Sciences philosophiques et théologiques* 77 (1993) 117.

122. On this combination, see Part 4, II, the section on the rituals.

repertory for the collectar, whether simple or augmented, evolved slowly toward a fixed and more or less definitive form. Precision in the assignment of collects and even short readings, and other *preces* was observed only from the twelfth century on and grew more rigorous during the second half of the Middle Ages.

The Manuscript Tradition

The numerous collectars of the High Middle Ages have been inventoried and described, at least in summary fashion, by P.-M. Gy, P. Salmon, and K. Gamber;[123] some of them have been the object of special studies. As a result of these efforts, the existence of independent collectars is well attested as early as the tenth century, and the typological diversity of the book can be uncovered thanks to the manuscripts that have come down to us.

The oldest documents attesting to the existence of the collectar are fragments from the eighth century: St. Gall, Stiftsbibl., cod. 349, pp. 5–36 (second half of eighth century, from the region of Constance), covering the portion of the year from Easter Sunday to the feast of Sts. Peter and Paul;[124] Karlsruhe, Bad. Landesbibl., Fragm. augien. 22 (35 fols.; about 800, Reichenau), fragments of a pure Gregorian collectar, with the orations for funerals.[125] In the St. Gall fragments, the collects are arranged into formularies corresponding to the days of the week after Easter (Vespers only), the Annunciation, Ascension, Pentecost, the feasts of John the Baptist and Peter and Paul (Lauds and Vespers). Every formulary is interspersed with a series of *Aliae orationes paschales* ["other paschal orations"].

For the ninth century, the Collectar of Prüm (Trier, Stadtbibl., cod. 504 [1245]; fols. 129v–138v),[126] which is attached to a martyrology-tonary, offers a more complete collection comprising a part of the Sanctoral with daily collects *ad matutinas*, *ad vesperas*, and *post evangelium*.

123. Gy, "Collectaire," especially 452–454, for the collectars before the twelfth century; Salmon, *Office divin*, 50–60; Gamber, *CLLA*, 548–559.

124. See Gamber, *CLLA*, no. 1501; O. Heiming, "Das Kollektar fragment des Sangallensis 340, pp. 5–36, Saec. VIII," *Mélanges liturgiques offerts au R. P. dom Bernard Botte* (Louvain, 1972) 175–203; Corréa, *Durham Collectar*, 22–25.

125. See Gamber, *CLLA*, no. 1502, and *CLLA, Supplementum*, 144; Corréa, *Durham Collectar*, 25–28.

126. See Gamber, *CLLA*, no. 1506; P. Siffrin, "Der Collectar der Abtei Prüm im neunten Jahrhundert (Trier, Stadtbibliothek, 1245/597, Bl. 129 v.–138 v.," *Miscellanea Liturgica in honorem L. Cuniberti Mohlberg*, vol. 2 (Rome, 1949) 223–244; Corréa, *The Durham Collectar*, 54–63.

At that period, the terms and expressions *collectarium, liber collectar-ius, collectaneum,* or else *orationale* appear to designate the collectar.[127]

In the tenth century, one observes the multiplication of proper and complete collectars, often with readings, sometimes attached to other books, most frequently the ritual, psalter, and hymnal. Let us cite especially the following manuscripts:

—Rheims, B. M., ms. 304 (first half of tenth century, Rheims, Saint-Thierry), a ritual-collectar (*ordo* for the funeral service);[128]

—Vercelli, Bibl.capit., cod. 178 (beginning of tenth century, Vercelli), a ritual-collectar (*ordines* for baptism and penance); certain collects are accompanied by antiphons, responsories, and lessons;[129]

—Durham, Chapter lib., cod. A.IV.19 (middle of tenth century, Durham), a ritual-collectar (with blessings, rituals for marriage and confirmation);[130]

—Zurich, Zentralbibl., cod. Rh. 83 (about 1000, Kempten), a hymnal-martyrology-collectar, the collectar beginning at fol. 58v, with the title *In nomine DNI incipit liber officiorum expositus a Sco Gregorio papa de festis diebus vel dominicis seu cottidianis de circulo anni* ["In the name of the Lord, here begins the book of offices set forth by Pope St. Gregory for festive days and Sundays as well as for ferial days throughout the yearly cycle"].[131]

From the eleventh and twelfth centuries on, other books were joined to the collectar, such as the pontifical (Oxford, Bodl. Lib., ms. liturg. 359; end of eleventh century, Arezzo);[132] but in general, the final and often complex form of the collectar tended to evolve toward the early forms of the breviary.[133]

---

127. See the numerous references in Becker, *Catalogi,* and Bischoff, *Schatzverzeichnisse.* The terms *collectaneum* and *orationale* postdate *collectarium* and *liber collectarius.*

128. Gamber, *CLLA,* no. 1509, and *CLLA, Supplementum,* 145; Corréa, *Durham Collectar,* 63–68.

129. Gamber, *CLLA,* no. 1510.

130. Ibid., no. 1517; Corréa, *Durham Collectar.*

131. Gamber, *CLLA,* no. 1525.

132. Ibid., no.1550b.

133. See the manuscripts described by Salmon, *Office divin,* 53–60, and VI, the section on the breviary, below.

IV. Reading at the Office

At the Office, there are three sorts of readings: scriptural, patristic, and hagiographic, to which correspond as many sorts of books, albeit not always clearly differentiated. At first, these books were joined together into the Office lectionary; later on, the lessons found their place in the breviary along with other parts of the Office. To make things easier, we shall treat of these three types of books separately, one after the other.

1. THE BIBLICAL READINGS AND THEIR BOOKS

In the prayer of the early Christians, the reading of and meditation on the Bible occupied a place of the greatest importance.[134] It is probable that the practice of *lectio continua* (reading the Bible in its entirety) yielded early on to that of choosing readings appropriate to the occasion. In his rule, Benedict directs several times that sacred Scripture be read at the Office. Every day at Vigils, the series of psalms is interrupted by three readings *(lectiones)* drawn from either the Old or New Testament. After the second series of psalms, a passage from the epistles is read. In summer, the nights being shorter, there are just three readings with only one from the Old Testament. But on Sunday, whatever the season, there are four readings at the end of each of the three nocturns, then, after the Te Deum, the presider reads the gospel. Lastly, Benedict prescribes for all the day Hours one reading after the psalmody (without specifying what kind). Benedict, following the Rule of the Master, already distinguishes long readings from short ones (chapters). It is certain that the custom of cutting a biblical passage into several readings existed at that period.

The oldest description of a true cycle of readings at the Office is found in *Ordo romanus* XIV, which seems to represent the usage at the

---

134. See *CP,* 4:220–222; Taft, *Liturgy of the Hours.*

basilica of St. Peter in the second half of the seventh century.[135] The liturgical year began with Quinquagesima and the great books of the Old Testament: Genesis, Exodus, Leviticus, Numbers, Deuteronomy, Joshua. During Holy Week, passages from Isaiah and Lamentations were read; at Easter, the epistles, the Acts of the Apostles, and Revelation; after Pentecost, the balance of historical books: Samuel, Kings, and Chronicles; in October and November, the Wisdom books: Proverbs, Ecclesiastes, Song of Songs, Wisdom; in December, Isaiah, Jeremiah, Daniel; after Epiphany, Ezekiel and the minor prophets. *Ordo romanus* XIII A, which in the eighth century formalizes the selection of biblical readings at the Lateran in Rome, shows some modifications of the preceding *ordo*.[136]

In its overall structure, the cycle of readings described in *Ordines* XIV and XIIIA is the one observed during the Middle Ages, with, of course, more or less important local adaptations depending on the places and customs (in particular, on the veneration of local saints since a hagiographic reading might replace the biblical one in a given monastery).

Given this scriptural framework, the liturgists of the Middle Ages engaged in a curtailing of all the readings at the Office, sometimes going as far as reducing a pericope to its incipit. Thanks to a certain flexibility in practice, the length of the readings varied from one Hour to the other, according to the time of year and the different places. The reasons for this curtailing were many. First, there was a general tendency during the Middle Ages to drastically shorten the readings in offices which had grown too long and increasingly enriched with singing (tropes, hymns, and so on). Second, there was the search for a balance between prayer and other forms of devotion, and even a certain alienation from Scripture—the exception to this disaffection was the Franciscan breviary of the thirteenth century in which the number of patristic and hagiographic readings was reduced in favor of Scripture, in agreement with the renewed esteem for meditation on the Bible.[137]

In the beginning and during a large part of the Middle Ages, it was customary to use a Bible for the readings. This was a simple proce-

135. See Andrieu, *OR*, 3:39–41; *Ordo* XIV goes back perhaps to the sixth century.
136. Andrieu, *OR*, 2:481–488.
137. On all these questions, see Martimort, *Lectures liturgiques*, 71–72; Gy, "Bible dans la liturgie," especially 550–552; Salmon, *Office divin*, 166–167.

dure: marginal notations written at the beginning of each biblical book allowed the reader to quickly find the pericopes for each day and each Hour.[138] Some rare manuscripts of the Bible present an entirely liturgical structure, the books being arranged not in the order of the Vulgate but according to the cycle of readings (Milan, Bibl. Ambrosiana, cod. E 51 inf.; eleventh-twelfth centuries).[139] The progressive abridgement of readings gave rise to smaller books with selected contents, such as the Salzburg manuscript (Museum Carolino-Augusteum, no. 2163) from the ninth century in which folios 2–10 contain only the readings from Isaiah for Advent;[140] another consequence of these shorter readings was the appearance of lectionaries, and then breviaries (see IV, 4, and VI of this part).

For the short readings or abbreviated readings dividing a biblical passage into several pericopes, it became customary early on to copy them into the collectar, following the collects for the whole of the liturgical year or inserted at their places in the celebration. The probable reason for this was that the presider at the Office had the task of reading and reciting both the brief lesson and the collect.[141] However, some collections of short readings (capitularies)[142] independent from the collectar are extant; they were used in monasteries for the day Hours and the night office during Eastertide and during the summer: Rome, Bibl. Vallicel., cod. A.3, fols. 1–85 (eleventh century); St. Gall, Stiftsbibl., cod. 423 (tenth century) and 428 (eleventh century).[143]

Finally, one can surmise that in addition to the lists of pericopes for the Mass,[144] there existed lists of biblical readings for the Office, although none has come down to our times. But in the Gallican liturgy, we have biblical lectionaries, written in the sixth and seventh centuries, that contain the Mass pericopes and the Office readings,[145]

138. See Salmon, *Office divin,* 26–27.

139. See Martimort, *Lectures liturgiques,* 73.

140. Gamber, *CLLA,* no. 1630a; for a general view of the manuscript witnesses of the books of biblical readings at the Office in the High Middle Ages, see *CLLA,* 588–592.

141. Gy, "Collectaire," 448–450; Martimort thinks—wrongly, in our opinion—that it is the presence of the little chapters in the collectar that led the presider to assume their reading, *Lectures liturgiques,* 75

142. See Baroffio, "Manoscritti liturgici," 162–163.

143. See Martimort, *Lectures liturgiques,* 74.

144. See Part 2, III, the section on the books of readings for Mass.

145. See Vogel, *Introduction,* 320ff.; Salmon, *Office divin,* 27; Martimort, *Lectures liturgiques,* 37–39.

either combined or in separate sections. One of the representative examples of this type of book is the Lectionary of Luxeuil (Paris, B. N., lat. 9427; end of seventh or beginning of eighth century, from the region of Paris).[146]

2. THE PATRISTIC READINGS AND THEIR BOOKS

In the West,[147] the practice of reading the works of the Church Fathers is attested by the Rule of Benedict who directs that, besides biblical texts, biblical commentaries be read every day at Vigils at the time of year when nights are long: *Codices autem leguntur in vigiliis divinae auctoritatis, tam veteris Testamenti quam Novi, sed et expositiones earum, quae a nominatis et orthodoxis Patribus factae sunt* ["Besides the inspired books of the Old and New Testaments the works read at the vigils should include explanations of Scripture by reputable and orthodox Fathers"].[148] But already in the *Decretum Gelasianum*—an Italian work from the fifth century which lists authors from the third, fourth, and fifth centuries and whose reading was recommended— the concern was to evaluate the authority of the Fathers in order to discern their suitability for liturgical reading.[149] Because this compilation utilizes Roman documents, one can suppose that the use of patristic readings in the liturgy was known in Rome before the sixth century. *Ordo romanus* XIV (second half of seventh century), representing the customs of monasteries serving the basilica of St. Peter, ends with these words: *Tractatus vero sancti Hieronymi, Ambrosi, ceterorum Patrum, prout ordo poscit, leguntur* ["Readings are taken from the treatises of Sts. Jerome, Ambrose, and other Fathers, as the *ordo* indicates"].[150] Concluding the yearly cycle of biblical readings, these texts were intended as commentaries on sacred Scripture. A little later, a homily on the gospel replaced the scriptural text every day; and by

146. On this manuscript, see Salmon, *Le lectionnaire de Luxeuil*, 2 vols., Collectanea biblica latina 7 and 9 (Rome, 1944, 1953).

147. There is a good summary of the state of the questions concerning the patristic readings in A.-G. Martimort, "La lecture patristique dans la liturgie des Heures," *Traditio et Progressio: Studi liturgici in onore Prof. Adrien Nocent, OSB*, Studia Anselmiana 95 (Rome, 1988) 311–331. See also Martimort, *Lectures liturgiques*, 77–80; *CP*, 4:222–225; Salmon, *Office divin*.

148. *The Rule of St. Benedict*, ed. T. Fry and others (Collegeville, Minn., 1980) 9.8, p.205.

149. See E. Schwartz, "Zum Decretum Gelasianum," *Zeitschrift für neutestamentliche Wissenschaft* 29 (1930) 161–168.

150. Andrieu, *OR*, 3:41.

the eighth century, the *cursus* of patristic readings can be regarded as fixed in the West for the duration of the Middle Ages, albeit with a good number of local variants.[151]

As for the practice of *lectio continua*, which was one of two ways of reading the Fathers at the Office,[152] no particular book was necessary. It was sufficient to make use of the monastery library and take out a manuscript of the works of Augustine or Jerome, for instance, and then simply add in the margins the divisions into readings. A representative example of this practice is furnished us by some collections of Augustine's sermons: Bibl. Vat., Pal., lat. 210 (sixth/seventh centuries, Lorsch); Pal., lat. 298 (tenth century, of unknown provenance).[153] However, the more and more rigorous assignment of proper readings to the Hours and feasts required the making of appropriate books. Thus were born the sermonaries and homiliaries offering to the celebrant a choice of patristic commentaries easily available for the patristic reading at the Office.[154] The great variety of these books attests to the many customs in force, depending upon the places and the diffusion of traditions.

In the Middle Ages, the distinction between sermonary and homiliary was artificial even though in the Latin usage, the word "homily" is reserved for the explanation of the Gospel. In both books, the Fathers' texts, divided into readings of varying length, were copied in the order in which they were used in the liturgical year, frequently with a separation between the winter part (from Advent to Easter) and the summer part (from Easter to Advent). Sometimes, the authors were identified by an alphabetic system in which each had his own letter. Some of these collections were simply used as an aid for the spiritual meditation of the monastics; others were a resource for the preparation of sermons; still others were intended for use at Mass.[155]

The work of several researchers has made it possible to reconstruct the Roman homiliary of the sixth and seventh centuries on the basis

151. On the later evolution, especially in the thirteenth century, of the organization of patristic readings in the West, see Salmon, *Office divin*, 93–94, 98, 166–167.

152. See Martimort, *Lectures liturgiques*, 79–80.

153. Ibid., 80.

154. See H. Barré, "Homéliaires," *Dictionnaire de Spiritualité ascetique et mystique, doctrine et histoire*, ed. M. Viller, F. Cavallera, J. de Guibert, vol. 7, pt. 1, cols. 597–606; Baroffio, "Manoscritti liturgici," 162; *Liturgica Vaticana*, 48–51.

155. On the multiple uses of the homiliaries, see Martimort, *Lectures liturgiques*, 81–82.

of more recent manuscripts (tenth to twelfth centuries).[156] Thanks to the comparison with other ancient Roman books, such as lectionaries (or rather lists of readings), it has become possible to reconstitute the original liturgical structure (respective organization of the Temporal and Sanctoral) of the homiliary of St. Peter. For each celebration, this homiliary offered a collection of sermons among which the presider was free to choose. So scholars have deduced that as with the sacramentary at Mass, each church or monastery had its own particularities. On the basis of the homiliary of St. Peter from the seventh century, four types took form in the eighth century: (1) the Homiliary of the Basilica of St. Peter (after Bibl. Vat., Arch. S. Pietro, cod. C.105; tenth century), overall faithful to its model but incorporating changes due to the evolution of the Roman liturgy in the eighth and ninth centuries; (2) Homiliary of Agimond for the Roman basilica of Sts. Philip and James, whose three volumes cover the whole liturgical year; (3) the Homiliary of Eginon of Verona (after Berlin, Deutsche Staatsbibl., Phillipps 1676), written for the cathedral of Verona about 796–799, under Eginon's episcopacy; (4) the Homiliary of Alain of Farfa (761–770), which can be reconstructed from two groups of manuscripts.[157] Other homiliaries preceding the Carolingian reform do not belong to the Roman tradition, and it is not sure that they were used for the Office.[158]

At the time of the adaptation of the Roman liturgical usages to the needs of the Gallican church, from the eighth century on, the *cursus* of patristic readings progressively became more precise, depending on local customs and the character of the offices, either long and needing complete readings or short and requiring the curtailment of all kinds of texts, among them the Fathers' sermons and homilies. As he had done in the case of the sacramentary, Charlemagne played a decisive role in the case of the books of readings at the Office by com-

156. See particularly the two basic publications of R. Grégoire, *Les homéliaires du Moyen Age: Inventaire et analyse des manuscrits* (Rome, 1966), and *Homéliaires liturgiques médiévaux* (Spoleto, 1980); A. Chavasse, "Un homéliaire liturgique romain du VIe siècle," *Revue bénédictine* 90 (1980) 194–233; J.-P. Bouhot, "L'homéliaire de Saint-Pierre du Vatican au milieu du VIIe siècle et sa postérité," *Recherches augustiniennes* 20 (1985) 87–115. On the oldest manuscript witnesses, see also Gamber, *CLLA*, 594–602.

157. On these four homiliaries, see Martimort, *Lectures liturgiques*, 84–85 (with a detailed bibliography).

158. Ibid., 86–87.

missioning Paul the Deacon to compose an "official" homiliary which rapidly gained acceptance throughout the empire.[159] This collection contained 244 sections corresponding to the liturgical year as it had been established by the Gregorian Sacramentary. This is a revealing fact, demonstrating that the authority of the official sacramentary at the time of the Carolingian period succeeded in imposing itself at the expense of the Roman model represented by the homiliary of St. Peter from the seventh century, whose influence endured but was transmitted through other channels. When compared to preceding collections, the homiliary of Paul the Deacon innovated on two essential points; first, it strictly assigned one patristic text to each day (with rare exceptions) and no longer a number of texts among which a choice could be made; second, it offered for all the Sundays of the year and many feasts a homily on the gospel of the day identified by one or two of the opening verses.

From the ninth century on, one sees particular traditions proliferate and become entrenched, depending upon the choice made by monasteries and churches with regard to patristic readings at the Office.[160] Here, one must not take into account either Alcuin's hypothetical homiliary[161] or the homiliaries of the School of Auxerre[162] composed for meditation (in close connection with exegetical teaching) and not for liturgical reading. Without going into a detailed description of each of the collections, on which we possess very many monographs,[163] let us simply note some important points in the evolution of the liturgical homiliaries between the ninth and fifteenth centuries. The ancient traditions, particularly the Roman homiliary of St. Peter, either persisted locally, especially in central Italy, or were supplanted by profound transformations occurring in particular churches. In the West as a

159. Ibid., 87–88 (with bibliography); Vogel, *Introduction*, 363–365. The commissioning letter of Charlemagne can be found in MGH, *Capitularia regum Francorum*, vol. 1, 80–81.

160. See a report on the state of this question in Vogel, *Introduction*, 364–365.

161. See *L'Ecole carolingienne d'Auxerre: De Murethach à Rémi, 830–908: Entretiens d'Auxerre 1989*, ed. D. Iogna-Prat, C. Jeudy, G. Lorichon (Paris, 1991), in particular, R. Etaix, "Les homéliaires carolingiens de l'Ecole d'Auxerre," 243–251; see also H. Barré, *Les homéliaires carolingiens de l'Ecole d'Auxerre*, Studi e Testi 225 (Vatican City, 1962).

162. See Martimort, *Lectures liturgiques*, 89–94.

163. See especially the basic studies of Etaix, "Homéliaires carolingiens," and Barré, *Homéliaires carolingiens*; see the references in Martimort, *Lectures liturgiques*, 89–94.

whole, one notes important interaction between liturgical and exegetical homiliaries, the latter nurturing the first, and also between different liturgical traditions. From the tenth and eleventh centuries on, texts from recent or contemporary authors were added to the readings drawn from the Fathers, and through these additions, the various traditions asserted more clearly their distinct identities. The new orders of the twelfth and thirteenth centuries (especially the Cistercians and Carthusians), imposed a standard model upon the different houses of their orders.

Lastly, let us mention that in the tenth and eleventh centuries, the liturgical homiliary was inserted into the Office lectionary, like that of Cluny (see section 4 below) in which the biblical, patristic, and hagiographic readings are grouped together. A little later, the Office lectionary was itself incorporated into the breviary,[164] but not without having been reorganized in relation to the other parts of the Office.

3. THE HAGIOGRAPHIC READINGS AND THEIR BOOKS

The reading of the lives of saints and the passions of martyrs during liturgical assemblies in antiquity is attested only in Christian Africa, for instance, at the time of Augustine for the vigil of a saint's feast. In the non-Roman liturgies of the seventh and eighth centuries there were hagiographic readings at Mass and the Office, as is proved by numerous Iberian, Gallican, and Ambrosian documents.[165] The liturgical character of the manuscripts pertaining to these traditions cannot be doubted: one proof among others is the existence of marginal notations for the division of the text into readings for the Office or Mass. For example, the Iberian passional, known through manuscripts written at the Abbey of Silos, offers a well-structured cycle of hagiographic readings following the rhythms of the offices and liturgical year.[166] For a long time, the Roman liturgy remained hostile to this type of reading in the liturgy. In their original state, *Ordines ro-*

---

164. See VI below, the section on the breviary.

165. On the history of hagiographic readings, see Martimort, *Lectures liturgiques,* 97–100; *CP,* 4:225–227. Concerning the list of manuscripts of the Iberian, Gallican, and Ambrosian traditions, see Gamber, *CLLA,* 181–183, 218–219, 286.

166. See B. de Gaiffier, "La lecture des Actes des martyrs dans la prière liturgique en Occident: A propos du passionnaire hispanique," *Analecta Bollandiana* 72 (1954) 134–166; more recently, R. Guerreiro, "Un vrai ou faux passionnaire dans le manuscrit 39 de la Real Academia de la Historia de Madrid?" *Revue Mabillon* 62, n.s. 1 (1990) 37–56, which contains an updated report on the manuscript tradition.

mani XIII and XIV ignore them; however, after their arrival in Gaul, they were submitted to modifications, one of them being the authorization to read hagiographical accounts: *similiter tractatus, prout ordo poscit, passiones martyrum et vitae patrum catholicorum leguntur* ["in the same way as the treatises, according to what the ordo prescribes, the passions of the martyrs and the lives of the Catholic Fathers are read"].[167] In Rome itself at the beginning of the ninth century, one observes a change of customs: from then on, it was recommended, at least for the vigil of Roman saints in their own churches, that their passions be read. In the twelfth century, the *ordo* of the Lateran provides for a hagiographic reading for all the big feasts of saints.[168] In the second half of the Middle Ages, passions and legends became predominant in the Office readings, contributing up to six, and even nine, lessons; certain people regarded them with grave reservations.[169]

The High Middle Ages left few manuscripts attesting to the Roman tradition concerning hagiographic readings. The early legendaries, whose production began in the eighth century and reached its climax in the eleventh and twelfth, were rarely intended for the celebration of the Office.[170] Their liturgical structure suggests rather that they were used for the reading in the refectory or for personal meditation.[171] Some medieval legendaries in which the texts are divided into three, six, nine, or twelve readings, were used in choir during the Office, for instance, Bibl. Vat., Vat., lat. 5771 (Bobbio, tenth century).[172] From the eleventh and twelfth centuries on, we know of a greater number of passionals—the passional was designated by the terms *passionarius, passionale,* or *liber passionalis* in medieval texts. They contained the acts of the martyrs and, by extension, any other hagiographic narrative.[173] It is possible that they were used in liturgical celebrations, but there

---

167. *Ordo romanus* XIV, see Andrieu, *OR,* 3:41, 29–30; also Dubois and Lemaître, *Sources et méthodes,* 161–190.

168. On all these questions, see Martimort, *Lectures liturgiques,* 99–100.

169. See Salmon, *Office divin,* 98; on the place of these readings in the Office of the Roman Curia in the thirteenth century, see ibid., 143–147.

170. See *Liturgica Vaticana,* 44–48.

171. See Martimort, *Lectures liturgiques,* 100–101. On the legendaries as a hagiographic literary genre, see G. Philippart, *Les légendiers latins et autres manuscrits hagiographiques,* Typologie des sources du Moyen Age occidental, fascs. 24–25 (Turnhout, 1977), and the fascicle updating them (1985).

172. See Gamber, *CLLA,* no. 1648.

173. In the Middle Ages, the boundary between legendary and passional was not a strict one.

is no certain proof of this. These passionals generally follow the order of the calendar *per circulum anni* ["through the yearly cycle"]; others are organized by categories of personages (apostles, saints, confessors of the faith). In the twelfth century, there appeared passionals presenting at the beginning of each life or passion of a saint a historiated initial, whether related or unrelated to a passage of the text; these are true treasures of hagiographic iconography.[174]

In fact, the hagiographic readings at the Office were most often written directly in the homiliaries, either in a distinct part of the book or inserted at their places in the succession of celebrations.[175] However, in many cases, the complete lectionary rearranged the cycle of readings, including the hagiographic ones, with a view to balancing the different kinds of texts according to the number of readings.

4. THE LECTIONARY OF THE OFFICE

In a way similar to that followed by the Mass lectionary, the Office lectionary brought together a large part of the readings (in general, only the incipit is written) for the Office as celebrated in a given place; its plan corresponded to each celebration for the whole of the liturgical year, most often divided into two parts (summer and winter).[176] Having come onto the scene in the tenth century, the Office lectionar-

174. See, for instance, the famous Passional of Zwiefalten, about 1120–1135 (Stuttgart, Würtembergische Landesbibl. Cod. Bibl. 2° 56–58), comprising three volumes; see *Katalog der illuminierten Handschriften der Würtembergischen Landesbibliothek Stuttgart: Die romanischen Handschriften der Würtembergischen Landesbibliothek Stuttgart*, vol. 2.1, Provenance of Zwiefalten, ed. S. von Borries-Schulten and H. Spilling (Stuttgart, 1987) nos. 34–36; and S. von Borries-Schulten, "Zur romanischen Buchmalerei in Zwiefalten: Zwei Illustrationsfolgen zu den Heiligenfesten des Jahres und ihre Vorlagen," *Zeitschrift für Kunstgeschichte* 52 (1989) 445ff. This passional was completed by the illustrated martyrology, about 1162 (Stuttgart, Cod. hist. 20 415); see Z. Haefeli-Sonin, *Auftraggeher und Entwurfskonzept im Zwiefaltener martyrolog des 12. Jahrhunderts* (Berne, 1992) *Katalog*, no. 64. See also the Passional of Weissenau, about 1200 (Geneva, cod. Bodmer 127); see S. Michon, *Le Grand Passionnaire enluminé de Weissenau et son scriptorium autour de 1200* (Geneva, 1990); at the end of this book there is a very helpful catalogue in which a fair number of illustrated passionals of the Middle Ages are featured.

175. See Martimort, *Lectures liturgiques*, 101, who gives a list of homiliaries with hagiographic readings, mostly from the tenth to twelfth centuries.

176. See the notices in Fiala and Irtenkauf, *Liturgische Nomenklatur*, 118; Baroffio, "Manoscritti liturgici," 161–162. See also Martimort, *Lectures liturgiques*, 103–105, where he—disappointingly—treats of the Office lectionary, to which he does not give a great importance. In the medieval texts (catalogues of ancient libraries, in-

ies diminished in number from the twelfth century on, in favor of the breviaries and even of other older forms of books of readings, such as homiliaries or biblical, patristic, and hagiographic manuscripts with marginal annotations. In his history of the formation of the breviary, Salmon rightly thinks that together with psalters and collectars, Office lectionaries, called enriched (for example, Paris, B. N., lat. 743, eleventh century, Saint-Martial of Limoges; Florence, Bibl. Marcel., cod. C.159, end of eleventh century, Tuscany), had acted as the nucleus around which certain primitive forms of the breviary had taken shape.[177]

One of the particularities of the Office lectionaries was their essentially local character; they were intended for one monastery or one religious order. The great diversity existing in both the arrangement of the Office readings and the other elements of the liturgy of the Hours prevented the emergence of a standard lectionary, authoritative throughout the whole West. An abbey or an order affirmed its identity in liturgical matters by establishing, among other things, its own original system of readings, the result of the combination of several homiliaries for instance.

Among the Office lectionaries which have been preserved, the most complete, in which Temporal, Sanctoral, and Common of the Saints succeed one another, contain the incipits of the biblical, patristic, and hagiographic readings for Sundays and big feasts (those with three nocturns and twelve readings) organized into formularies; but they do not provide for ferial days or feasts with three readings. We possess a representative example of this sort of lectionary in the Cluniac lectionary entirely reconstituted by R. Etaix on the basis of three manuscripts: Paris, B. N., lat. 13371 (fols. 87r–96v); n.a.l. 2390 (first half of eleventh century); n.a.l. 2246 (about 1100).[178] These attempts at reconstitution prove to be indispensable, not only for knowing the liturgy of a given place at a certain period of the Middle Ages, but also for reconstructing the Sanctoral of an outstanding abbey, like Cluny, and thus on the basis of one liturgical *cursus* of the office, the evolution of the cult of saints in general.

---

ventories of church treasuries, and so on) no particular distinction is made between Mass lectionaries and Office lectionaries.

177. See Salmon, *Office divin*, 60–61.

178. R. Etaix, "Le lectionnaire de l'office à Cluny," *Recherches augustiniennes* 11 (1976) 91–159.

Other similar efforts have been successfully made by taking as a point of departure documentation often incomplete (fragments of lectionaries) but nonetheless helpful because it can be compared with other sources like customaries and ordinaries (in which ceremonies are described), breviaries, and also biblical manuscripts with marginal annotations.[179]

179. Among studies of this sort, that of A. Davril is exemplary, "Le lectionnaire de l'office à Fleury: Essai de reconstitution," *Revue bénédictine* 89 (1979) 110–164.

V. The Books of the Office of Prime

Long neglected by liturgists, the books used for the office in chapter [the room where a community of monastics or canons assemble] after Prime have of recent years been the object of a renewed interest, especially on the part of historians. In fact, only the martyrology had been studied previously by many liturgists. The rediscovery (in certain cases, one can even speak of discovery) of the other books, such as necrologies or obituaries, *libri memoriales, libri vitae,* and even the book of the chapter, was stimulated by the historians' research on the commemoration of the dead in the Middle Ages.[180]

From the Carolingian period on, new forms of commemoration of the dead developed in the medieval West, perhaps induced by another vision of death and the hereafter. New liturgical practices arose at Mass and the Office during which one commemorated all deceased religious (clerics, abbots, abbesses, monastics) as well as certain laypersons whose names were kept in books (or other necrological documents) owing their origin to these practices.[181] The commemoration of the dead was the ideal setting for the emergence of new forms of social intercourse, in particular confraternities, between ecclesiastical communities, abbeys, churches, cathedrals, and chapters of canons.[182] In the Carolingian period, the recitation of the names of the dead to

180. See in particular the work of the German school of Münster, and especially the book of essays *Memoria: Der Geschichtliche Zeugniswert des liturgischen Gedenkens im Mittelalter,* ed. K. Schmid and J. Wollasch, Münstersche Mittelalter Schriften 48 (Münster, 1984). See also O.G. Oexle, *"Memoria* und Memorialüberlieferung im frühen Mittelalter," *Frühmittelalterliche Studien* 10 (1976) 70–95.

181. Concerning the many necrological documents of that period—books, wax tablets, or anything else, not necessarily having a liturgical character—see N. Huyghebaert, *Les documents nécrologiques,* Typologie des sources du Moyen Age occidental, fasc. 4 (Turnhout, 1972), with 15 pages of update by J.-L. Lemaître.

182. See K. Schmid and J. Wollasch, "Die Gemeinschaft der Lebenden und Verstorbenen in Zeugnissen des Mittelalters," *Frühmittelalterliche Studien* 1 (1967)

be commemorated during the liturgy did not wait for specific books to be created. Before the appearance of true necrological documents, mention of the names of deceased persons, singly or in groups, are found in a great number of medieval documents. Limiting ourselves to the liturgical field, we find such names in sacramentaries, at the canon of the Mass where they are added to certain prayers *(Memento, Nobis quoque)*, and in calendars.[183] The creation of new types of books attests to the massive development of these practices and of their codification within a precise liturgical setting, the office in chapter, where they were placed next to the commemoration of the saints and martyrs of the Church.

When read in a methodical way, these liturgical documents give precious information on the life of medieval society, in particular in monasteries, where the commemoration of the dead was particularly flourishing.[184] Finally, the work of the School of Münster has shown the richness of these texts, or rather of these lists, for the study of the relationship between monasteries and for prosopography.

1. THE OFFICE IN CHAPTER AFTER PRIME

From the eighth century on, the custom of reading the names of the dead whose commemoration was made at the office in chapter after Prime became widespread. The Hour of Prime was the last to have been introduced into the *cursus* of the Divine Office, probably in the fifth century.[185] But it was only in the eighth century that the first tangible elements of this office make their appearance. Written in a little monastic community following the Luxeuil observance, *Ordo romanus* XVIII, going back to the end of the eighth century, sets the office of Prime, which takes place in the dormitory, at the first or second hour of the day: 3. *Ista prima ibi cantatur ubi dormiunt et ibidem pro invicem, capitolo dicto, orant. 4. Statim, ibi sediunt prior cum ipsis, et ibi legunt regulam sancti Benedicti et a priore, vel cui ipse iusserit, per singolos*

365–405, and by the same authors, "'Societas et fraternitas': Begründung eines kommentierten Quellenwerkes zur Erforschung der Personen und Personengruppen des Mittelalters," *Frühmittelalterliche Studien* 9 (1975) 1–48.

183. See Part 2, I, the section on sacramentaries.

184. See especially the study by J.-L. Lemaître, *Mourir à Saint-Martial: La commémoration des morts et les obituaires à Saint-Martial de Limoges du XIe au XIIIe siècle* (Paris, 1989), and the article by J. Wollasch, "Les obituaires, témoins de la vie clunisienne," *Cahiers de Civilisation médiévale* 22 (1979) 139–171.

185. See Huglo, "Office de prime."

sermones exponitur, ita ut omnes intellegant ut nullus frater se de ignoran-
tiam regole excusare possit ["3. This hour of Prime is sung where they
sleep; and once the little chapter has been recited, they pray in the
same place. 4. Immediately afterward, they sit there, the prior being
with them, and read the Rule of St. Benedict; all the words are explained one by one by the prior or anyone charged with doing so in
order that no brother may excuse himself by invoking his ignorance
of the Rule"].[186] The Rule that Chrodegang, bishop of Metz, imposed
on the canons of the cathedral marks an important step in the formation of Prime since it shows a well-organized Office.[187]

At that time, Prime comprised the reading of one chapter from the
Rule (according to local customs), a sermon or homily (on Sunday,
Wednesday, Friday, and solemn feasts), and the reading of the martyrology. But there was nothing yet about commemorating the dead.
One canon of the Council of Aachen in 817 describes a similarly
structured office of Prime, and stresses the importance of the martyrology,[188] but it also alludes to the commemoration of the dead.[189]

By the ninth century, the office in chapter after Prime was completely established and presented the following structure: (1) office of
the readings, (2) chapter of faults, (3) assignment of manual labor.

Only the office of readings had a strictly liturgical character since
the other two parts were concerned rather with the organization of
life within the monastery. There was a special emphasis on penance
with the chapter of faults, during which the monastics publicly con-
fessed their faults, accused one another, and received the penances
necessary for the atonement of faults.

Because of the first section, the office of readings, a particular book
came into existence, the chapter book, first attested in the ninth century.[190] Thus, we once more observe the same process, repeated

186. Andrieu, *OR,* 3:195–208.
187. Two redactions of Chrodegang's Rule with two different titles are extant: *In
hora prima* ["at the first hour"] in the first (*PL* 89, col. 1067) and *Ut ad capitulum quo-
tidie veniat* ["that one should come to chapter everyday"] in the second (*PL* 89, col.
1102).
188. See B. de Gaiffier, "De l'usage et de la lecture du martyrologe: Témoignages
antérieurs au XIᵉ siècle," *Analecta Bollandiana* 79 (1961) 40–59.
189. See Huglo, "Office de prime," 13–14; Ph. Hofmeister, "Das Toten gedächtnis
im Officium Capituli," *Studien und Mitteilungen zur Geschichte des Benediktinerordens
und seiner Zweige* 70 (1959) 189–200.
190. On the origin and history of the chapter book in the Middle Ages, see the
basic article of J.-L. Lemaître, "'Liber capituli': Le livre du chapitre, des origines

throughout the Middle Ages: a liturgical action, once firmly implanted, brings about the creation of an appropriate book, tailored for use in a specific rite.

In monasteries and cathedral chapters, another consequence of the office in chapter after Prime was that a particular space reserved for its enactment was provided, the chapter hall, early indications of which are already attested in the eighth century.[191]

2. THE CHAPTER BOOK

A composite book if there was ever one since it is made up of other books in juxtaposition, the chapter book was used in the Middle Ages for just the first part (devoted to the readings) of the office in chapter after Prime.[192] The oldest complete manuscripts go back to the ninth century. The best known among them is the martyrology of Usuard, an inaccurate title since this book also includes the other texts of the office of Prime (Paris, B. N., lat. 13745; Saint-Germain-des-Prés, after 858),[193] whose contents are as follows:

—prologue by Usuard, a monk of Saint-Germain-des-Prés, the author of the book (fols. 1–2);

—martyrology, composed by Usuard (fols. 3–38);

—hymns in honor of St. Germain (fols. 88v–89r);

—list of the abbots of Saint-Germain-des Prés (fols. 89v–90v);

—Rule of St. Benedict (fols. 90v–156);

—necrology (fols. 157–183).

The majority of medieval manuscripts used at the office in chapter are made up of the Rule (Benedictine, Augustinian, and so on), martyrology, and necrology (or obituary). Sometimes, a lectionary is added, most often reduced to the mention of the liturgical day and gospel pericope followed by the incipit of the homily.[194]

---

au XVIᵉ siècle: L'exemple français," *Memoria: Der Geschichtliche Zeugniswert,* 625–648.

191. On this topic, see the texts collected by Lemaître, "Aux origines de l'office du chapitre et de la salle capitulaire: L'exemple de Fontenelle," *La Neustrie: Les pays au nord de la Loire de 650 à 850, Colloque historique international,* ed. H. Atsma, 2 vols., Beihefte der Francia 16 (Sigmaringen, 1989) 2:365–369.

192. Concerning the history of this book, see Lemaître, "Liber capituli"; Baroffio, "Manoscritti liturgici," 165.

193. See J. Dubois, *Le martyrologe d'Usuard,* text and commentary (Brussels, 1965).

194. The lists of pericopes are only an accessory part of the composition of the book and function only as a reminder of the biblical passages to be read at other

In the texts of the Middle Ages, the mention of the *Liber capituli* is rare and according to the study of J.-L. Lemaître, is not found before the thirteenth century.[195] During the High Middle Ages, the chapter book was often designated by the title of one of the texts composing it *(martyrologium, regula)* or on occasion both.

Let us now turn to the history and contents of the two principal liturgical books contained in the chapter book.

3. THE MARTYROLOGY

J. Dubois devoted a large part of his scholarly labors to the study of martyrologies, in which the historians of medieval liturgy are highly interested, especially because these documents help us understand the cult of saints[196] and retrace its history.

While the liturgical calendar cited only the names and qualities of the saints, the martyrology, which followed the Roman (calends, nones, and ides) not the liturgical calendar,[197] announced the anniversaries of the saints celebrated in the different churches. Along with names, the places where the saints were venerated, their quality, their time, and sometimes a summary of their actions, their "history," were mentioned; hence the term "historical martyrology." These texts were read every day during the first part of the office in chapter after Prime, sometimes with several saints on the same day, therefore several "stories." Compiled from diverse sources (legends, passions, lives of the saints, chronicles, and so on), the notices in the martyrology

---

Hours of the Office or at Mass. For a complete survey of the manuscripts, their contents, their codicological aspect, their chronological and geographical repartition, see Lemaître, "Liber capituli," 637–648.

195. The oldest known mention is in the chapter book of the Abbey of Cluny containing the list of the manuscripts commissioned by the abbot Yves I of Vergy (1257–1275), Paris, B. N., lat. 10938: *Item collectarium . . . et librum novum capituli* ["likewise, a collectar . . . and the new chapter book"]; see Lemaître, "Liber capituli," 626–627.

196. See J. Dubois, *Le martyrologe du Moyen Age latin,* Typologie des sources du Moyen age occidental, fasc. 26 (Turnhout, 1978), with 7 pages of update; see also the collection of the main articles which he has devoted to this book, *Martyrologes: D'Usuard au martyrologe romain* (Abbeville, 1990). See also the notice in *Liturgica Vaticana,* 44–48, with bibliography; J. M. McCulloh, "Martyrology," *Dictionary of the Middle Ages,* ed. J. R. Strayer, vol 7 (New York, 1987) 161ff.; and recently, Dubois and Lemaître, *Sources et méthodes,* 103–134.

197. See Part 2, I, 1, the section on the calendar, and J. Hennig, "Kalendar und Martyrologium als Literaturformen," *Archiv für Liturgiewissenschaft* 7 (1961) 1ff.

are the best sources of information on the cult of the saints, the topography of places in antiquity and the High Middle Ages, the discovery and translation of relics, the dedications of altars and churches, the relationship between monasteries and chapters of canons. The medieval martyrologies, whether integrated into the chapter book or not, allow us to reconstitute the history of the different known traditions (based on the Hieronymian Martyrology [fifth century], the Martyrology of Ado [858], the Martyrology of Usuard [after 858–before 875], and so on).

The majority of medieval manuscript sources contain, more or less modified, the text of the Martyrology of Usuard (which has no empty day). Usuard composed his martyrology, using several textual traditions.[198] A good number of local types derive from the Martyrology of Usuard, recast to a greater or lesser extent.[199] The relative unity of different martyrologies is due to their drawing from a common store; in the manuscripts, this forms a structure on which are arranged elements either particular to one religious house or shared by other monasteries of the same family. This blend of unity and diversity is one of the riches of these liturgical documents. They enable us to fathom, even to reconstitute, the history of a particular cult, to get the feel of the evolution of hagiography in the Middle Ages, thanks to helpful comparisons with other liturgical books and various texts. True witnesses to the liturgical life of an abbey, they bear the traces of new cults in the numerous marginal additions visible in almost all manuscripts. The great number of sources which have come down to us prove that each church wanted to possess "its own" martyrology, indispensable because of its use at the office. The martyrologies were not only employed to announce the saints of the day; above all they were meant to instruct and spiritually edify the members of the community by describing the saints' virtues and miracles.

The public reading of the martyrology at the office influenced the material aspect of the manuscript, especially the layout of the pages, which needed to be clear in order to facilitate the reader's task.

4. THE NECROLOGY AND OBITUARY

Like the martyrology, the necrology followed the Roman calendar; it contained for each day the anniversaries of the deceased whose

198. See Dubois et Lemaître, *Sources et méthodes*.
199. See the collected articles in Dubois, *Martyrologes*, 43–159.

memory was to be recalled at the office in chapter after Prime. In the Carolingian *liber memorialis,* used at Mass,[200] membership in a religious community, lineage, and other criteria determined the order in which the names were placed, whereas, in the necrology, the date of death was the sole factor determining the structure of the book. The advent of necrologies in the course of the ninth century, along with the chapter books in which they generally were included, did not spell the demise of the *libri memoriales,* which continued to be used until the twelfth century, as the manuscripts that have been kept show. As early as the Carolingian period, the necrology was augmented by the transcription, into the margins of the original text, of mutual agreements between confraternities by which two communities pledged to commemorate the other's deceased monks in the same way as their own.

In the thirteenth century, Mass endowments for the commemoration of the dead necessitated the creation of a new book, the obituary,[201] whose contents were akin to those of the necrology. Instead of commemorating a dead person during the office of Prime, one celebrated a Mass for that person. The structure of the obituary was not affected by this change of practice since, like the necrology, it remained a list of names classified in the order of the anniversaries of the days of death. The only sizable difference between the two books was that the obituary also contained the legal will setting up the endowment for anniversary Masses; thus, as much as a liturgical book, the obituary is a book of accounting since the income from the foundation was entered there.

In most chapter books in the Middle Ages, the necrology and obituary part follows, each day, the martyrology or the Rule.

---

200. It was also possible to consult the sacramentaries at the canon of the Mass to find the names of the deceased whose anniversaries were commemorated.

201. See Lemaître, *Mourir à Saint-Martial,* 174, and "Les obituaires français: Perspectives nouvelles," *Revue d'Histoire de l'Eglise de France* 64 (1978) 69–82.

VI. Genesis and Development of the Breviary

The history of the breviary has benefited from the assiduous work of many liturgists so that today we are able to retrace the steps of the genesis and development of this book during the Middle Ages and the following centuries.[202]

Like the missal for the Mass, the breviary contains all the liturgical texts for the Office, whether said in choir or in private. In the beginning, the word *breviarium*, which means digest, designated any type of work presenting a summary *(summarium)* of a text, juridical for instance.[203] Before the first half of the thirteenth century, *breviarium* did not yet designate a precise liturgical book. It is the Franciscan breviary deriving from the second rule of the order approved by Innocent III in 1223 that for the first time expressly bears the name *breviarium: Clerici facient divinum officium secundum ordinem sanctae Romanae Ecclesiae excepto Psalterio, ex quo habere poterunt breviaria* ["The clerics will celebrate the Office according to the *ordo* of the holy Roman Church, except for the psalter which they may use in shortened forms"].[204] From the thirteenth century on, the manuscripts often bear the title of *breviarium*, a term, however, that does not reflect the diversity of the sources. The first examples go back to the eleventh and twelfth centuries, and the

202. Among the historians of the breviary, let us cite in the first place S. Bäumer, *Histoire du bréviaire*, 2 vols. (Paris, 1905); then, P. Batiffol, *Histoire du bréviaire romain*, 3rd ed. (Paris, 1911); H. Bohatta, *Bibliographie der Breviere, 1501–1850* (Leipzig, 1937); and Leroquais, *Bréviaires*. The last author studied a large number of manuscripts in order to write the introduction to his catalogue (pp. L–CXXXIII), which has become indispensable to any study of the breviary. Later on, we have Salmon, *Office divin*, with the telling subtitle, "Histoire de la formation du bréviaire du IXe au XVIe siècle"; Van Dijk and Walker, *Origins*. See also the short notices in Fiala and Irtenkauf, *Liturgische Nomenklatur*, 116–118; Baroffio, "Manoscritti liturgici," 164; Thiel, "Liturgische Bücher," 2380–2381.

203. See Huglo, *Livres de chant*, 118–119.

204. See Salmon, *Office divin*, 152–157.

book spread like wildfire during the thirteenth, then during the rest of the Middle Ages.[205] In contrast to the missal, the breviary does not seem to have been prepared by *libelli*, except perhaps for complete offices of saints which were circulated as independent booklets.[206] A few fragments of manuscripts from the ninth and tenth centuries suggest the existence of first attempts at breviaries (with juxtaposed rather than blended parts) before the eleventh century, but their fragmentary state precludes any definitive conclusions.[207] Like the first missals, the first breviaries juxtaposed the different elements of the Office: psalter, hymnal, antiphonal, lectionary, collectar, and so on. This type with juxtaposed parts was more commonly called *Liber officialis*, according to the expression found in the manuscript sources, especially those of the eleventh century from Germanic regions.[208] One group of breviaries from the eleventh century written in St. Gall (for example, St. Gall, Stiftsbibl., cod. 414) is representative of this type in which the pieces (antiphons, chapters, prayers, readings) are not abbreviated but grouped into sections.[209]

Among the earliest breviaries with juxtaposed parts are some masterpieces of medieval illumination, such as Paris, Bibl. Mazarine, ms. 364 (written by Oderisius, abbot of Monte Cassino between 1099 and 1105).[210] It comprises, in succession, all the books necessary for the

205. Lists of manuscripts are found in Leroquais, *Bréviaires;* Van Dijk and Walker, *Origins,* 528–542; Salmon, *Office divin,* 64–79.

206. Salmon, *Office divin,* 62–63.

207. See especially the fragments published by Gamber, *CLLA,* 606–614, and *CLLA, Supplementum,* 164–166. The author considers the earliest two attestations to the breviary to be the 21 folios of Basel, Universitätsbibl., N I 6 (nos. 8 and 20–22) (end of tenth century, from Switzerland or northern Italy), *CLLA,* no. 1690, and two folios kept in Nuremberg, Germanisches Museum, Küpferstichkabinett, Kapsel 536, SD 2815 (first half of ninth century, from southern Germany); see K. Gamber, "Ein Brevier fragment aus der 1. Hälftedes 9. Jahrhunderts," *Revue bénédictine* 95 (1985) 232–239. Gamber's hypotheses in this domain, as in that of the genesis of other liturgical books, are not unanimously accepted by specialists; here as elsewhere, the reproach is that his theories on the formation of the books are based on fragments from which no certain conclusions can be deduced.

208. See Huglo, *Livres de chant,* 117–118. The expression *Liber officialis* frequently appears in the library catalogues of Germanic regions from the eleventh century on; see Gy, "Premiers bréviaires," 108, n. 12.

209. Gy, "Premiers bréviaires," 104–113.

210. See H. Toubert, "Le bréviaire d'Oderisius (Paris, Bibl. Mazarine, ms. 364) et les influences byzantines au Mont-Cassin," *Un art dirigé: Réforme grégorienne et Iconographie* (Paris, 1990) 311–362.

celebration of the Office and, at the end, the list of incipits of the pieces arranged in the order of the celebration. This last part, entitled *breviarium sive ordo officiorum* ["breviary or order of the Office"] seems to be a sort of breviary within a breviary.

In the eleventh and twelfth centuries, breviaries with their different parts combined and inserted into their proper places in the celebration, made their appearance. The tendency was to shorten considerably all pieces in order to diminish the thickness of the books. In the breviaries used in choir, the readings retained a reasonable length, whereas in all the other types, they were reduced to a few lines or even a few words. This principle of reduction facilitated the use of breviaries when traveling, and the size of the books proves that they were sometimes taken along on a journey.[211] Being of small dimensions and as a consequence very thick, the breviaries were divided into two parts (summer, from Easter to Advent, and winter, from Advent to Easter; not Temporal–Sanctoral). The psalter, in general written separately in the beginning of breviaries with combined parts, was often omitted in the pocket type. The manuscripts present a great range of choices for the breviaries: they could be in one or two volumes;[212] format, arrangement of the text, musical notation, decoration were varied, depending above all on the kind of use for which they were intended.[213] Thus, there exist breviaries especially destined for the abbot, others for the reading of the Hours to the sick in the infirmary, others for traveling, others for the Office in choir, and so on.

One encounters "missal–breviaries" from the eleventh and twelfth centuries; their purpose was not to superpose a breviary on a missal but to group into one book the whole liturgy of one day or one feast, not that of the whole year.[214] In these manuscripts, Italian or French in origin, Masses were inserted into breviaries after Terce, their proper liturgical place.

The examination of the many manuscript sources from the eleventh and twelfth centuries leads to the conclusion that the breviary was

---

211. The term *portiforium,* designating pocket breviaries, for instance those to be taken along when traveling, continued to be used in England from the twelfth century to the time of printed breviaries.

212. See Salmon, *Office divin,* 80–85.

213. See P.-M. Gy, "La mise en page du bréviaire," *Mise en page et mise en texte du livre manuscrit,* ed. H.-J. Martin and J. Vezin (Paris, 1990) 127–120.

214. Concerning this type of breviary and the manuscripts pertaining to it, see Salmon, *Office divin,* 64–67.

regarded as a practical book into which one attempted to gather together as many elements of the Office as possible, without always succeeding in including everything. At the same time, the breviary was considered a model book and was destined to reorganize the monastic and canonical liturgy in the second half of the eleventh century. The study of Cluniac breviaries composed between the eleventh (for instance, Paris, B. N., lat. 12601)[215] and thirteenth centuries (for instance, the Breviary of St.-Victor-sur-Rhins)[216] reveals the persistence of a local tradition peculiar to the Cluniac Order, which influenced the churches depending upon the great Burgundian monastery. In the thirteenth century, the breviary used by the Roman Curia, and subsequently widely diffused because of its adoption by the Franciscan Order, became the instrument wielded by ecclesiastical authorities to impose a standard liturgy of the Office bearing an official stamp.[217] After the Middle Ages, breviaries printed in different regions demonstrate in a striking manner the persistence of the medieval tradition, especially for the Liturgy of the Hours.[218]

215. See J. Hourlier, "Le bréviaire de Saint-Taurin: Un livre liturgique clunisien à l'usage de l'Echelle-Saint-Aurin (Paris, BN, lat. 12601)," Etudes grégoriennes 3 (1959) 163–176.

216. A. Davril, "A propos d'un bréviaire manuscrit de Cluny conservé à Saint-Victor-sur-Rhins," Revue bénédictine 93 (1983) 108–122.

217. See Salmon, Office divin, 152ff.; S.J.P Van Dijk, "The Breviary of St. Francis," Franciscan Studies 9 (1949) 13ff.

218. See Davril, "Un bréviaire manuscrit de Fleury de 1598, témoin de la liturgie médiévale," Revue bénédictine 86 (1976) 154–162.

Part Four

The Books of Sacraments and Rites

For any cultic celebration, one needs sacred texts and guidelines for conducting the rites. In the Christian liturgy, orations, organized into formularies, biblical readings, and sung pieces, appear in books intended for the different ministers having a part in the worship service.[1] It is equally necessary to have at one's disposal books descriptive (even prescriptive) in character, which specify the order the ceremonies are to follow, the roles, movements, and postures of the actors, and give the list of the required liturgical objects, and so on. According to its proper liturgical meaning, an *ordo* is a description of the sacred rites, a directory, a sort of guide for the use of priests and their assistants, describing in detail the order of the ceremonies and the manner of their performance.

From the earliest times of Christianity (second to fifth centuries), the description of the rites—known for that period through the catechesis and preaching of bishops and priests—plays a preeminent role in the transmission of the faith because, in the last analysis, what is involved is the search for liturgical norms destined to be imposed first on one community, then on a diocese, and finally on the whole of Christendom.

In the fifth and sixth centuries, the first rulings for the principal Christian celebrations appeared: baptism, Eucharist, dedications of churches, offices of Holy Week, and so on. In the Middle Ages, these documents (in general small booklets, *libelli*) gave rise to the main descriptive and prescriptive books of the Latin liturgy, in which the place given to the rubrics, written in red or orange, is important: the *ordines*

---

1. On this topic, see Part 2.

romani, the rituals, and the pontificals, and on another cultic plane, the customaries, the ordinaries, the ceremonials, the processionals.

We turn now to the description of the history of these different books. By reason of their content and character, *ordines romani,* rituals, and pontificals must be placed in the same category: they are liturgical books in the strict sense because they are used during celebrations by the officiants. In contrast, customaries, ordinaries, ceremonials, and processionals belong rather to the category of books *pertaining to* the liturgy, regulating the rites (or describing their performance) of a religious order or a diocese, for instance, but playing no part whatsoever in the liturgy itself. These books, which appear in the second half of the Middle Ages, will be presented later in other sections. As for the *ordines romani,* rituals, and pontificals, it seems judicious to classify them according to their respective users: priests, monks, bishops, pope. Indeed, it will soon become obvious that the type of texts they contain does not always make it easy to distinguish them from one another. Finally, let us add that all these books, in some degree and despite their typological differences, sometimes important—as the distinction between liturgical books and books *pertaining to* the liturgy—made an essential contribution to the Church's purpose to order its liturgy, to set down rules and usages and then diffuse them so that the liturgy might be the sacramental expression of the Church's doctrine.

I. The *Ordines Romani*

An *ordo* concerns a precise liturgical action for which it assembles together both the sacred texts to be spoken (incipits of the orations, readings, chants, and so on) and under the form of rubrics, the rules governing, sometimes to the slightest detail, the performance of this action.[2] In general, these texts are rather short, hence it behooves one to be prudent when interpreting the medieval terminology used to designate them. Although this is not the place to elaborate on the terms proper to each of the books dealt with in this part, a preliminary word of caution is necessary if one is to correctly interpret the medieval references to the *ordines*, references that correspond but faintly to the actual contents of the manuscripts.[3] In the manuscripts, the *ordines* are very rarely given a title, still less are they introduced by the mention of *ordo* or *ordo romanus*. Conversely, the term *ordo* (or even *ordo romanus*) appears time and time again in the catalogues of medieval libraries in which, although it sometimes designates a real *ordo*, episcopal for example, it applies as much to a modest *libellus* as to the large volume of a pontifical or parish ritual.[4] However, certain *ordines romani* (called *OR* from now on) bear titles disclosing their contents with precision: *De officiis in noctibus* ["The night offices"], *Instructio ecclesiastici ordinis* ["Exposition of the ecclesiastical order"] *Ordo vel denuntiatio scrutinii* ["Order and explanation of the scrutinies"].

2. First of all, one must distinguish between *ordines* in general and *ordines romani*, which are so called because of their Roman origin. It will quickly become obvious that several *ordines* of the Middle Ages have nothing in common with the *ordines romani*.

3. Here too, we lack an overall study of the concordance, or absence of it, between the terminology employed by medieval texts and the actual contents of the manuscripts that have been preserved.

4. On the different medieval meanings of the word *ordo*, see Vogel, *Introduction*, 135–136.

Still other titles underline the Roman character of the text: *Ordo ecclesiasticus romanae ecclesiae vel qualiter missa celebratur (OR I)* ["Ecclesiastical order of the Roman Church and how Mass is celebrated"].

1. HISTORY OF THE *ORDINES ROMANI*

The *ordines* of Roman origin *(OR)* appear in the research on ancient liturgical books with the publication of Melchior Hittorp's book *De divinis catholicae Ecclesiae officiis* ["The Divine Offices of the Catholic Church"] in 1568 in Cologne; in this book, the author edited a compilation of *ordines* under the title *Ordo romanus vulgatus* ["The Roman order promulgated"]. In the following century, E. Martène[5] and especially J. Mabillon, who published a selection of fifteen *ordines* from the ninth to the fifteenth centuries,[6] pioneered a critical edition of these texts on the basis of the manuscript witnesses of the Middle Ages. Without forgetting the numerous studies done in the meantime, we owe to the great liturgist M. Andrieu (1886–1956)[7] the critical edition in which he sorts, dates, and localizes the *OR* on the basis of the oldest manuscripts.[8] Since Andrieu, many partial studies and editions have complemented the work of the great Strasbourg liturgist by adding specific details to his hypotheses, even correcting them, without however questioning either the classification he adopted or the work he did on the manuscripts.[9] Before presenting this classification, we must specify that Andrieu had circumscribed his task to the study of *ordines* of Roman origin *(OR)*, and he gave relatively little attention either to the fate of these texts, especially after their introduction into Gaul, or to non-Roman *ordines*;[10] this, others coming after him have done.

---

5. In his *De antiquis Ecclesiae ritibus libri tres* (1700–1702).

6. *Museum italicum*, 2 vols. (Paris, 1687–1689); the second volume bears this title: *Musei italici, t.II, Complectens antiquos libros rituales sanctae romanae Ecclesiae cum commentario praevio in Ordinem romanum* ["Volume 2 of the Italian Museum, containing the ancient books of rituals of the holy Roman Church, preceded by a commentary on the Roman Ordo"]. See *PL* 78, cols. 851–1408.

7. On this liturgist, see p. 14.

8. Andrieu, *OR*; we must regret that this monumental work has to this day gone without a volume of tables. On Andrieu's edition, see Martimort, *Ordines*, 17–47; C. Lambot, "Les *ordines romani* du haut Moyen Age édités par Mgr Michel Andrieu," *Revue bénédictine* 62 (1952) 302–306.

9. See a list of these works in Vogel, *Introduction*, 139–144; Martimort, *Ordines*.

10. On these collections as a whole, see especially the summary of Martimort, *Ordines*.

2. NATURE OF THE *ORDINES ROMANI*

Varying in length from a few folios to more than sixty pages, the *OR* have been classified according to the many liturgical actions which they describe (one can almost say that there are as many kinds of *ordines* as rites) and especially according to the type of liturgy they pertain to. Distancing himself from Mabillon's classification, Andrieu grouped the *OR* (a total of fifty, without counting the doublets, see table of *OR*)[11] in accordance with the sort of liturgy they refer to: papal, episcopal, monastic, and so on; the one exception is the noteworthy *OR* 50, which concerns the liturgical year and is thus a particular case. Among the most important for the history of the liturgy, one finds *OR* for the pope's or the bishop's Mass, Christian initiation, the office of Holy Week, ordinations, the dedication of churches, the blessing and coronation of sovereigns, funerals.

3. THE *ORDINES ROMANI* IN THE MANUSCRIPTS[12]

Before going on to the examination of the different collections, their history, and their contents, let us see briefly how the texts were used and circulated in the Middle Ages. Those *libelli* which contained one *ordo* each, gathered together at a given period (sixth and seventh centuries), gave rise to more or less organized collections of *ordines* (see pp. 182–185). This grouping into more important codicological entities—attested by the manuscripts of *ordines* from the eighth to tenth centuries—never really supplanted the writing and circulation of *ordines* (especially those of non-Roman traditions) as independent booklets. For instance, booklets concerning the dedication of a church continued to exist and were not necessarily inserted afterward into an older manuscript or one contemporary with the booklet itself.[13] But a good number of *libelli* were added at a later date to a preexisting manuscript; an example of this sort of thing is the *ordo* for the

11. On Andrieu's classification and numbering, see Andrieu, *OR*; and Vogel, *Introduction*, 191–197, with a useful concordance table between Mabillon's classification and Andrieu's; see also Martimort, *Ordines*, 110–123.

12. See the first volume of Andrieu, *OR*, entirely devoted to the manuscripts he used for the edition of the texts. He has detailed reports on the fragments, the isolated *ordines*, and of course, the collections.

13. As perhaps for the four folios of the *libellus*, from the eleventh century, of the Ambrosian *ordo* for the dedication of a church (Lucca, Bibl. Capit., cod. 605); see P. Borella, "L'*ordo* ambrosiano de G. Mercati per la dedicazione della chiesa," *Ephemerides liturgicae* 72, (1958) 48–50.

dedication of a church written on six folios and, subsequently tacked onto a sacramentary produced in the second half of the ninth century in the circles of Charles the Bald (Paris, B. N., lat. 2292). M. Gros has demonstrated that the Italian calligraphy of this *ordo* from the eleventh century as well as its text, independent from the Romano-Gallican tradition, lead to the conclusion that this *libellus* was composed to adapt the Carolingian manuscript to the local liturgy.[14]

Whether Roman or not, one *ordo* or several *ordines* not infrequently end up being transcribed on blank pages of manuscripts, whether liturgical or not. Or else, and with more serious consequences for the history of the liturgy, they are inserted perfectly from the viewpoints of both codicology and liturgy into sacramentaries.[15] The sacramentaries of the Leonine type do not contain any *ordo*,[16] whereas the Gelasian and Gregorian[17] have included texts (rubrics and prayers) for the rites of baptism, confirmation, penance, anointing of the sick, and funerals. In parishes and monasteries, priests needed these texts which enabled them to celebrate baptism or funerals with the sacramentary, the book pertaining to their function. We must also mention manuscripts of monastic origin in which one encounters supplementary *ordines*, for the dedication of a church or the consecration of an altar, for instance. These sacramentaries with "enlarged" contents did not prevent the advent and development of rituals (see II of this part).

The collections of OR were most often transcribed into independent manuscripts. At first, the contents of these manuscripts were organized in various ways depending on the different collections, but later on, the material was classified according to the different types of liturgy in which the *ordines* were to be used. The manuscripts of this second category, which are sometimes collections of *libelli*, mark a decisive step in the formation of the pontifical, to such a point that they are called "primitive pontificals."[18]

---

14. M. Gros, "L'*ordo* pour la dédicace des églises dans le sacramentaire de Nonantola," *Revue bénédictine* 79 (1969) 368–374.

15. See Martimort, *Ordines*, 37–39.

16. Concerning the Leonine Sacramentary, see Part 2, I, section on sacramentaries.

17. Concerning these two great families of sacramentaries, see Part 2, I, section on sacramentaries.

18. See III, 1, below, on the "primitive pontificals."

4. HISTORY AND CONTENT OF THE COLLECTIONS OF *ORDINES ROMANI* AND OTHER *ORDINES*[19]

List of the *ordines romani* (the numbering is Andrieu's):

1. *Ordo* for a papal Mass (Rome, about 690–700).
2. First supplement to the *ordo* (Rome, about 690–700).
3. Second supplement to *Ordo* I (Rome, about 690–700 and Frankish lands about 750).
4. Frankish revision of *Ordo* I (Frankish lands, 750–800).
5. Second revision of *Ordo* I (Rhine region, about 850–900).
6. Third Frankish revision of *Ordo* I (Metz? 850–900).
7. Prayers and signs of the cross at the Canon of the Mass (Frankish lands, ninth century).
8. Vestments of the pontiff (Frankish lands, 850–900).
9. First *ordo* for an episcopal Mass (Frankish lands, 880–900).
10. First *ordo* for an episcopal Mass (Mainz? 900–950).
11. *Ordo* for baptism (Rome, seventh century, perhaps 550–600).
12. *Ordo* for the Office (Rome, 775–850).
13A. *Ordo* for the night office readings (Rome, 700–750).
13B. *Ordo* for the night office readings (Frankish lands, 775–800).
13C. *Ordo* for the night office readings (Frankish lands, about 1000).
13D. *Ordo* for the night office readings (Frankish lands, eleventh century).
14. *Ordo* for the readings at the Vatican basilica (Rome, 650–700).
15. *Capitulare ecclesiastici ordinis* ["Charter of the ecclesiastical order"] (Frankish lands, 775–780).
16. *Instructio ecclesiastici ordinis* ["Exposition of the ecclesiastical order"] (Frankish lands, 775–780).
17. *Breviarium ecclesiastici ordinis* ["Summary of the ecclesiastical order"] (Frankish lands, 780–800).
18. The monastic Divine Office (Frankish lands, 775–780).
19. *Ordo* for monastic meals (Frankish lands, 775–780).
20. *Ordo* for the feast of the Purification (Frankish lands, eighth century, after a Roman source).
21. Procession of the Greater Litanies (Frankish lands, eighth century).
22. *Ordo* for Lent (Frankish lands, 780–800).
23. *Ordo* for Holy Thursday to Holy Saturday (Rome, 700–750).

19. For more details on the contents of each of the *OR*, see Andrieu, *OR*, and Vogel, *Introduction*, 155–188.

24. *Ordo* for the offices from Wednesday in Holy Week to Holy Saturday (Frankish lands, 750–800).[20]

25. Blessing of the Easter candle (Frankish lands, 800–850).

26. *Ordo* for the night office from Holy Thursday to Easter (Rome, 750–775).

27. Appendix to *Ordo* XXVI (Frankish lands, 700–750, after a [Roman] source dating from about 650–700).

28. *Ordo* for middle Sunday [fifth Sunday of Lent] to the octave of Easter (Frankish lands, about 800).

29. Monastic *ordo* for the last four days of Holy Week (Frankish lands, 870–890).

30A. *Ordo* for Holy Thursday to the Saturday after Easter, *in albis* (Frankish lands, 750–800).

30B. *Ordo* for Holy Thursday to the Saturday after Easter, *in albis* (Frankish lands, 775–800).

31. *Ordo* for the Divine Office from the middle Sunday [fifth Sunday of Lent] to the octave of Easter (Frankish lands, 850–900).

32. *Ordo* for the last three days of Holy Week (Frankish lands, 880–900).

33. *Ordo* for the last three days of Holy Week (Frankish lands, tenth century).

34. Roman *ordo* for ordinations (Rome, about 750, after a source from the fourth century).

35. Modified *ordo* for ordinations (Frankish lands, 900–925).

35A. Episcopal ordination (Rome, Frankish lands, about 970).

35B. Episcopal consecration (Rome, Frankish lands, 975–1000).

36. The degrees of the Roman hierarchy (Rome, 880–900).

37A. *Ordo* for ordinations on Ember Days (Frankish lands, 800–900).

37B. *Ordo* of ordinations on Ember Days (Frankish lands, Rhine region, about 825).

38. *Ordo* for ordinations on Ember Days (Frankish lands, Rhine region, about 940).

39. Ordinations in the Roman Church (Rome, 790–800).

40A. Ordination of the pontiff (Rome, sixth century).

40B. Ordination of the pontiff (Rome, sixth century).

---

20. On the historical interest of this *ordo*, see M. Klockener, "Die 'orationes sollemnes' am Mittwoch der Heiligen Woch (*OR,* XXIV, 1–4): Eine Neuerung aus Karolingerzeit," *Archiv für Liturgiewissenschaft* 34 (1992) 84–101.

41. Gallican *ordo* for the dedication of a church (Frankish lands, about 750–775).
42. Roman *ordo* for the dedication of a church and the deposition of relics (Rome, about 700–750).
43. *Ordo* for the translation of relics (Frankish lands, 790–800).
44. *Ordo* for the *diligentia* [rite of ablutions and incensation used in the *confessio*] in St. Peter's (Rome, about 790).
45. *Ordo* for the coronation of the emperor (Rome, Frankish lands, about 900).
46. *Ordo* for the coronation of the Emperor (Frankish lands, Cambrai, about 1050).
47. *Ordo* for the coronation of the Emperor (Frankish lands, about 1050).
48. Mass for the coronation of the Emperor (Frankish lands, about 1050).
49. *Ordo* for funerals (Rome, eighth century).
50. *Ordo* for the liturgical year (Germany, about 950).

We have seen above that the collections, made for obviously practical reasons, did not put an end to the circulation of certain isolated *OR*. The dominant concern of the liturgists who compiled these collections was to make available in a minimum number of volumes the many texts describing the rites of the Roman Church. Moreover, it is significant that the creation of collections of *OR* accelerated, not to say was entirely achieved, when they spread beyond the Alps, to Gaul in particular, from the beginning of the eighth century on. The analysis of the structure of the collections demonstrates that they are imperfectly organized gatherings of documents, not yet deserving to be called books in the exact sense of the word. The gap separating them from books really organized to respond to a specific type of liturgical action and especially to the needs of their users, would not be bridged before the appearance of the "primitive pontificals."

The purpose, first of Martène and Mabillon, then closer to us of L. Duchesne and to a lesser degree M. Andrieu, was to rediscover through the *OR* the authentic Roman liturgy in antiquity and to follow its adaptations and transformations, particularly in Gaul.[21] This point of historiography sheds light on the prodigious favor these *OR* texts enjoyed with people of the Middle Ages. In their eyes, the rites

21. Concerning these questions, see Martimort, *Ordines*, 26–30.

of the Roman Church were models to be imitated, and this goal necessitated the availability of written descriptions. Here, we come close to
seeing the conditions under which the *OR* were produced in Rome in
the fifth and sixth centuries. At that time, there developed a more
structured view of liturgical time, resulting in a process of the organization of the Mass orations into formularies and of readings and sung
pieces into systems as reflected in the sacramentaries, the books of
readings, and the antiphonals; and in parallel fashion, the practices
and usages proper to the different rites were progressively codified in
the *OR* so as to endow them with official status. In their work, Andrieu and also liturgists like A. Chavasse and V. Saxer have described
very well the historical and liturgical setting in which the *OR* arose.[22]
As an example, let us simply recall the pivotal role the *OR* played in
the process of the development of the urban environment in the city
of Rome (setting up of parishes, platting of neighborhoods and so on).

5. THE ROMAN COLLECTION OR COLLECTION A

Collection A was put together in Gaul between 700 and 750 from
purely Roman *ordines* and made it possible to conduct celebrations according to the Roman rite. We no longer have any document containing this collection, deriving from a Roman scriptorium. The oldest
attestation is Montpellier, Bibl. Fac. Méd., ms. 412 (Tours, beginning
of ninth century).[23] Several manuscripts from the tenth and eleventh
centuries prove that the collection was circulated after the Carolingian period.[24] It puts together the following *ordines:* (1) papal Mass
(about 690–700); (11) *ordo* for Christian initiation (about 700–750);
(13A) *ordo* for the readings at the night office (about 700–750); (27)
Holy Week (about 650–700); (42) *ordo* for the deposition of relics

22. See in particular, A. Chavasse, "L'organisation stationnale du Carême romain,
avant le VIIIe siècle: Une organisation pastorale," *Revue des Sciences religieuses* 56
(1982) 17–32; "Les grands cadres de la célébration à Rome *in urbe* et *extra muros*
jusqu'au VIIIe siècle," *Revue bénédictine* 96 (1986) 7–26; "Aménagements liturgiques
à Rome au VIIe et au VIIIe siècle," *Revue bénédictine* 99 (1989) 75–102; "A Rome le
Jeudi saint, au VIIe siècle, d'après un vieil *ordo*," *Revue d'Histoire ecclésiastique* 50
(1955) 21–35; V. Saxer, "L'utilisation par la liturgie de l'espace urbain et suburbain: L'exemple de Rome dans l'Antiquité et le haut Moyen Age," *Actes du XIe
Congrès international d'Archéologie chrétienne, Lyon, Vienne, Grenoble, Genève, et
Aosta, 21–28 septembre 1986*, 2 vols. (Rome, 1989) 2:917–1031

23. See Andrieu, *OR*, 211–213.

24. On these manuscripts from the tenth and eleventh centuries, see Vogel, *Introduction*, 145.

(about 700–750); (34) ordinations (about 750, but from a much more ancient source, perhaps fourth century). Very probably each *ordo* of the collection was introduced into Gaul in the first half of the eighth century through the intermediary of individuals returning from Rome and fascinated by Rome and its liturgy. It is only at the time of the first romanization of the Gallican liturgy by Pepin the Short,[25] that the *ordines* bearing the strongest Roman stamp were gathered into collections.[26]

6. THE GALLICANIZED COLLECTION OR COLLECTION B

Like the gallicanized Roman sacramentaries, for instance, the Gelasian of the Eighth Century,[27] Collection B contains *OR* already largely adapted to the liturgy of Carolingian Gaul. Indeed, as in the case of the Roman sacramentaries which were too strongly marked by their origin (Sanctoral, local places, type of celebration), it was necessary to modify the contents of the *OR* in order to render them suitable for use in the churches of Gaul. Collection B contains most of the *ordines* already present in Collection A, but modified, and some other texts as well: (1) papal Mass with Gallican adaptations (like the movements and place of the celebrant); (11) *ordo* for Christian initiation, with changes; (13B) *ordo* for the readings at the night office used in Gaul; (28) *ordo* for Holy Week; (37A) *ordo* for ordinations on the Ember Days, comparable to that in the Gelasian (purely Frankish, about 800–900); (41) Gallican *ordo* for the dedication of a church (about 750–775); (42) *ordo* for the deposition of relics, under a form identical to that of Collection A. Although it dates from the second half of the eighth century, the complete Collection B is found in some manuscripts from the first half of the ninth century (the best manuscript witness is Verona, Bibl. capit., cod. 92)[28] which already look like first drafts of pontificals because they contain the texts of some formularies for sacraments and blessings. Collection B clearly expresses the compromise between the adaptation of Roman sources, at the time they were being adopted by a large portion of the medieval West, and the will to preserve local usages.

25. See Part 2, I, section on sacramentaries.
26. See Vogel, *Introduction*, 146–150.
27. See Part 2, I, section on sacramentaries.
28. See Andrieu, *OR*, 1:367–372.

7. THE GALLICAN COLLECTIONS

Two collections contain *ordines* which are almost exclusively theirs and have no posterity. The St. Amand Collection, so called from the scriptorium of the abbey in northern France where it was done, is preserved in one single manuscript (Paris, B. N., lat. 974; tenth century).[29] In all likelihood, this collection was compiled about 770–790 and contains a Frankish recension of the *ordo* for the papal Mass, and other *ordines:* (30B) for the Easter Triduum and Easter Week (about 775–780); (21) for the procession of the Greater Litanies (eighth century); (39) for ordinations (Rome, about 790–800); (43) for the deposition of relics; (20) for the procession on the feast of the Purification (eighth century, after a Roman source).[30]

The St. Gall Collection (named after St. Gall, Stiftsbibl., cod. 349; end of eighth century),[31] or according to its title in the manuscript, *capitulare ecclesiastici ordinis* ["charter of the ecclesiastical order"], was written about 775–780 by a Burgundian or Austrasian monk. The anonymous author made use of Roman sources which he adapted to local needs. The list of *ordines* in this collection, obviously destined for monastic use, is as follows: (14) *ordo* for the readings at the night office at the basilica of St. Peter (Rome, about 650–700); (15) the *capitulare ecclesiastici ordinis*, a Roman ceremonial for the liturgical year (about 775–780); (16) *instructio ecclesiastici ordinis* ["exposition of the ecclesiastical order"], a monastic ceremonial for the liturgical year (about 775–780); (18) the monastic Divine Office (about 775–780); (19) *ordo* for monastic meals (about 775–780).

Let us conclude this brief presentation of the principal collections with *ordines* which were circulated in an independent manner without ever becoming part of a homogeneous collection.[32] The small group of *ordines* transcribed in Brussels, Bibl. royale, cod. 10127–10144 (end of eighth century),[33] forms not so much a collection as a sort of ritual for the priest's use. There, one finds the following *ordines:* (3) second supplement to the *ordo* for the papal Mass (about 690–700); (13B) *ordo* for the readings at the night office; (24) *ordo* for

29. Ibid., 1:255–256.
30. See Vogel, *Introduction*, 152, and Martimort, *Ordines*, 24.
31. See Andrieu, *OR*, 1:330–333, 491–492.
32. Concerning the *ordines romani* that were discovered and then added to Andrieu's, and represent variants of unequal importance to the known texts, see Martimort, *Ordines*, 36–37.
33. See Andrieu, *OR*, 1:91–96; Gamber, *CLLA*, no. 856, pp. 392–393.

the Offices from Wednesday in Holy Week to Holy Saturday (about 750–800); (26) *ordo* for the night office from Holy Thursday to Easter (about 750–775); (30A) *ordo* for Holy Thursday to Saturday *in albis*. Some of these texts are taken up later on in manuscripts of the ninth and tenth centuries.[34] Rare *ordines* were circulated independently from any collection (such as Andrieu's numbers 35B, 37, 45, 47), see the list of *ordines* just above) before being integrated into the vast compilation of the Romano-Germanic Pontifical in the second half of the tenth century.[35]

To simplify, one could say that the history of the *OR* stops in the tenth century with the appearance of the "primitive pontificals," and especially the Romano-Germanic Pontifical. Nevertheless, the *ordines*, and not just those of Roman origin, continued to have a life after the creation of the pontifical, if only in the many rituals which are true typological prolongations of the prescriptive texts found in the *OR*.

Their historical interest no longer needs any demonstration so important was their impact on the Latin liturgy in the West, especially at the time they made their way into the Frankish Empire.[36] I shall simply limit myself to recalling the unique testimony of the nine small ivory plaques attached to the back cover of the Drogon Sacramentary (Paris, B. N., lat. 9428; middle of ninth century), showing nine scenes of the Eucharist celebrated by the bishop in the cathedral of Metz. The different scenes, presented with a meticulous attention to detail (number and placement of the officiants, gestures, liturgical objects, and so on), reflect the historical fact that Metz adopted the *ordines romani* during the Carolingian period under the episcopacy of Chrodegang (742–766); this is incontrovertible proof of the romanization of the Gallican liturgy in one of its bastions, the cathedral of Metz.[37]

34. See Martimort, *Ordines*, 23.

35. See III, 3, in this part, the section on the Romano-Germanic Pontifical.

36. On all these questions, see Martimort, *Ordines*, 42–47.

37. See R. E. Reynolds, "Image and Text: A Carolingian Illustration of Modifications in the Early Roman Eucharistic *Ordines*," *Viator* 14 (1983) 59–75.

II. The Rituals

The history of the rituals failed to arouse the interest of a large number of liturgists, either those of the seventeenth to nineteenth centuries or those of the twentieth century. The particular status of this liturgical book explains for a large part this relative historiographic void. Indeed, at its origin, the history of the book is one with that of the *ordines romani* and, from the Council of Trent on, one with that of the printed rituals. Between the two, the confusion of the rituals with the parish manuals (*pastorale, manuale curatorum* ["pastoral guide," "manual for the clergy in charge"]), which are rather guides and collections of counsels addressed to pastors, has contributed to render even more obscure the exact identity of the rituals.[38] The medieval manuscript rituals are the true ancestors of the printed rituals, in particular of the official Roman edition of 1614.[39] They have been partially disentangled from other books by P.-M. Gy in an article which has left its stamp on the research in this field.[40] Besides this overall study, there exist monographic analyses on a multitude of manuscripts.

38. The definitions of the ritual given in good dictionaries of liturgical books are generally not clear enough to elucidate the essential characteristics of the book; see, for instance, Fiala and Irtenkauf, *Liturgische Nomenklatur,* 127, and Thiel, *Liturgische Bücher,* 2392.

39. On the connection between manuscript rituals of the Middle Ages and printed rituals of modern times, see J.-B. Molin and A. Aussedat-Minvielle, *Répertoire des rituels et processionaux imprimés en France* (Paris, 1984).

40. Gy, "Collectaire," 441–469, repeated, with some corrections and additions, in *La liturgie dans l'histoire* (Paris, 1990) 91–126. It will prove helpful to consult also J.-B. Molin, "Un type d'ouvrage mal connu, le rituel: Son intérêt et ses caractéristiques bibliographiques." *Ephemerides liturgicae* 63 (1959) 218–224, and W. von Arx, "Zur Entschungsgeschichte des Rituale," *Zeitschrift für Schweizerische Kirchengeschichte* 63 (1969) 39–57.

1. DEFINITION AND FUNCTION OF THE MEDIEVAL RITUAL

The ritual contained everything that was necessary (rubrics and texts) for the performance of one or several liturgical actions, in particular those which were not exclusively reserved for the bishop. This leads us to speak of the ritual as the book of the priest, indispensable for a certain number of rites he presided over, sometimes as the sole officiant if he was involved in parish ministry; it was also one of the books of the monks and priest-monks which enabled them to carry out properly monastic rites. Centered on the administration of the sacraments, the rituals of the High Middle Ages contained the texts of certain *OR* or those of other *ordines* which never qualified as *OR* and remained independent from any collection, whether Roman or Gallican.

In order to understand correctly the typological specificity of the rituals of the High Middle Ages, one must place them within their historical and ecclesiological context. Several historians have shown that from the ninth century on, the parish emerged as an administrative and ecclesiastical entity; this promoted a specifically presbyterial liturgy within the multiple priestly functions.[41] Conversely, it is interesting to note that the process of codification and uniformization of the liturgy during the Carolingian period strongly influenced the development of the medieval parish's consciousness of itself. This all-important role of the liturgy in the formation of the parish community was especially decisive in the diffusion of the different liturgical books or texts proper to a specific rite. The ceremonies and formulas of the sacred acts having been fixed in writing, the clergy, secular or regular, played its role with increased authority in their religious

41. See the inclusive report of H. Platelle, "La paroisse et son curé jusqu'à la fin du XIIIᵉ siècle," *L'encadrement religieux des fidèles au Moyen Age et jusqu'au Concile de Trente: La paroisse, le clergé, la pastorale, la devotion*, Actes du 109ᵉ Congrès national des sociétés savantes, Dijon, 1984, vol. 1 (Paris, 1985) 11–26; the important study of A. Angenendt, "Die Liturgie und die Organisation des Kirchlichenlebens auf dem Lande," *Cristianizzazione ed organizzazione ecclesiastica delle campagne nell'alto Medioevo: Espansione e resistenze, 10–16 aprile 1980*, 2 vols., Settimane di studio del Centro italiano di studi sull'alto Medioevo 28 (Spoleto, 1982) 1:169ff.; J. Avril "La paroisse médiévale: Bilan et perspectives d'après quelques travaux récents," *Revue d'Histoire de l'Eglise de France* 74 (1988) 91–113. See also the particular example treated by A. Dierkens for the diocese of Liège, "La christianisation des campagnes de l'Empire de Louis le Pieux: L'exemple du diocèse de Liège sous l'épiscopat de Walcaud (ca.809–ca.831)," *Charlemagne's Heir: New Perspectives on the Reign of Louis the Pious (814–840)*, ed. P. Godman and R. Collins (New York, 1990) 311–329.

ministry to the populations.[42] And in fact, a large number of rituals reflect certain aspects of this role.

2. THE RITUAL IN THE *LIBELLI:* FORMS AND FUNCTIONS

In his article published in 1960, Gy established a meticulous typology for the different forms of manuscript rituals of the High Middle Ages.[43] Within this typology, *libelli* occupy a place of honor because of their number and their importance in the development of the ritual as a liturgical book. Rituals contained the description of the acts (in the rubrics) and the sacred formulas (orations, readings, and so on). From the tenth century on, booklets meant to be used in a specific liturgical action appeared. The main attestations adduced by Gy—to which one must add the many *libelli* studied since his article was written—demonstrate that they were intended principally for the rites of penance,[44] the anointing of the sick,[45] and funerals.[46] Such a specialization should not surprise us because it corresponds to the essential duties of a priest in his parish during the High Middle Ages; these duties were second only to the celebration of the Eucharist and the administration of baptism.[47] For these last two, the priest, regular or secular,

---

42. On the active part taken by monks in liturgical and pastoral matters in certain parishes, in "competition" or coordination with the secular priests, see especially G. Devailly, "Le clergé régulier et le ministère paroissial," *Cahiers d'Histoire* 20 (1975) 259–272; G. Constable, "Monasteries, Rural Churches and the *Cura animarum* in the Early Middle Ages," *Cristianizzazione*, 1:340–389.

43. See Gy, *Collectaire.*

44. The sacrament of penance underwent modification during the Carolingian period; see C. Vogel, *Le pécheur et la pénitence au Moyen Age* (Paris, 1969); R. Kottje, "Busspraxis und Bussriten," *Segni e riti nella Chiesa altomedievale occidentale, 11–17 aprile 1985*, 2 vols, Settimane di studio del Centro italiano di studi sull'alto medioevo 33 (Spoleto, 1987) 1:360–395.

45. See A. Triacca, "Le rite de l'*impositio manuum super infirmum* dans l'ancienne liturgie ambrosienne," *La maladie et la mort du chrétien dans la liturgie*, Conférences Saint-Serge, 21e Semaine d'Etudes liturgiques, 1er–4 juillet 1974, Bibliotheca "Ephemerides liturgicae," Subsidia 1 (Rome, 1975), 339–360.

46. See P.-A. Février, "La mort du chrétien," *Segni e riti*, 2:881–942; D. Sicard, *La liturgie de la mort dans l'Eglise latine des origines à la réforme carolingienne*, LQF 63 (Münster, 1978); F. Paxton, *Christianizing Death: The Creation of Ritual Process in Early Medieval Europe* (New York, 1990).

47. To be convinced of this, it is sufficient to study, just as an example and ever so briefly, the episcopal cartularies of the ninth and tenth centuries; these were a sort of code of internal regulations proper to each diocese, directly ordered by the bishop and expressing his desire to insist on a given aspect of the parish pastoral

used the sacramentary, which very often included the ritual of baptism. Since this sacrament was administered in the course of a celebration, it made no sense to separate its texts from the sacramentary. The rituals of penance and those destined to help the sick and dying were an altogether different case. In the parishes of the High Middle Ages, these rites, then in the midst of development, necessitated a mobile practice of the liturgy, and, therefore, demanded appropriate documents which were easy to carry and not costly. A significative sample of this kind of booklet is preserved in Paris, B. N., lat. 13764 (fols. 90–116v), written in the scriptorium of St. Amand about 900 and incorporated into a collection coming from St. Remi in Rheims.[48] With its two rituals, one for penance and another for the anointing of the sick (with the Mass for the sick, including the readings and sung pieces), it no doubt was intended for the priest going to visit the sick in the countryside surrounding his parish.[49] Others serve only for funerals, like the *libellus* from the tenth century (Rome, Bibl. Vallicel., cod. C.10; fols. 133–138) from the monastery of San Eutizio in Valcastoriana in Umbria, today included in an evangeliary from the twelfth century.[50]

The variety of parish and monastery rituals, which arose in the tenth century, would continue to the end of the Middle Ages. In the twelfth and thirteenth centuries, the typology of these easy-to-carry booklets was enriched with new rites, such as marriage,[51] and this

---

care. See P. Brommer, *Capitula episcoporum: Die bishöflichen Kapitularien des 9 und 10 Jahrhunderts*, Typologie des sources du Moyen Age occidental, fasc. 43 (Turnhout, 1985); G. Devailly, "La pastorale en Gaule au IXe siècle," *Revue d'Histoire de l'Eglise de France* 59 (1973) 25–54; see also J. Avril, "A propos du *'proprius sacerdos,'* quelques réflexions sur les pouvoirs du prêtre de paroisse," *Proceedings of the Fifth International Congress of Medieval Canon Law, Salamanca, 21–25 September 1976*, ed. S. Kuttner and K. Pennington, Monumenta iuris canonici, series C, subsidia 6 (Vatican City, 1960) 471–486; and J. Chélini, *L'aube du Moyen Age: Naissance de la chrétienté occidentale, la vie religieuse des laïcs à l'époque carolingienne* (Paris, 1991).

48. See E. Palazzo, "Les deux rituels d'un *libellus* de Saint-Amand (Paris, B. N., lat. 13764," *Rituels: Mélanges offerts au P. Gy, OP* (Paris, 1990) 423–436.

49. For other *libelli* of the same kind, see E. Palazzo, "Le rôle des *libelli* dans la pratique liturgique du haut Moyen Age: Histoire et typologie," *Revue Mabillon* 62, n.s. 1 (1990), 9–36, especially 26–28.

50. Gamber, *CLLA*, no. 1025, p. 436; R. Amiet, "Catalogue des livres liturgiques manuscrits conservés dans les archives et les bibliothèques de la ville de Rome," *Studi Medievali* 27 (1986) 955.

51. See J.-B. Molin and P. Mutembe, *Le rituel du mariage en France du XIIe au XVIe siècle* (Paris, 1974).

caused an increasing specialization of the *libelli*. Let us recall that in the thirteenth century, the definitions of diocesan liturgy and administration of the sacraments were changed in the synodal statutes; this favored the definitive institution of special booklets for the priests.[52] At the time of the Renaissance, the parish ritual would be combined with the manual for the administration of the sacraments; and the texts for baptism, marriage, anointing of the sick, and funerals would continue to be the core of this book.

In the monasteries also, the rituals continued to be more and more specialized in order to adapt to the evolution of the most diverse liturgical practices. The abbatial rituals (especially in the second half of the Middle Ages) for rites that only the abbot could perform[53] are among the most interesting because they became a peculiar category of composite books—they could contain texts for other rites—specifically designed for the status and functions of the abbot.[54]

3. THE COMPOSITE RITUALS

Whether associated with other types of liturgical books or inserted into more important books, principally the sacramentary, the composite rituals of the High Middle Ages are as numerous as the independent *libelli*. They have been very well studied by Gy,[55] who distinguishes essentially the collectar-ritual and the sacramentary-ritual (or even the missal-ritual). The combination of the collectar[56] and ritual was born in monastic milieux in the tenth century and persisted at least until the twelfth and thirteenth centuries. The collectar contained all the collects the celebrant needed for the Liturgy of the Hours, whereas the ritual associated with it most often comprised the texts necessary for the liturgy of the sick and of the dead, as well as rites peculiar to monasteries (such as the *ordo ad faciendum monachum* [*"ordo* for the making of a monk"]). The celebrant used the collectar-ritual for the liturgical actions at the Office and for others that took place in various parts of the monastery. This book, of which we possess

52. O. Pontal, *Les statuts synodaux*, Typologie des sources du Moyen Age occidental, fasc.11 (Turnhout, 1975), and A. Vauchez, *Histoire de la France religieuse*, ed. J. Le Goff and R. Remond, vol. 1: *Des origines au XIVe siècle* (Paris, 1988) 368–381.

53. Such as the blessing of sacred vestments.

54. See Gy, *Collectaire*, 465–466; see also III below, the section on pontificals, including 2, on benedictionals.

55. See Gy, *Collectaire*.

56. On the history of this Office book see Part 3, III, the section on the collectar.

a large number of witnesses from the tenth century[57] and afterward, did not prevent the inclusion of rites (baptism, penance, funerals) in sacramentaries, as was the custom in the manuscripts from the ninth century. The contents of certain collectar-rituals were augmented by the addition of texts of a strictly monastic usage, such as the blessing of various parts of the monastery, monastic profession, and even, in rare instances, partial hymnals.[58] The sacramentary-ritual (and the missal-ritual) combined in a balanced way the texts of certain *ordines* (penance, baptism, funerals) and the sacramentary, here reduced to the formularies for the Masses corresponding to the ritual part of the book and to those of votive Masses, depending on the devotion of the user, whether monk or secular priest. In a word, it was a sort of votive sacramentary-ritual. This book of a very particular type had little in common with the sacramentary properly so called in which were inserted within the liturgical year rituals for baptism, anointing of the sick, funerals, and so on. These two forms of association between the ritual and the sacramentary were primarily favored by monasteries, where the need for *libelli* was less than in parishes because monks were not as itinerant as parish priests in their practice of liturgy. This type of manuscript, of which we have several attestations dating from the tenth and eleventh centuries,[59] is typologically closer to juxtaposition than to internal combination. Paris, Bibl. Mazarine, 525 (northern Italy, end of tenth century),[60] has a ritual at the beginning (*ordines* of baptism, penance, and so on) and, as a second part, formularies for votive masses similar to those of the *libelli missarum*. Paris, B. N., lat. 5251 (St. Martial of Limoges, end of tenth century), is similarly structured with juxtaposed parts and also contains a martyrology.[61] This type of composite book progressively disappeared from the twelfth century on when the missal and ritual parted company and evolved separately.

4. THE MEDIEVAL DESIGNATIONS OF THE RITUAL

The variety of terms used in medieval texts perfectly reflects the typological evolution of the ritual. During the High Middle Ages, the

57. See the non-exhaustive list given by Gy, *Collectaire*, 455–456.
58. A good example of this rather rare combination is Bibl. Vat., Ottob., lat. 145 (southern Italy, second half of eleventh century); see Gamber, *CLLA*, no. 465 a, p. 248.
59. See Gamber, *CLLA*, 566–575.
60. See Gy, *Collectaire*, 458, and Gamber, *CLLA*, no. 1585, p. 569.
61. See Gamber, *CLLA*, no. 1598. p. 572.

library catalogues make room for the small-sized *libelli*, each of them intended for one specific action. *Libello continentur orationes sufficientes ad sepulturam fratrum et orationes per singulas officinas monasterii et lectiones tractatus ad vigilias defunctorum recitandas:* this title clearly designates a *libellus* for funerals, the blessing of various places in a monastery, and the readings to be recited at the office of the dead.[62] Other references are less explicit: *Defunctorum ordines volumen unum* [*"ordo* for the liturgy of the dead in one volume], perhaps a *libellus* for funerals.[63] In the twelfth century—and even more in the thirteenth—the ritual became a truly independent book with more substantial contents; it appears as *manuale* in the synodal statutes: *Librum qui dicitur manualis habeant singuli sacrerdotes parochiales ubi continetur ordo servitii extremae unctionis, catechismi, baptismatis et huiusmodi* ["Let all parish priests each have the book that is called manual, containing the *ordo* of extreme unction, catechism, baptism, and other rites of the same kind"] (Statutes of Eudes of Sully, bishop of Paris [1200–1208]).[64] The terms *agenda, baptisteria, obsequium* ["Mass," "baptism," "funerals"], which one frequently encounters in medieval texts from the eleventh century on,[65] designate most often complete rituals identified by the liturgical act whose text is the first in the manuscript; in general they are not *libelli.* The relatively unstable condition of the ritual prior to the twelfth and thirteenth centuries was thus accentuated by designations that are variable and vague. The word *rituale* appeared only in the sixteenth century in Italy in the printed editions; at the same time, terms like *agenda* and *obsequiale* would persist in certain countries such as Germany.

The medieval rituals, by mirroring the evolution of the sacramental practices in the Middle Ages, also enable us to trace the history of the priestly function in its liturgical and pastoral attributions and to

62. Catalogue of the Abbey of Reichenau set up during the episcopacy of Regimbert (835–842), *Mittelalterliche Bibliothekskatalog, Deutschlands und der Schweitz,* vol. 1 (Munich, 1918) 261, lines 3–6.

63. Becker, *Catalogi,* no. 36, p. 81. For other references to the probable *libelli* of the rituals of the Middle Ages, see E. Palazzo, "Rôle des *libelli*," 16–20.

64. See O. Pontal, *Statuts synodaux,* 16–20.

65. Like the catalogue of the library of Wissenburg from 1043: *Baptisteria VI* (Becker, *Catalogi,* 73); or that of the Library of Pfäfers from 1151: *Baptisteria in quibus benedictio ferri et aquae et alia continentur et in uno obsequium mortuorum* ["Rituals in which are contained the blessings of iron and water and other things and in the same book the rite of funerals"] (Becker, *Catalogi,* 208).

compare it with that of the bishop, who was the user of the pontifical while the priest was the user of the ritual.

Few books have had a more eventful life than the rituals, unceasingly adapted to the changes affecting the rites, hence the multitude of possible forms the rituals could take. As it was rarely a pawn in ecclesiastical politics—in contrast to the pontifical and breviary—the ritual eludes almost entirely any strict typological classification.

The manuscripts attest to this state of affairs, because they sometimes offer combinations unheard of in other books; for example, there is the collectar-ritual from the abbey of Lagrasse (Paris, B. N., lat. 933; second half of eleventh century), to which a *libellus* for the dedication of a church was appended (fols. 155–162v), written by a scribe who was probably an Italian working in the southwest of France, perhaps on the occasion of a papal visit.[66]

66. On this manuscript, see Gy, *Collectaire*, 454 and 456, and *Catalogue général des manuscrits latins de la Bibliothèque nationale*, vol. 1 (Paris, 1839) 330–331; the *ordo* for the dedication of a church is that of the Roman pontifical from the twelfth century.

III. The Pontifical, the Book of the Bishop

The history of the pontifical in the Middle Ages has been made almost entirely clear thanks to the research of C. Vogel and R. Elze on the Romano-Germanic Pontifical dating from the tenth century (from now on referred to as RGP);[67] that of M. Andrieu on the pontificals from the second half of the Middle Ages;[68] and that of N. K. Rasmussen on the pontificals called "primitive" (that is, from the ninth and tenth centuries),[69] which are the intermediary link between the *ordines romani* and the RGP. We are therefore in possession of excellent editions of the texts, accompanied by studies on the history of the liturgy authored by the best experts in this field.[70]

By analyzing the evolution of the primitive forms of the pontifical down to the time when it acquired the status of an official book (RGP and then Roman Pontificals), it is in fact the evolution of a part of the episcopal, and even papal, liturgy that we shall follow from the ninth to the fifteenth century.

1. THE FIRST PONTIFICALS OR "PRIMITIVE PONTIFICALS"

Up to Rasmussen's work, historians of the liturgical books did not really comprehend how the transition between the *ordines*, whether isolated or organized into collections, and the RGP, from the second half of the tenth century, had happened. It was the more important to elucidate this point of the history of liturgical books since the RGP, produced in the circles of the Ottonian court between 950 and 962, appeared as the first official book intended for the bishop and enabling

67. Vogel and Elze, *PRG*.
68. Andrieu, *Pontifical.*
69. Rasmussen, *Pontificaux.*
70. Concerning the history of the pontifical, worthwhile information can still be found in the introduction of Leroquais, *Pontificaux*, 1:I–CLIV.

him to celebrate "his" liturgy; indeed, the contents of the book are devoted to the actions which are the bishop's exclusive province. How did things come to this point? Had the RGP been prepared by first drafts of pontificals, or on the contrary, was it the result of changes in collections of *ordines,* which came about empirically through practice? Were the Ottonian compilers of the RGP inspired by prior experiences in the matter of pontificals, or else were they the inventors of this new book, born solely from their genius and imagination? These are all questions to which Rasmussen has given definitive answers.[71]

The Gathering of Libelli *of Episcopal* Ordines

On the basis of the "primitive" pontificals, Rasmussen proposed a new approach to the problems the different types of celebration in the High Middle Ages presented for the liturgists. The author tried to systematize a way to look at the manuscripts based on a simple principle: their contents and material aspect supply clues to the effective use of the document. Reviewing one by one the manuscripts prior to the year 1000, Rasmussen established as refined a typology as he could of the episcopal liturgical document before the advent of the RGP. Through the systematic examination of the contents (which *ordines?* which rituals?) and of the external form of the manuscripts, types as different as the travel copy and the cathedral sample became discernible, living witnesses to the various forms of the celebration of the rites by the bishop. In many cases, these manuscripts are of small format, of modest make, and contain only the texts necessary (rubrics and prayers) for the celebration of one specific action of the episcopal function, like clerical ordinations, the chrism Mass on Holy Thursday, the *ordo* for a council, the consecration of a church. They may also contain rites not exclusively reserved for the bishop but pertaining to

---

71. In addition to Rasmussen's *Pontificaux,* readers can consult the following articles by the same author: "Le 'Pontifical' de Beauvais (IXe–Xe siècle)," *Papers Presented to the Fifth International Conference on Patristic Studies, Oxford, 1967,* ed. F. L. Cross, vol. 1, Studia Patristica 10, Texte und Untersuchungen zur der altchristlichen Literatur 107 (Berlin, 1970) 413–418; "Unité et diversité des pontificaux latins aux VIIIe, IXe et Xe siècles," *Liturgie de l'Eglise particulière et de l'Eglise universelle,* Conférences Saint-Serge, 22e Semaine d'etudes liturgiques, Paris, 30 juin–3 juillet 1975, Bibliotheca "Ephemerides liturgicae," subsidia 7 (Rome, 1976) 393–410; "Célébration épiscopale et célébration presbytérale, un essai de typologie, *Segni e riti,* 2:581–607; to these one must add what Rasmussen wrote in Vogel, *Introduction,* 226–230.

the priestly charge which the bishop exercised in his cathedral, as the priest did in his parish. At first (perhaps already in the second half of the ninth century), there were as many *libelli* as rites to be performed; and no special geographical region appears to have been their privileged place of origin. Besides the independent *libelli*, there were a few *rotuli*, whose contents were equally limited to a specific rite (in general, ordinations); some of these date back to the eleventh century, after the appearance of the RGP.[72] The "pontifical" scrolls that have been preserved come for the most part from southern Italy, a region where the use of scrolls in the liturgy was held in high favor.[73] Textual attestations prove that these scrolls were in use as early as the Carolingian period. For instance, in a letter addressed in 869–870 to Adventius, the bishop of Metz, who was to travel to Trier on the occasion of the consecration of the new archbishop of that city, Hincmar of Rheims supplies us with many details on the order of the ceremony and speaks of using a *rotulus* for the consecratory rite.[74]

The following references probably designate as many small-sized *libelli* of this kind, whether modest or luxurious, depending on where they would be used and for what type of rite: *ordo romanus; ordo romani concilii* ["*ordo* for a Roman council"];[75] *ordo romanus in duo quaternionibus* [*ordo romanus* in two quires of eight folios"];[76] *Quaternos cum letania; Quaternos I cum letania et duos de dedicatione; . . . quaterniones II* ["Quires of eight folios with litany. One quire of eight folios with litany and two quires (for the dedication of a church) . . . "];[77] *ad ecclesiam*

---

72. Rasmussen, *Pontificaux.*

73. See in particular the many *Exultet* scrolls from the eleventh and twelfth centuries; see Part 2, II, 7, on the other forms of books. A good example of the pontifical scroll is supplied by ms. Asti, Bibl. Capit., cod. XIII (eleventh century); see F. Dell'Oro, "Frammento di rotolo pontificale del secolo XI," *Traditio et Progressio: Studi liturgici in onore Prof. Adrien Nocent, OSB,* Studia Anselmiana 95 (Rome, 1988) 177–204.

74. See M. Andrieu, "Le sacre épiscopal d'après Hincmar de Reims," *Revue d'Histoire ecclésiastique* 48 (1953) 22–73. For other testimonies of the same kind, see Rasmussen, *Pontificaux.*

75. Catalogue of the library of the Archbishop of Salzburg, about 959–990; Becker, *Catalogi,* no. 34, p. 77.

76. Catalogue of the Abbey of St. Gall, ninth century; Becker, *Catalogi,* no. 22, p. 51.

77. It is easy to recognize the *libelli* for the dedication of a church, but the others are more difficult to identify; catalogue of the episcopal library of Vich; E. Junyent, "La biblioteca de la Canonica de Vich en los siglos X–XI," *Spanische Forschungen der Görresgesellschaft,* 1/2 (Münster, 1963) 136–145, especially 139–140.

consecrandam quaterniones duos, ad visitandum infirmum quaterniones duos, ad ordinationes ecclesiasticos quternione uno ["two quires of eight folios for the dedication (of a church), two quires of eight folios for visiting the sick, one quire of eight folios for ecclesiastical ordinations"].[78] Already in the tenth century, but especially in the eleventh and twelfth, the term *ordo* in library catalogues, either with added specific details on the rites or not, is used to designate preferably a pontifical: *ordo episcopalis . . . ordo pontificalis* ["episcopal *ordo . . .* pontifical *ordo*"],[79] *ordo I argenteus* ["one silver-covered *ordo*"].[80]

The next step toward the pontifical was to assemble several *libelli* into an artificial collection, which did duty as a "primitive" pontifical. The liturgical and codicological composition of a number of those studied by Rasmussen betrays the compilation of *libelli*. Noteworthy in that respect are the pontificals of Beauvais (Leiden, Bibl. Rijskunivers., BPL 111.2; ninth–tenth centuries),[81] of Rheims (Rheims, B. M., ms. 340; ninth or tenth century),[82] and a Benevento manuscript (Bibl. Vat., Vat., lat. 7701; tenth century).[83]

In all the pontificals he studied, Rasmussen observed that any fixed structure in the contents was lacking as well as any stable nucleus on which other *ordines* could have been grafted. This fact proves the empirical character of their formation. The great diversity of the results, usually modest in appearance, is the consequence of their being a compilation of *libelli*, even though one finds in almost every case *ordines* for the dedication of churches, clerical ordinations, and penance. Rare are the more carefully executed samples, such as the famous Pontifical of Sens from the tenth century (St. Petersburg, Publ. Bibl.

78. *PL* 132, col. 468: a list of episcopal *libelli* bequeathed by the bishop of Elne to his cathedral in 915, included in his testament, rather than a collection of *libelli* forming a little pontifical, as Rasmussen thinks; if his opinion were right, the reference would have been much shorter and would not have enumerated the different quires of eight folios.

79. Catalogue of the church of St. Martin in Tournai, twelfth century; see L. Delisle, *Le cabinet des manuscrits de la Bibliothèque nationale*, vol. 2 (Paris, 1874) no. 134, p. 500, and no. 286, p. 503.

80. Inventory of the books and liturgical objects of the cathedral of Bamberg, second quarter of twelfth century; since this document (probably a pontifical, given the date) is in a cathedral treasury, its binding must have been precious, see Bischoff, *Schatzverzeichnisse*, 57.

81. Rasmussen, *Pontificaux.*

82. Ibid.

83. Ibid.

im M. E. Saltykova-Schredina, lat. Q.v.I., no. 35)[84] for the use of the metropolitan, containing the pledges of obedience sworn by the suffragan bishops of the province of Sens, the ordinary episcopal functions, and royal rites (coronation of the king and queen) whose historical significance is still a matter of controversy. Let us recall also that these "primitive" pontificals appeared almost simultaneously in several different places, a fact demonstrating that there were no deliberate "politics" involved in their creation.

In order to explain the genesis and development of the pontificals, one must first have recourse to reasons of a practical order: the bishop had at hand, gathered into one slim volume, all he needed outside the eucharistic liturgy. When he celebrated in the cathedral, he could also use the sacramentary in which certain episcopal rites were at first transcribed before being "detached" to constitute the pontifical. The bishop's increasingly prominent role in the liturgy of his church from the ninth century on contributed to a historical process attested to by the "primitive" pontificals. In the ninth and tenth centuries, the episcopal function becomes more clearly defined within Christian society and grows more and more important in the social and religious as well as in the liturgical spheres.[85] The advent of the pontifical as an independent book demonstrates this momentous evolution of the bishop's position in his diocese and his liturgical responsibility.[86] The RGP will be a sort of fulfillment of this recognition of the bishop as a major figure in Western Christendom.

84. Ibid. The date (ninth century) and the importance of this manuscript were recently reviewed, in less than convincing a manner, by P. Konakov, who is preparing an edition with commentaries.

85. See J.-C. Picard, "L'ordre carolingien," *Histoire de la France religieuse*, 1:171–281; M. Parisse, "Princes laïques et/ou moines: Les évêques du Xe siècle, *Il secolo di ferro: mito e realtà del secolo X, 19–25 aprile 1990*, 2 vols., Settimane di studio del Centro italiano di studi sull'alto Medioevo 38 (Spoleto, 1991) 2:449–516.

86. See, for example, B. Guillemain, "L'action pastorale des évêques en France aux XIe et XIIe siècles," *Le Istituzioni ecclesiastiche della Societas Christiana del secoli XI–XII, Diocesi, pievi et parrochie*, Atti della sesta settimana internazionale di studio, Milano, 1–7 settembre 1974, Miscellanea del Centro di studi medievali 8 (Milan, 1977) 117–135; M. Mostert, "L'abbé, l'évêque et le pape: L'image de l'évêque idéal dans les oeuvres d'Abbon de Fleury," *Religion et culture autour de l'an mil: Royaume capétien et Lotharingie* (Paris, 1990) 39–45. On the bishops' role in the art of the High Middle Ages, see F. Heber-Suffrin, "L'oeuvre architecturale des évêques de Metz autour de l'an mil," *Haut Moyen Age: Culture, éducation et société: Etudes offertes à Pierre Riché* (La Garenne-Colombes, 1990) 409–410; and X. Barral i Altet, "Les moines, les évêques et l'art," *Religion et culture autour de l'an mil*, 71–80.

2. A CATEGORY BY ITSELF: THE BENEDICTIONALS

There were blessings[87] in both sacramentaries and pontificals, in which they generally formed a distinct part; otherwise, they were made into a separate book called a benedictional. In the sacramentaries, the blessings were essentially for monastic use. When joined to a pontifical, either being a part of the book or inserted among the *ordines,* they concerned more specifically the episcopal function. As for the independent book, Rasmussen has proved the existence of *libelli,* sorts of embryos which he names "simple benedictionals,"[88] preceding the appearance of the complete benedictionals.[89] For the most part, these simple benedictionals are *libelli* containing especially episcopal blessings for the entire liturgical year and votive Masses; some are for military or royal functions. Let us cite as an example a manuscript in Munich (Bayer. Staatsbibl., clm. 6430; fols. 1–14), produced in Freising in the ninth or tenth century.[90] Other manuscripts juxtapose the benedictional and pontifical, as in the sumptuous manuscript in Rouen (B.M., ms. Y.7 [369], written in Winchester about 980 for Archbishop Robert.[91] Finally, the complete benedictional makes its appearance in the tenth century or thereabouts, when it becomes an independent book in the typology of the liturgical documents pertaining to the bishop. But history of this book as distinct from the pontifical has not yet been the object of the thorough study it deserves.[92] One of the best specimens of this once independent book is the Benedictional of Bishop Warmundus, written in northern Italy at the end of the eleventh century (Ivrea, Bibl. capit., cod. 10 [XX]).[93]

87. Concerning this particular sort of liturgical piece, see Part 2, I, 1, the section on the content of the sacramentary, and E. E. Moeller, *Corpus benedictionum episcopalium,* 4 vols., CCSL. 162 (Turnhout, 1971–1973).

88. Rasmussen, *Pontificaux.*

89. These *libelli* containing blessings are attested in the library catalogues like that of St. Mary Major in Cremona, from the year 984: *Episcopalium benedictionum libelli auro inscripti volumen unum* ["One volume of booklets of episcopal blessings written in gold"]. In this case, the *libelli* are perhaps already bound into one volume? See Becker, *Catalogi,* no. 36, p. 81.

90. See Gamber, *CLLA,* no. 280, p. 184; J. Deshusses, "Le bénédictionnaire gallican du VIIIe siècle," *Ephemerides liturgicae* 77 (1963) 169–187.

91. E. Temple, *Anglo-Saxon Manuscripts, 900–1066* (London, 1976) no. 24, pp. 53–54.

92. Probably, as we have seen, because of its frequent association with other books; however, see Fiala and Irtenkauf, *Liturgische Nomenklatur,* 128–129.

93. F. Dell'Oro, "Le benediziones episcopales del codice Warmondiano (Ivrea, Bibl. Cap., Cod. 10 (XX)," *Archiv für Liturgiewissenchaft* 12 (1970) 147–254.

There also exist some "enlarged benedictionals" into which prayers and *ordines* were inserted within the body of blessings without changing the structure of the book in the least. Being inseparable from the history of the pontifical and to a lesser degree from that of the sacramentary, the benedictional gained its autonomy because of the development of the episcopal liturgy and because it is in some way the second textual instrument, after the pontifical, needed by the bishop in his cathedral. Since the greatest number of them were intended for bishops, the independent forms of this book are frequently referred to as episcopal benedictionals.[94]

3. THE ROMANO-GERMANIC PONTIFICAL

Vogel considers the Romano-Germanic Pontifical "one of the two main cultic monuments of the Ottonian renaissance in the second half of the tenth century" (the other being the Fulda Sacramentary);[95] indeed, with it, the history of the liturgical books of the High Middle Ages takes a new turn. In the first place, it consecrates the episcopal liturgy, which now has an official book with which obviously all the other books used in worship must be in accord. In the second place, the RGP thrusts us into another period of the history of the liturgy and its books, for it is the point of departure, if not the progenitor of the books called the "second generation." Together with the missal and the breviary, it puts an end to the "first generation," born of the Carolingian liturgical reform (notably with the sacramentary and *ordines*).

Having been the object of many studies and of a "definitive" edition by Vogel and Elze,[96] the RGP and its history are well known today.

Nature and Content of the RGP

Although they are an extensive compilation of liturgical texts— sometimes called disparate—the contents of the RGP nevertheless present an organized structure so that they form a true book free from the randomness and gropings that characterized the gatherings

---

94. For studies on other benedictionals of the High Middle Ages, see in particular the works of Dell'Oro, among which it will be helpful to consult "Il Benedizionale di Novara (Novara, Bibl. Cap. S. Maria, Cod. LXXXVIII (Colombo 4)," *Novarien* 6 (1974) 53–138; "Un benedizionale ad uso della cattedrale di Aosta nel secolo XI (Aosta, Bibl. Capit., Cod. 15)," *Recherches* (1976) 5–84.

95. Vogel and Elze, *PRG* 3:3.

96. Vogel and Elze, *PRG*.

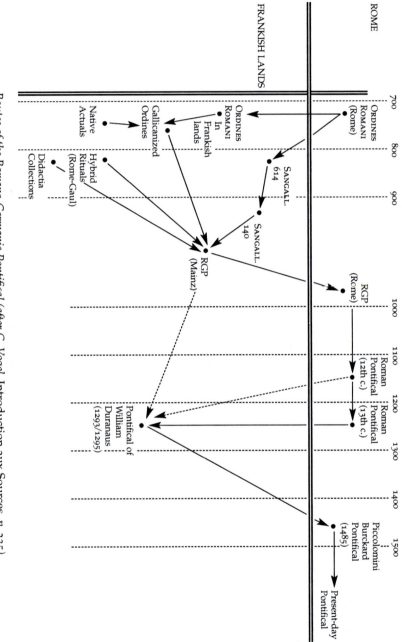

Routes of the Romano-Germanic Pontifical (after C. Vogel, Introduction aux Sources, p. 235)

of *libelli* into the primitive pontificals. The RGP is the fruit of a pro-
longed labor of carefully considered compilation (see pp. 204–207)
and did not grow haphazardly around the core of a few *ordines* transcribed in *libelli*. It comprises 258 sections, variable in length and containing ritual *ordines* (with rubrics, prayer texts, even blessings),
votive Masses with complete formularies, even *expositiones missae*
["explanations of the Mass"] as well as sermons for special occasions
(like the dedication of churches), juridical texts (relative to the consecration of a bishop) and canons of councils.

Focusing on the person of the bishop, the book contains everything
(or almost everything), he needed to celebrate in his cathedral and
diocese, with a special insistence on the texts that were exclusively
his. Therefore, the intent is crystal clear: the book was designed for
the bishop in the setting of "his" liturgy, and we see how at that time,
the episcopal status was increasing in prestige within the ecclesiastical
hierarchy.

Assembling *ordines*, Roman for the greatest part but also Gallican,
the RGP owes to its hybrid contents the modern designation which
Andrieu bestowed on it but which has no ancient foundation. In medieval sources, we encounter instead such terms as *ordo romanus,
ordo,*[97] *ordo episcopalis, ordo pontificalis,*[98] which may designate *ordines*
as well. Only in the second half of the Middle Ages will the terminology pertaining to pontificals become more particularized and exact.
Since the compilers did not give any title to their work, no designation became dominant, in contrast to what happened in the case of
the sacramentary.

The Manuscript Tradition

The examination of the numerous manuscripts of the RGP, produced between the tenth and twelfth centuries, led Vogel and Elze to
trace their descent from one unique archetype whose original has disappeared.[99] Out of the fifty or so samples studied by the two editors
of the book, thirty-eight have been divided between four principal

97. See the numerous references drawn from the medieval library catalogues,
Becker, *Catalogi,* and the inventories of church treasuries, in the Germanic world
in particular, see Bischoff, *Schatzverzeichnisse.*
98. Catalogue of the books of the church of St. Martin in Tournai, twelfth century; one of the two references alludes perhaps to a benedictional; see Delisle,
Cabinet des manuscrits, 2:500 and 503.
99. See Vogel and Elze, *PRG* 3:6–11; Vogel, *Introduction,* 230–239.

groups: (1) Germanic (26 mss.); (2) Italian, whose manuscripts were copied from Germanic models (7 mss.); (3) French (3 mss.); (4) English (2 mss.). The oldest source dates from the second half of the tenth century (Lucca, Bibl. capit., cod. 607);[100] in all likelihood copied in Lucca itself from a model produced in Mainz, the very place where the RGP originated, it is considered the manuscript most faithful to the original state of the book.[101] All the copies that have been preserved derive from one common archetype which an examination of the manuscript tradition authorizes us to place in the Romano-Germanic Empire, more precisely in Mainz. The variants proper to the different regional groups can be explained in two ways: several recensions may have been produced in the scriptoria of Mainz, or these regional variants attest that the hypothetical archetype rapidly underwent adaptations when it was diffused throughout a large part of the West (see pp. 207–209).

Origin, Date, and Historical Circumstances of the Creation of the RGP

The RGP is a book that was brought to completion through the emperor's will; it was for the Ottonian sovereigns what the Gregorian Sacramentary of the *Hadrianum* type had been for the Carolingian rulers.[102] On the political plane, this carefully planned and organized compilation seems to have been undertaken to support the Ottonians' attempt at a liturgical reunification of the Empire in imitation of

100. The date assigned to the Lucca manuscript is not unanimously accepted by the specialists. Some think it goes back to the very first years of the eleventh century; see recently R. E. Renolds, "The Ritual of Clerical Ordination of the Sacramentarium Gelasianum Saec. VIII: Early Evidence from Southern Italy," *Rituels*, 437–445, especially 439. The analysis tips the scale in favor of the tenth century.

101. The wording of the question in the ceremonial of bishops, *Vis sanctae Mogotiensi Ecclesiae, mihi et successoribus meis fidem et subiectionem exhibere?* ["Do you resolve to show fidelity and submission to the Church of Mainz, to me, and to my successors?"], which the metropolitan addressed to the bishop to be ordained (his suffragan), as well as the insertion of the names of the saints proper to Lucca in the litany favor the hypothesis that this is an Italian copy of a manuscript from Mainz; see Vogel, *Introduction*, 234 and 244. However, the morphology of the calligraphy does not seem to me to exclude a scribe of German origin. Could this be perhaps a Germanic (from Mainz) copy brought to Italy by Otto I on one of his visits to that country between 962 and 964? (see p. 206). In his extensive inventory of Ottonian manuscripts, H. Hoffmann did not take this manuscript into account, *Buchkunst und Königtum im ottonischen und frühsalischen Reich*, 2 vols. (Stuttgart, 1986).

102. See Part 2, I, 3, section on the Gregorian sacramentary.

Charlemagne a century earlier. This undertaking coincided with the establishment of the *Reichskirchensystem* ["imperial ecclesiastical system"] by Otto I. This system linked the bishops directly to his person while granting them the means of exercising their power in their territories. The rapid diffusion of the RGP was due less to its intrinsic value than to the renown of the place where it was composed, the see of the archbishopric of Mainz, whose eighteen suffragan dioceses made up the middle part of the empire. At that time, the archbishop of Mainz often combined with his charge the function of archchancellor of the empire, which contributed to enhance the importance of the city of Mainz, then regarded as the true religious capital. From 954 to 968, the archbishop-archchancellor was William, son of Otto I and brother of Otto II. The specialists of the RGP see in him the principal protector (perhaps even the artisan) of the undertaking, if not its inspirer.

Ordo L, which covers the entire liturgical year (Vogel-Elze, *PRG*, section XCIX), does not seem to depend on an independent tradition antedating the RGP. In this *ordo*, a Sangallian hymn (*Humili prece et sincera devotione* ["With humble prayer and sincere devotion"] from about 925) sung on Rogation Days gives variants characteristic of Mainz: *Ottmarus pater* ["our father Ottmar"], founder and protector of the Abbey of St. Gall, is replaced by *Albanus pater* ["our father Alban"]; mentions of Sts. Boniface and Disibod, the patrons respectively of the city of Mainz and the Abbey of Disibodenberg near Mainz. It is not plausible that these additions and substitutions were done elsewhere than in the scriptorium of St. Alban in Mainz.[103]

The work of Vogel and Elze allows us to assign a date between 950 and 962 to this compilation. The principal sources of *Ordo* L (practically all the texts are from the first half of the tenth century) furnish the *terminus ante quem non*. A thorough examination of the oldest manuscript witnesses (in particular ms. 607 of Lucca) furnish the terminus ad quem. These arguments are confirmed by the analysis of the *ordo* for the royal coronation (Vogel-Elze, section LXXII, *ordo ad regem benedicendum* ["*ordo* for the blessing of a king"]) which appears in this exact form for the first time in the RGP.[104] The contents of this *ordo* do

103. For a more developed treatment of the arguments in favor of the Mainz origin of the RGP, see Vogel and Elze, *PRG* 3:11–14.

104. On the history of the *ordines* for the coronation in Germany, see P. E. Schramm, "Die Krönung in Deutschland bis zum Beginn des Salischen Hauses (1028)," *Zeitschrift für Rechtsgeschichte*, Kanonistische Abteilung 24 (1935) 310–322. This piece was reprinted along with other articles on the same topic in *Kaiser, Könige und*

not correspond to the description of the royal coronation of Otto I in Aachen on August 7, 936, which is known to us through a chronicler's account.[105] On the contrary, they are in perfect agreement with the description of the royal coronation of Otto II on May 26, 961, also in Aachen.[106] Presiding over this ceremony was the archchancellor of the empire and primate of Germany, William of Mainz; it is plausible that he might have composed an *ordo* especially for this occasion.

Its powerful influence and its prestige designated Mainz as the natural place of origin for a new liturgical book intended to serve the religious politics of the Ottonian dynasty. The success of the book was immediate as shown by its widespread diffusion throughout a large part of the Empire. However, because it had been conceived for a limited use, exclusively episcopal, the book did not succeed in supplanting in the hierarchy of liturgical books the sacramentary, the symbol of the Carolingian liturgical reform. Upon William's death in 968, the abbey of Fulda, the great rival of the see of Mainz, recovered its political and religious supremacy in the empire. The scriptorium of Fulda then began to produce a series of sacramentaries; the most important was conceived as a sort of "liturgical monument," a compilation of the types of sacramentaries from the Carolingian period, as if to obstruct the other compilation of the Ottonian period, emanating from the rival city of Mainz, the RGP,[107] or to complete it. Favorable political circumstances because of the *renovatio imperii* ["restoration of the Empire"] promoted by the Ottonians, secured a good measure of success—albeit temporary—for the RGP. It also benefited from a certain liturgical decline in Rome, where it received a warm welcome. Otto I, accompanied by many dignitaries of his church, made several sojourns in Italy with the intent of remedying the liturgical void which at that time afflicted Rome along with a large part of Italy. Under these conditions, the RGP appeared as the ideal instrument for revitalizing the Roman liturgy. This was the principal reason for its rapid implantation in Rome, where even

---

Päpste, 4 vols. (Stuttgart, 1968–1971); see also the up-to-date report by J. Flori, *L'idéologie du glaive: Préhistoire de la chevalerie* (Geneva, 1983) 84–102.

105. Korvei von Widukind (c.925–c.973), *Res gestae Saxonicae*, vol. 2, pts. 1–2, MGH, Sc, 3:54–57.

106. On all these questions, see Vogel and Elze, *PRG* 3:14–28.

107. See E. Palazzo, *Les sacramentaires de Fulda, étude sur l'iconographie et la liturgie à l'époque ottonienne*, LQF 77 (1994).

under Gregory VII (1073–1085), so reticent toward anything coming from the empire, it became authoritative as one of the tools for the renewal of liturgical books.

Therefore, the RGP serves as a hinge in the typology of liturgical books and occupies a primordial place in the development of Christian worship during the second half of the Middle Ages. It was both a compilation of usages and texts older than itself and a point of departure for the making of new books. It can be said that owing to the RGP's implantation in Rome, the *ordines romani,* organized at last into one homogeneous book and no longer assembled into collections, came back to their original homeland after a long peregrination beyond the Alps, which started at the beginning of the eighth century.

4. THE ROMAN AND NON-ROMAN PONTIFICALS[108]

The posterity of the RGP, especially in Italy, was considerable as early as the eleventh century. By the twelfth, the Mainz compilation had been so intimately melded with the Roman usages that liturgists and canonists had even forgotten its origin. About 1150, when quoting the RGP, Prior Bernard[109] in his *ordo officiorum Ecclesiae Lateranensis* [*"ordo* for the offices of the Church of the Lateran"] simply calls it *ordo romanus.*[110] In fact, the RGP quickly became the essential source for the composition of Roman pontificals in the twelfth century. The process consisted in substantially pruning the Mainz book in order to adapt it to the conditions of the Roman liturgy. The liturgists of the different churches of Rome acted as their Frankish confreres had done a few centuries earlier when they had had to adapt the Roman sources (sacramentary, antiphonal, *ordines romani*) to the needs of the Gallican church. The reworking of the RGP in Rome resulted especially in the deletion of the coronation *ordines,* purely monastic pieces and rituals, strictly Gallican usages, and didactic compositions. Thus,

108. A good survey of the history of the pontifical after the RGP has recently been published by M. Klockener, *Die Liturgie der Diözesansynode: Studien zur Geschichte und Theologie des "Ordo ad synodum" des "Pontificale Romanum,"* LQF 68 (1986) especially 25–38.

109. As Gy has shown, the historical importance of this *ordo* is considerable since it describes, for the twelfth century, the complex relationship between the papal chapel and the Lateran basilica, "Interactions entre liturgies: Influence des chanoines de Lucques sur la liturgie du Latran," *Revue des Sciences religieuses* 58, Hommage à M. le P\^r Chavasse (1984) 537–552; reprinted in *Liturgie dans l'histoire,* 127–139.

110. See Vogel and Elze, *PRG* 3:50–51.

as modifications proceeded, the RGP itself progressively receded into the background, yielding to more "practical" books directly intended for the liturgy.[111]

Andrieu's work on the Roman pontificals of the twelfth century[112] led to the conclusion that the RGP is their common source. The nine manuscripts used by Andrieu for his edition of the pontifical of the twelfth century present a structure very close to that of the RGP and are the expression of the liturgy of several churches in Rome.[113] After the First Lateran Council, 1123, the papacy recovered its sovereignty in the government of the Church and in particular in its liturgical expression. It was decided to send throughout Europe papal legates with the mission of reorienting local liturgical usages and aligning them according to Roman practices. In this operation, the new pontificals, born from the revision of the RGP, played a prominent role.

Under the pontificate of Innocent III (1198–1216), a new impulse was given to the Roman pontifical within a thoroughgoing reform of the Latin Church initiated by the pope. The liturgists at the pontifical court composed books reflecting the official liturgy of the Curia and destined to be imposed on the whole West.[114] Among these new books, the ordinary,[115] the missal, and the pontifical occupied the foremost positions within a system aiming at the ecclesiological identification of the *ecclesia romana* and the *curia romana*. The pontifical, which the terminology of the time often confused with the ordinary, resulted from the recasting of the different versions of the Roman pontifical of the twelfth century. There also, the very root of the book is the RGP. The edition of the archetype, which we also owe to Andrieu, has made it possible to distinguish several recensions throughout the thirteenth century.[116] Already widely circulated in Italy, this official pontifical of the Roman Church was, in its third recension, made the norm in France at the time the papacy moved to Avignon in the fourteenth century. At that point, it competed with the pontifi-

111. On all these questions, see ibid., *PRG* 3:51–55.

112. Andrieu, *Pontifical*, vol. 1.

113. On these manuscripts, see ibid., and Vogel, *Introduction*, 250–251.

114. See P.-M. Gy, "L'unification liturgique de l'Occident et la liturgie de la curie romaine," *Revue des Sciences philosophiques et théologiques* 59 (1975) 601–612, and "La papauté et le droit liturgique aux XIIᵉ et XIIIᵉ siècles," *The Religious Roles of the Papacy: Ideal and Realities*, Papers in Mediaeval Studies 8 (Toronto, 1989) 229–245.

115. See V below, section on the ordinaries.

116. Andrieu, *Pontifical*, vol 2.

cal written around 1293–1295[117] by the eminent liturgist of the thirteenth century, William Durandus (1230–1296), bishop of Mende.[118] After "struggles" for influence and reciprocal contaminations, the Pontifical of William Durandus—itself partially inspired by the Roman pontificals of the twelfth century since the author had sojourned in Italy—finally triumphed, thanks to a highly unstable situation in Rome at the time of the Great Schism in the West. Partially descended from the RGP, the work of Durandus served as a basis for the first printed edition of the *Pontificale romanum* in 1485[119] (see stemma, p. 202). The threefold division[120] adopted by Durandus for his pontifical became the normative structure for all future printed editions. The different sources used by Durandus, pontifical from the twelfth century, pontifical of the Curia from the thirteenth century, and even a few pieces from the RGP that had not been retained in the Roman books, make this pontifical a true summa of the episcopal liturgy, attesting to the abundant posterity of the RGP, the progenitor of works that were the symbols of a specific period in the history of the Church during the Middle Ages.

5. ILLUSTRATION OF THE PONTIFICAL[121]

"It would seem that for four centuries (down to the thirteenth century), the miniaturists did not dare to directly approach the decoration of the pontifical."[122] This statement from the great French liturgist Leroquais is still valid for modern research even though it deserves

117. Andrieu, *Pontifical*, vol. 3. Andrieu, *Pontifical*, vol. 4, offers tables and a general index of the three volumes of edited texts.

118. On the work and influence of William Durandus, see *Guillaume Durand: Evêque de Mende (vers 1230–1296), canoniste, liturgiste et homme politique*, ed. P.-M. Gy, Actes de la table ronde du CNRS, Mende, 24–27 mai 1990 (Paris, 1992).

119. On the different versions of the printed pontificals down to Vatican II, see Vogel, *Introduction*, 255–256.

120. *In prima parte de personarum benedictionibus, ordinationibus et consecrationis [sic.] agitur. . . . In secunda parte de consecrationibus et benedictionibus aliarum tam sacrarum quam prophanarum rerum agitur. . . . In tertia parte de quibusdam ecclesiasticis officiis agitur. . .* ["The first part treats of the blessings, ordinations, and consecrations of persons. . . . The second part treats of the consecrations and blessings of other things, both sacred and secular. . . . The third part treats of some ecclesiastical offices. . ."] (Andrieu, *Pontifical*, 3:327, 328, 331).

121. Concerning the illustration of the pontifical in the Middle Ages, see the recent up-to-date summary in *Liturgica Vaticana*, 40–43.

122. Leroquais, *Pontificaux*, 1:CXXX.

to be qualified and even partially corrected. Leroquais made the accurate observation that the pontifical properly so called was not illustrated before the middle of the thirteenth century. Within the confines of a book focusing on the history of liturgical books during the High Middle Ages, we must renounce analyzing the circumstances of the rise and development of iconographic cycles specifically intended for the pontifical in the second half of the thirteenth century. Let us simply mention that to date, the vast study which this subject requires has not yet been undertaken. Such a study will have to elucidate the role which the Roman pontifical composed under Innocent III and reflecting the liturgy of the Curia in the thirteenth century seems to have played in the elaboration of an iconography proper to the new official book of the bishop. Let us recall also that the establishment of a specific iconography for the pontifical cannot be dissociated from the evolution of the decoration of other liturgical books, such as the missal, and that the links with the iconography of theological books or books paraliturgical in character, such as the *Rationale divinorum officiorum* ["The Rationale of Divine Offices"] by Durandus, must not be overlooked either.[123]

Therefore, before the thirteenth century, the *OR* and the rituals show no specific illustrations. For the collections of *OR* and the rituals, there was no iconographic tradition although certain rites described in these texts were represented in the sacramentaries if we consider only the domain of illumination. In the part of this book devoted to the history of the sacramentary, allusions have been made to those liturgical scenes, painted in the books themselves or carved on the ivory plaques of their covers.[124] In most cases, these are representations of the rite of baptism, of moments of the eucharistic celebration, and of ordinations to the clerical ranks. These scenes portraying the enactment of liturgical actions and in general painted on only part of the page or, more rarely, inside historiated initials[125] also appear in some illustrated pontificals of the High Middle Ages. The episcopal scroll of Bishop Landulf, a great protector of the arts, written in the second half of the tenth century in the Benevento region, contains a cycle of twelve scenes of clerical ordinations. Reynolds has

123. See C. Rabel, "L'illustration du *Rational des Divins Offices* de Guillaume Durand," *Guillaume Durand*, 171–181.

124. See Part 2, I, section on sacramentaries.

125. Starting with the thirteenth century, there would again be a large number of these in the pontificals.

satisfactorily demonstrated that this cycle reflected the ordination liturgy of southern Italy (independent from the RGP, circulated in the region at that time) and that the images closely followed the rubrics of the *ordo*. This cycle is thus situated outside the Carolingian iconographic tradition of these rites as found in other books than the pontifical.[126] Concerning this Italian *rotulus,* one already notices that one of the most striking characteristics of the illustration, first of the *ordines,* then of the pontifical, is as faithful a representation as possible of the descriptive part of the rites and in particular of the rubrics.

The RGP was never endowed with an iconographic cycle on a par with the official role which Ottonian politics assigned to it in liturgical matters. The reasons are perhaps to be sought, in the first place, in the absence of any iconographic tradition for the sort of pieces contained in this book and, in the second, in the will of the Mainz compilers to avoid any reference, even through images, to the sacramentary—the symbol of the Carolingian liturgical unity—in which illustration traditionally held an important place. Only a limited number of pontificals from the end of the tenth and beginning of the eleventh centuries were decorated with cycles borrowed from the sacramentary. As examples, let us cite the luxurious Pontifical of Archbishop Robert (Rouen, B. M., ms. Y. 7 [369]), made in Winchester about 980,[127] and the Pontifical of St. Dunstan (Paris, B. N., lat. 943), perhaps written in Canterbury, with four full-page drawings whose Trinitarian iconography is exceptional and remained without posterity.[128] Pontificals of Germanic origin from the same period and from circles where RGP and Ottonian art were dominant contain images having an official character: they show the bishop in the exercise of his ecclesiastical function or in his position within Ottonian politics. These images show the bishop's power through the liturgical badge of his charge, the pontifical. Paris, B. N., lat. 1231 (between 1060 and 1084), opens with a full-page painting representing the bishop of Regensburg, Otto of Riedenburg, offering his book to St. Peter, patron of his church, in the iconographic tradition of the dedication scenes.[129] This is the one

126. Reynolds, "Image and Text: The Liturgy of Clerical Ordination in Early Medieval Art," *Gesta* 22 (1983) 27–38.

127. Temple, *Anglo-Saxon Manuscripts,* 53–54.

128. See F. Avril and P. Stirnemann, *Manuscrits enluminés d'origine insulaire (VIIe–XXe siècle),* Bibliothèque nationale, CRME (Paris, 1987) no. 16, pp. 13–14; Rasmussen, *Pontificaux.*

129. See *Regensburger Buchmalerei* (Regensburg, 1987) 37–38, pl. 16.

painting in this manuscript. The copy of the RGP kept in Bamberg (Staatsbibl., lit. 53; 1007–1024) contains a representation of King Henry II flanked by two bishops who obviously appear here as upholding the legitimacy of the sovereign.[130] The Pontifical of Schaffhausen (Schaffhausen, Stadtbibl., Ministerialbibl., Min. 94; 1080–1090) also shows—inserted into the text of the *ordo coronationis* (fol. 29v)—an image of two bishops in the act of putting the crown on the king's head; this is in accordance with the Salic tradition of representing coronations.[131]

These formal images belong to the tradition of official portraits in Ottonian and, later on, Salic art and are not specific to the pontifical.[132] One also sees this episcopal iconography on ivory plaques, such as the one recently acquired by the Louvre Museum; executed between 1100 and 1110, it represents two bishops, Hervé (987–997) and Roger (997–1016), who succeeded one another in the see of Beauvais.[133] The iconography belongs to the tradition of official portraits of abbots and bishops in the Romanesque period: the dignitaries are clad in formal garments and carry the insignia of their functions, among which are books. D. Gaborit-Chopin has demonstrated that this plaque had been affixed to a pontifical of the Beauvais cathedral which contained the formula of coronation and a reference to Robert the Pious (reigned 987–1031). The ceremonious representation of the two Beauvais bishops is then explained by the historical tradition that associated them with the coronation of the first two Capetians.

The decoration of the pontifical in the High Middle Ages, illuminations and bindings, conveys the notion that the episcopal power and historical authority of bishops are legitimate guarantees, of the foundation of a dynasty for instance. Although sparse, this decoration is nevertheless of great interest, on the one hand, for studying religious and political history and, on the other, for tracing the evolution of the episcopal function throughout the Middle Ages.

---

130. See *Das Evangeliar Heinrichs des Löwen und das mittelalterliche Herrscherbild* (Munich, 1986) 46–47 and pl. 21.

131. See *Das Reich der Salier (1024–1125)* (Sigmaringen, 1992) 421–424.

132. See the many examples presented in *Evangeliar Heinrichs des Löwen*.

133. D. Gaborit-Chopin, "La plaque d'Hervé et Roger, évêques de Beauvais," *Bulletin de la Société nationale des antiquaires de France* (1989) 279–290.

IV. The Customaries

In the typology of the liturgical books of the Middle Ages, the customaries occupy a place apart because of their mixed status as books *of* and *for* the liturgy on the one hand and as collections of the usages of daily life on the other hand. Although it was not a liturgical book in the strict sense, that is, it was not used during the worship services, the customary nevertheless contained the rules governing the liturgical life of a monastic community. In this capacity, it deserves the full attention of historians of Christian worship and logically takes its place beside the *ordines romani* in the category of documents prescriptive in character.

On account of the renewed interest the customaries have benefited from in recent decades, in particular on the part of specialists in monasticism, we can avail ourselves today of a twofold documentation (editions and studies) that lay the groundwork for further research. German historians have distinguished themselves by their work in this field. Their trail blazer has been K. Hallinger, preceded by B. Albers. The latter wrote a pioneering thesis on monastic life in Cluny and Gorze in the tenth and eleventh centuries,[134] before launching the collection *Corpus Consuetudinum Monasticarum*, which has completely renewed the study of customaries, as well as that of other related documents, such as the statutes.[135]

---

134. K. Hallinger, *Gorze-Kluny: Studien zu den monastischen Lebensformen und Gegensätzen im Hochmittelalter*, 2 vols. (Rome, 1950, reed. 1971); today, this book should be used very cautiously, see Th. Schieffer, "Cluniazensische oder gorzische Reformbewegung?" *Cluny*, ed. H. Richter (Darmstadt, 1975) 60–90.

135. K. Hallinger, ed., *Corpus Consuetudinum Monasticarum*, 12 vols. in 16 (Siegburg, 1961–1987). On this collection and its importance, see R. Schieffer, "*Consuetudines monasticae* und Reformforschung," *Deutsches Archiv* 44 (1988) 161–169.

1. HISTORY OF THE MEDIEVAL CUSTOMARIES

In the background of the customaries, we find the notions of rule and custom. From its origins, monasticism has been based on a series of rules, legislated by the founders, which define the regular life of the monastics. These rules—some thirty of them between the fifth and the eighth centuries—organize the monastics' daily life with its manual, intellectual, and liturgical activities.[136] Being locally adapted, the rule became custom which, not written at first, was transmitted principally by the usages of communal life.[137] During the Carolingian period, one sees some individual monastery or religious order give a definitive form to many customs based on ancient rules (for instance those of St. Benedict and St. Augustine). Modifications to the Benedictine Rule, then dominant, and the subject of a commentary by Smaragdus (first half of ninth century) were proposed at various councils, like that of Aachen in 816–817, during which attempts were made to impose the customs of Benedict of Aniane.[138] But the local usages held their ground, and thus a monastic geography is discernible in the ninth century determined by the kinds of customs observed in monasteries.[139] At that time, there were no customaries properly so called, but rather texts describing the usages of some monasteries (like Aniane and Fulda) in order to allow other monasteries to adopt them. Once the daily routine of monastic life and liturgical usages were written down, custom started to be codified. However, it was only in the tenth century that customaries properly so called came into existence. They were well-organized collections of all the aspects, whether material or

136. See A. De Vogüe, *Les règles monastiques anciennes (400–700)*, Typologie des sources du Moyen Age occidental, fasc. 46 (Turnhout, 1985).

137. On the notion of custom, see the fundamental article of K. Hallinger, "Consuetudo: Begriff, Formen, Forschungsgeschichte, Inhalt," *Untersuchungen zu Kloster und Stift*, Veröffentlichungen des Max-Planck-Instituts für Geschichte 68 (Göttingen, 1980) 140–166; see also J. F. Angerer, "Zur Problematik der Begriffe Regula-Consuetudo-Observanz und Orden," *Studien und Mitteilungen zur Geschichte des Benediktinerordens und seiner Zweige* 88 (1977) 312–323.

138. J. Semmler, "Die Beschlüssesdes Aachener Konzils im Jahr 816," *Zeitschrift für kirchengeschichte* 74 (1963) 15–82. In the field of monastic architecture, Benedict of Aniane appears also as a reformer; see especially C. Hertz, "Saint Benoît d'Aniane réformateur, bâtisseur," *Etudes sur l'Hérault*, n.s. 5–6 (1989–1990) 35–44.

139. See J. Wollasch, "Questions clés du monachisme européen avant l'an mil," *Saint-Sever, millénaire de l'abbaye, Actes du Colloque international, Saint-Sever, 25–27 mai 1985* (Mont-de-Marsan, 1986) 13–26.

liturgical, of the life of a monastery.[140] What happened then was that the tradition proper to one monastery spread to a more or less extensive region, thus creating zones of influence for important monasteries such as Fleury (Saint-Benoît-sur-Loire), Fulda, Cluny, St. Emmeram of Regensburg, St. Gall, Monte Cassino, Canterbury. Although sharing a common background, traditions nevertheless developed in a relatively independent manner so that differences appeared, notably in the internal organization of a monastery and liturgical practices.

Finally, where and when various traditions recorded in the customaries came into contact, different political, social, economic, and religious ideas confronted one another, as we are going to see.

2. NATURE AND CONTENT OF THE CUSTOMARIES

By studying the Cluniac customs and statutes between the tenth and twelfth centuries, D. Iogna-Prat has picked out three essential characteristics of this sort of document, applying to all the customaries of the High Middle Ages.[141] Before going into more detail concerning each of these characteristics, let us recall that medieval terminology does not really distinguish between customaries and statutes; the boundary between *consuetudines, statuta, instituta* is sometimes blurred. However, the customs recorded in customaries described all the practices in the life of a monastery, whereas the statutes, decreed by the abbot or abbess, concerned only particular points. Some authors, like G. Constable,[142] regard the preeminence of statutes over customs as the expression of increasing abbatial power in the twelfth century; others, without rejecting this hypothesis, grant a lesser importance to the statutes, pointing out that they were before all else corrections—on specific points of the customs in force—of already existent customaries.

140. See the historical report of L. Donnat, "Les coutumes monastiques autour de l'an mil," *Religion et culture autour de l'an mil,* 17–24; and "Les coutumiers monastiques: une novelle entreprise et un territoire nouveau," *Revue Mabillon* 64, n.s. 3 (1992) 5–21.

141. D. Iogna-Prat, "Coutumes et statuts clunisiens comme sources historiques (ca 990–ca 1200)," *Revue Mabillon* 64, n.s. 3 (1992) 23–48.

142. G. Constable, "Cluniac Administration and Administrators in the twelfth Century," *Order and Innovation in the Twelfth Century: Essays in Honor of Joseph R. Stayer* (Princeton, 1976) 17–30, 417–424; "Monastic Legislation at Cluny in the Eleventh and Twelfth Centuries," *Proceedings of the Fourth International Congress of Medieval Canon Law, Toronto, 21–25 August 1972,* Monumenta iuris canonici, series C, subsidia 5 (Vatican City, 1976) 151–161.

Both types of document definitely belong to the category of descriptive texts among which one must distinguish the customs concerning liturgical usages, the customs dealing with the material life of the community, and the "mixed" customs addressing both.

In these customaries, liturgical ceremonies were scrupulously described. In general following the order of the liturgical year, every rite (Mass, Office, sacraments, and various ceremonies) was itemized with an enumeration of the liturgical pieces and objects (often the incipits of the prayers, chants, and readings were listed; and the chalice and chasuble to be used was indicated) and with the description of the movements within the church, such as processions as well as the officiants' gestures.[143] The depiction of each ceremony was often preceded by the enumeration of the preparations required, with a particular insistence on the respective responsibilities of the officiants. On occasion, within one single monastery, several customaries could succeed one another, and as a consequence, it is possible to follow the evolution of worship in a given monastic community for several decades, even centuries.[144]

Besides the customaries, whose contents were extensive, the monastics needed more convenient documents intended for a precise liturgical action, in other words, some excerpts from the customaries. These guides for the liturgy, on a par with the customaries and the ordinaries, could take the shape of small lists for the refectory readings, based on what the monastery library[145] held, or else lists of exceptional food allotments arranged *per circulum anni* ["throughout the year"]. We possess a good example from Corbie, a sort of paraliturgical memory aid, which could well suggest that the administration of the monastery was being put back into order; this is on folios 23v–26v of Paris, B. N., lat. 13908, and could be placed in parallel with other diplomatic documentation. In all likelihood written under Abbot Maingaud (985/986–c.1014), the list is arranged in two cycles: the first concerns almost exclusively the meals served the monks in commemoration of their de-

143. See R. Grégoire, "La communion des moines-prêtres d'après les coutumiers monastiques médiévaux," *Sacris erudiri* 18 (1967–1968) 524–549.

144. See Iogna-Prat, "Coutumes et statuts clunisiens," and *Liber tramitis aevi Odilonis,* ed. P Dinter, *Corpus Consuetudinum Monasticarum,* vol. 10 (Siegburg, 1984).

145. See D. Nebbiai-Dalla Guarda "Les listes médiévales de lectures monastiques: Contribution à la connaissance des anciennes bibliothèques bénédictines," *Revue bénédictine* 96 (1986) 271–326.

ceased abbots; the second deals with the meals accompanying the celebration of certain feasts of the Sanctoral and Temporal.[146] Here, the daily life of the community in the course of the year accords with its paraliturgical activities and is regulated in one of its aspects (diet) according to the liturgical calendar.[147]

Customs and statutes were also regulatory texts, for they could impose on all the establishments of the same religious order a new rule of life. Their normative character in this case depended upon the juridical value of the compilations. For the authority of the customaries and the statutes to assert itself within a religious order or group of monasteries, they had to emanate from an important abbey which exercised its influence over a good number of priories. As early as the end of the tenth century, the sovereignty of Cluny was measured especially by the many "handwritten works,"[148] among which customaries occupied a large place.

Lastly, these documents are, on occasion, also reform texts concerning both internal usages and their diffusion outside the motherhouse. The example of the Abbey of Cluny is again very revealing since most of the Cluniac customs in our possession are copies made in other monasteries. The *Liber tramitis*,[149] which is such an important source of information on monastic and liturgical life in the tenth and eleventh centuries, has come down to us thanks to the reform undertaken by Abbot Hugh of Farfa (998–1039) in his Italian monastery, apparently inspired by the example of Cluny although he preserved the usages of Farfa. Let us also observe that from one abbey to another, the adoption of a particular custom coming from a monastery of prestigious authority could concern every facet of life in the place which adopted the custom or else could be only a partial borrowing that left intact the preeminence of local traditions. The end result was that the customs were more or less composite depending upon whether the adoption of imported usages was total or partial.

146. L. Morelle, "La liste des repas commémoratifs offerts aux moines de l'abbaye de Corbie (vers 986–989), une nouvelle pièce au dossier du 'Patrimoine de saint Adalhard'?" *Revue belge de Philologie et d'Histoire* 69 (1991) 279–299.

147. Other aspects of the daily life of monastics have been studied on the basis of liturgical books, for example, the organization of the infirmary library; see D. Nebbiai Dalla-Guarda, "Les livres de l'infirmerie dans les monastères médiévaux," *Revue Mabillon* (1993).

148. This is the expression of Iogna-Prat in "Coutumes et statuts clunisiens."

149. See note 144.

3. HISTORICAL AND LITURGICAL INTEREST OF THE CUSTOMARIES

The customaries are a source of inexhaustible richness for all medievalists, be they archaeologists or historians of religious life, social and economic practices, political ideology, or art. A comparative study of the different liturgical traditions proper to different monasteries can be achieved in large part only on the basis of the clues supplied by monastic customaries. The greater or smaller degree of codification of liturgical usages from place to place enables researchers to distinguish steps in the establishment of a specific liturgy and determine what are its links with the diocesan liturgy. This codification should be studied monastery by monastery and often would reveal its roots in the usages of the Carolingian tradition, strongly influenced by the reform movement of Benedictine monasticism promoted by Benedict of Aniane.[150] The medieval customaries are especially important witnesses to the persistence, or lack of it, of the liturgical modes established during the Carolingian period. We know, for instance, thanks to the work of L. Donnat,[151] that the Carolingian foundations were particularly well developed in the Cluniac zone of influence, whereas to the contrary—to speak only of the territory of early France—Fleury's (Saint-Benoît-sur-Loire) zone of influence maintained liturgical usages more definitely rooted in the Frankish tradition—imbued with ancient practices and local customs—antedating the monastic reform of Benedict of Aniane.

The liturgical characteristics, among others, of each tradition, tending either to conservatism or innovation, allow us to discern more precisely the different roles played by specific monasteries (or groups of monasteries) in political and social life between the tenth and twelfth centuries.[152] For instance, the traces observed in Cluny of usages coming from the Germanic world highlight the central position of that Burgundian monastery situated on the border between French territory and that of the empire. This corroborates what is known of the

---

150. See J. Semmler, "Benedictus II: Una regula, una consuetudo," *Benedictine Culture (750–1050)* (Louvain, 1983) 14ff.

151. See Donnat, "Coutumes monastiques."

152. See J.-F. Lemarignier, "Structures monastiques et structures politiques dans la France du Xe et des débuts du XIe siècle," *Il monachesimo nell'alto Medioevo e la formazione della civiltà occidentale, 8–14 aprile, 1956,* Settimane di studio del Centro italiano di studi sull'alto Medioevo 4 (Spoleto, 1957) 357–400.

actions by some Cluniac abbots, in particular Odilo and Hugh, in favor of a rapprochement with the empire.[153]

The particulars of the daily life and administrative system proper to each community or group of monasteries appear clearly through an attentive examination of the customaries. Questions such as the conditions of admission to the monastery, with their implications for social history;[154] the evolution of the ecclesiastical hierarchy, notably with the insistence on the abbot's power, are elucidated by several chapters in the customaries. Economic wealth can also be evaluated by comparing account books and charts with the passages in the customaries that deal with the possessions of the monastery and the distribution of its goods, especially under the form of food for the poor.

Finally, the customaries have enabled us to reconstitute through the comparative study of textual sources and archeological sources the architectural and artistic history of many monasteries and churches of the Middle Ages, some of which have entirely disappeared. The monastery of Cluny and its church (Cluny II), key edifices of Burgundy about the year 1000 and built under the abbacies of Maiolus and Odilo,[155] or the abbatial church of Fruttuaria in Lombardy, established in the eleventh century by William of Volpiano,[156] can be reconstructed thanks to such investigations. For the history of liturgical objects, vestments, and altars, the customaries supply a documentation of exceptional interest, still under-exploited.

To sum up, three main steps marked the history of the customaries: (1) the setting down of customs and usages derived from monastic rules in the Carolingian period; (2) the codification of usages in

153. Among the many studies of J. Wollasch on the relationships between Cluny and the empire, see, for example, "Kaiser Heinrich II. in Cluny," *Frühmittelalterliche Studien* 3 (1969) 327–342.

154. G. Constable, "Entrance to Cluny in the Eleventh and Twelfth Centuries according to the Cluniac Customaries," *Mediaevalia Christiana, XIe–XIIIe siècle: Hommage à Raymond Foreville* (Paris, 1989) 334–354.

155. See K. J. Conant, *Cluny, les églises et la maison du chef d'ordre,* Mediaeval Academy of America 77 (Mâcon, 1968); C. Sapin, "Cluny II et l'interprétation archéologique de son plan," *Religion et culture autour de l'an mil,* 85–89; N. Stratford, "Les bâtiments de l'abbaye de Cluny à l'époque médiévale: Etat des questions," *Bulletin monumental* 150 (1992) 383–411.

156. See L. Pejrani Barico, "I resultati dell'indagine archeologica sulla chiesa abbaziale di Fruttuaria, prime considerazioni," *Dal Piemonte all'Europa: Esperienze monastiche nella società medievale, 34 Congresso storico subalpino, Torino, 27–29 maggio 1985* (Torino, 1988) 587–606.

individual monasteries (appearance of customaries properly so called) in the tenth and eleventh centuries; (3) from the twelfth century on, the creation of new codifications in the new orders, aiming at regulating the relationships between the "mother-house" and the houses depending upon it (an example of this is the Cistercian Order's *charta caritatis*, dating from 1118–1119).

V. The Ordinaries[157]

Ordinaries belonged to the same category of books concerned with the liturgy as the customaries, the collections of rules, and even the reading guides (for the refectory, for example) of which we spoke above. The ordinaries answered the need for codification of the liturgical usages of the clergy, whether religious or diocesan, and therefore were, even more than the customaries, indispensable complements of the liturgical books properly so called.[158]

In a recent summation of the subject, A.-G. Martimort establishes a clear distinction between customary and ordinary: "Practically, what differentiates the one type from the other is that the ordinary describes the course of the liturgical year with its celebrations: Office, Mass, processions, whereas the customary enumerates (I would add 'also') the usages and rites of the life of the community, thus particularizing and complementing in the case of monastics and canons the prescriptions of the Rule. . . ."[159] Nonetheless, there exists a real, almost genetic, link between these two types of documents. One could say that in some way, the ordinary was already contained in the customary. Compared with the latter, it did not include what concerned the daily life of the monasteries. Because of its strictly liturgical character, the ordinary devoted a much larger place to the description of rites. Although it was not a liturgical book in the strict sense, it must be regarded as a book pertaining to the liturgy, since it codified, regulated the usages of a monastic community, a cathedral, a diocese. Some authors even call it, and rightly, a book used in the preparation of

157. This section is inspired in large part by my attempt to bring all results together; "Les ordinaires liturgiques comme sources pour l'historien du Moyen Age: A propos d'ouvrages récents," *Revue Mabillon* 64, n.s. (1992) 233–240.

158. Concerning the historiography of the research on ordinaries, see Martimort, *Ordines,* 51ff.

159. Ibid., 66–67.

worship services,[160] for from the twelfth century on, it was this book that outlined the way in which each celebration ought to be conducted and established connections between the different actors and their respective books.

Let us examine the three main traits which characterized an ordinary. First of all, it very exactly followed the unfolding of the liturgical year in which, depending on the cases, the Temporal and the Sanctoral were either combined or separate, and it was generally preceded by a calendar whose contents might agree or not with its own. It was within this time frame that all liturgical actions for each day were described, the Mass as well as the Office. Second, as a general rule, the ordinary gave only the incipits of the liturgical pieces (chants, prayers, readings, and so on) in the order in which they occurred in the celebration; these incipits were interspersed with rubrics of variable length which described the ceremony. These descriptions were intended for the master of ceremonies who also had to use this book. In the third place, it described the essentially local usage of a cathedral, a monastery, or a canons' church; of a diocese, a monastic family, an order of canons, monastics, or mendicants.

1. HISTORY OF THE ORDINARY AND ATTEMPT AT TYPOLOGY

There have been general studies as well as monographs written on the history of the ordinary. The recent writings of Martimort and E. Foley[161] complement older works such as the introduction of A. Hänggi to the Ordinary of Rheinau from the twelfth century,[162] the study of B. Schimmelpfennig on the books of ceremonies in the Roman Church in the Middle Ages,[163] and especially the unpublished paper of J. Dufrasne on the manuscript ordinaries of diocesan churches

160. See E. Foley, "The *Libri ordinarii:* An Introduction," *Ephemerides liturgicae* 102 (129–137).

161. See Martimort, *Ordines;* E. Foley is above all the author of a study accompanying the publication of the first ordinary of the Abbey of St. Denis (Paris, Bibl. Mazarine, ms. 526), dating from the second quarter of the thirteenth century, which will be mentioned below: *The First Ordinary of the Royal Abbey of Saint-Denis in France,* Spicilegium friburgense 32 (Fribourg, 1990).

162. A. Hänggi, *Der Rheinauer Liber ordinarius,* Spicilegium friburgense 1 (Fribourg, 1957).

163. B. Schimmelpfennig, *Die Zeremonienbücher der römische Kirche im Mittelalter* (Tübingen, 1973).

kept in the Bibliothèque nationale in Paris.[164] In addition, there exists a vast number of monographic studies,[165] usually preceded by a historical introduction on the place under consideration and its liturgical usages.

While the *ordines romani* were centered on actions, the ordinary focused rather on the liturgical organization of a specific place throughout the year. It was an instrument of codification and search for unity among the liturgical traditions proper to a religious family, monastery, cathedral, diocese. In order to acquire this authority, it needed to be separated from the customary in which it would have been submerged in the mass of the usages of the monastic or canonical life described in the latter. The appearance of the independent ordinary in the twelfth century can also be explained by practical reasons, as is often the case with liturgical books: it sorted out, reorganized, classified the numerous pieces (chants, prayers, readings) that were gradually added to the Church's prayer.

The golden age of the ordinary was the thirteenth century, in the course of which one observes a sort of extreme individualization of the local liturgies, whether monastic or diocesan. This phenomenon became even more accentuated in the fourteenth and fifteenth centuries with the result that the ordinary gained a major importance for liturgical and religious history in general. Often, the composition of an ordinary was not fortuitous: it accompanied a reform of the liturgy or set down a tradition in writing during a period (essentially the thirteenth century) in which many new offices—formerly added to customaries and liturgical books on extra pages or in the margins— had to be included in a manuscript. In this case, whether locally or within a whole religious order, a revision was undertaken: liturgical practices were updated in order to remedy uncertainties, facilitate the performance of the ceremonies, and prevent errors. The ordinary took its place among the "second generation" of books, along with the pontifical (the one deriving from the RGP of the tenth century), breviary, and missal. In this group, it appears as a central element

164. J. Dufrasne, *Les ordinaires manuscrits des églises séculières conservés à la Bibliothèque nationale de Paris,* typewritten memoir, Institut supérieur de Liturgie (Paris, 1959).

165. See the list—non-exhaustive—given by Martimort, *Ordines,* 53–61, which embraces the ordinaries of France, Germany, Switzerland, England, Italy, and Spain.

around which the other books organized themselves within a new ec-clesiology of the liturgy, hence its historical importance.[166]

If one wants to describe more accurately and precisely the typol-ogy of the ordinaries, one must of necessity take into account the character of the community they pertained to and therefore distin-guish the ordinaries of the cathedrals—and the churches depending upon them—from those of monasteries and also from those destined for a whole congregation of monastics or canons. Within these main categories, one must meticulously examine the manuscripts them-selves in order to discern the types, a work to which Dufrasne ap-plied himself, and arrive at a characterization of each ordinary based on the manner of celebration. Some ordinaries furnish lengthy and detailed rubrics enabling us to reconstruct the offices or the Mass as they were celebrated in a given place; others on the contrary are short on rubrics (in this case the rubrics are only the connecting link between the different pieces) and give scant information on celebra-tions and processions. The ordinaries with long rubrics and those with short ones are not specific to one type of ordinary: they can be found in cathedrals or monasteries alike. It must be added that the ordinaries of the fourteenth, fifteenth, and even sixteenth centuries, had a tendency to be overloaded with extraordinarily detailed rubrics. The earlier ordinaries, that is, mainly those from the thir-teenth century, give rather sparse information in the way of rubrics and average only sixty to eighty sheets, whatever the liturgical con-text in which they were used.

The careful examination of the manuscripts makes it possible to re-fine the typology of the ordinaries, which reflects the variety of the celebrations. One encounters cases of textual juxtaposition lending themselves to historical interpretation. Let us cite that of a customary and an ordinary combined into one perfect paleographic and codico-logical unity, like that in Paris, B. N., lat. 13874 (Corbie, first half of twelfth century); in this document the Customary of Cluny coexists with the Ordinary of Corbie. Another example is found in Paris, B. N., lat. 1237 (Tours, fifteenth century); there also one homogeneous whole results from the juxtaposition of a cathedral ordinary (fols. 1–51r) and the synodal statutes of the diocese (fols. 51v–83v). A third example is in Paris, B. N., lat. 1234 (Uzès, beginning of fourteenth century); in

---

166. See P.-M. Gy, "Typologie et ecclésiologie des livres liturgiques médiévaux," *Liturgie dans l'histoire*, 81.

this case, we note that it was intended for use in the diocese, without mention of any particular place, not even the cathedral—which one would have expected—and was simply meant to be used in a variety of ways within the diocese. Perhaps this was a pocket copy which the bishop would have taken on his travels to the parishes; thanks to his ordinary, he could follow the usages of his cathedral and adapt them to the parish he was visiting. The small size of the manuscript (19.5 by 15 centimeters), its limited number of folios (thirty-two), and its casual appearance would support this hypothesis. Overall, the ordinary appears to have been an essentially utilitarian book which was regularly consulted (as proved by the pages often worn out or damaged) and whose modest aspect contrasts with the magnificence of the calligraphy and decoration of the liturgical books containing sacred texts. However, a few manuscripts are exceptions, but in general these emanate from royal or pontifical circles. Thus Paris, B. N., lat. 1435 (50.5 by 11.5 centimeters, end of fourteenth or beginning of fifteenth century), the ordinary of the chapel of the king of France (the Sainte-Chapelle), is written in a clean hand with, at the beginning of each celebration, a handsome initial letter adorned with fine filigree. There exists another one, Paris, B. N., lat. 4162 A (central Italy, 1365), made for Cardinal Albornoz; it is one of the rare medieval samples that has a richly decorated frontispiece specifying that it contains the text of the ordinary of the Roman Curia at the time of Innocent III (1213–1216). The handwriting is carefully executed, but in contrast to the king's copy, it was obviously heavily used as shown by its worn condition.

The medieval designations of the ordinaries are often approximate and lacking in precision.[167] The generic terms most frequently encountered, with no distinction whatever between types, are the following: *liber ordinarius* (the most frequent in the titles of manuscripts), *ordinarium, ordo, ordo ecclesiasticus, ordo officiorum, officium ecclesiasticum, breve, observantiae, consuetudines, liber ceremoniarum, directorium chori*. Often, the mere title is insufficient to establish a distinction between the types of ordinaries, hence the need to study the actual text of the manuscripts in order to discover what contents a particular title covers. Consequently, in the vast undertaking of refining the typology of

167. See Foley, *Libri ordinarii*, 134–136, and Martimort, *Ordines*, 62–63. See also the classic lists of Fiala and Irtenkauf, *Liturgische Nomenklatur*, 119; Thiel, *Liturgische Bücher*, 2383, 2389.

the ordinaries, many specific kinds are still overlooked, such as the abstracts or condensations of ordinaries, which are simply made up of lists.

2. HISTORICAL AND LITURGICAL INTEREST OF THE ORDINARIES

Like the customaries, the ordinaries are indispensable for historians of Christian worship, in particular liturgists, but also for theologians—notably in their study of the forms taken by the celebration of the sacraments in the course of centuries. Indispensable also for historians of music, who, thanks to the ordinaries, are able to perfect their knowledge of the evolution of the repertory proper to a given feast and also their knowledge of the history of musical notation. Indispensable, finally, for historians of architecture and archeology, who can find in the ordinaries precious information on the history of a building and its interior plan. The historical and archeological study of a church should systematically include that of the ordinaries because it is highly probable that architectural remodelings and interior rearrangements, even new constructions have entailed the composition of an ordinary. For instance, the ordinary of the Abbey of St. Denis written about 1234,[168] is the most important source not only for our rediscovery of the manner of worship in the monastery and its surroundings in the thirteenth century, but also for our evaluation of the degree of persistence, at a time when the royal influence regained its strength, of the liturgical tradition inherited from Suger (d. 1151), in spite of the architectural modifications worked on the Carolingian and Romanesque parts of the edifice between 1231 and 1281.[169] Lastly, let us add that for their part, experts in the topography of the towns and villages of the Middle Ages find in the ordinaries precious pieces of information, especially because of the many descriptions of processions through towns.

For the fourteenth, fifteenth, and even sixteenth centuries, the ordinaries shed light on certain aspects of popular religiosity and sacred drama, on occasion through the description of superstitious practices.[170] Sometimes, especially in the manuscripts of the fifteenth century

168. See Foley, *First Ordinary.*

169. See also E. Foley, "Saint-Denis Revisited: The Liturgical Evidence," *Revue bénédictine* 100 (1990) 532–549.

170. For a history of superstitions in medieval times, see the survey of J.-C. Schmitt, "Les superstitions," *Histoire de la France religieuse,* 1:420–551.

which feature more and more developed rubrics, one comes across unexpected details, like the enumeration of the beverages offered to the clergy on the occasion of lengthy processions.

The study of ordinaries also contributes to a better knowledge of certain moments in the history of the Church and the liturgy. We give only two examples. First, the new conception of the Church elaborated by the Roman Curia at the beginning of the thirteenth century in which an official ordinary plays an important role.[171] In the first half of the thirteenth century, Innocent III and his successors gave a fresh importance to the liturgy of the papal chapel; the concrete expression of this new emphasis was the composition of reshaped liturgical books with, in the first place, the ordinary of the Curia (1213–1216), regulating both the Office and the Mass, and then the pontifical and missal. In this new system, the ordinary, which in the contemporary references is often confused with the pontifical, occupied an important place because it was the basic book according to which all the other books pertaining to the liturgy were organized. At the same time, the idea that the liturgy of the papal chapel was the most authentic in the Roman Church gained widespread acceptance; as a result, the way was open to the ecclesiological identification between the *ecclesia romana* and the *curia romana*. In this context, it is possible that a standard ordinary—whose oldest attestation is Paris, B. N., lat., 4162 A[172]—was composed in order to spread abroad the model of the papal chapel throughout the West.

The second example concerns the restoration of the diocesan church and the redefinition of the liturgy. The liturgical renewal at the diocesan level was made possible only by the strengthening of the power of bishops and that of the local churches. The concrete expressions of this increase of episcopal power were the development of the cathedral chapters (which elected the bishops), the rise of real episcopal curias in dioceses, the growth of economic power, and a more effective influence of bishops on the urban scene (especially in the construction of vast cathedrals).[173] The diocesan synods, already reactivated at the

171. See Gy, "Papauté et droit liturgique," 229–245.

172. This manuscript no longer entirely reflects the original state of the papal ordinary between 1213 and 1216; see J. P. Van Dijk, *The Ordinal of the Papal Court from Innocent III to Boniface VIII and Related Documents*, Spicilegium friburgense 22 (Fribourg, 1975).

173. See A. Vauchez, "Le christianisme roman et gothique," *Histoire de la France religieuse*, 1:283–415.

end of the twelfth century, were instruments of reform and action in the bishops' hands. Thus, there was an undeniable relationship between the synodal statutes of the thirteenth century and the redaction of ordinaries.[174] It was for this reason that both texts were often joined in one manuscript.[175] In Paris at the beginning of the thirteenth century, the statutes of Eudes de Sully stipulated that the ordinary of parish priests must be in conformity with that of the cathedral, the first church in the diocese. In 1261 in Angers, the statutes of Nicolas Gellent specify that "priests should have the ordinary and follow it. We order that each church be in possession of the book called the ordinary, which the priests will consult everyday before starting Vespers in order to perform these same Vespers, Matins, and the office of the following day according to the directions in the ordinary."[176] As we can see, the prescriptions of synodal statutes often enable us to determine accurately the date of composition for the ordinaries. It happens that the ordinaries not only describe what was usually done, but also reveal that the selection of pieces and rites was due to a decree coming from a higher authority.[177] By regulating the liturgy of the diocese, the ordinary legislated in matters of worship in the same way as the synodal statutes did for the overall diocesan administration.

Therefore, the convening of a synod may well have been the occasion for the composition of an ordinary or even the revision of an already existing book, or indeed, its reworking of the latter with a view to establishing liturgical legislation.

174. Concerning the synodal statutes, see O. Postal, *Les statuts synodaux*, Typologie des sources du Moyen Age occidental, fasc. 11 (Turnhout, 1975).

175. See p. 224, Paris, B. N., lat. 1237.

176. The translation is that of J. Avril, *Les statuts syodaux français du XIIIe siècle*, vol. 3: *Les statuts synodaux angevins de la seconde moitié du XIIIe siècle* (Paris, 1988) 73.

177. We possess a representative example of this in the Ordinary of Mende by William Durandus, see P.-M. Gy, "L'ordinaire de Mende: Une oeuvre inédite de Guillaume Durand l'Ancien," *Liturgie et musique, IXe–XIVe siècle*, Cahiers de Fanjeaux 17 (Toulouse, 1982) 239–249.

VI. The Processionals

Situated at the boundary between several other books pertaining to the liturgy, the processional has not yet gained the attention it deserves on the part of historians because it is commonly associated with other books.[178] However, the fact that it is frequently joined to an antiphonal or a collectar has resulted in its being studied, albeit partially, by those specializing in these books. Gy devoted fundamental pages to the processional.[179] Huglo pondered the role of the processional in the history of liturgical chant.[180] What follows is essentially based on these works.

Content and History of the Processional

At its beginning, the processional was exclusively a book of chant and contained the procession antiphons for the Office and, more rarely, for the Mass. Its existence is attested at least as early as the tenth or eleventh century in manuscripts we shall come back to later, but before this period, we have no reliable information. R.-J. Hesbert, opposing the hypotheses of H. Leclercq,[181] supposed that convenient booklets containing procession chants already existed in the Carolingian period.[182] Unfortunately, no example supports Hesbert's idea, so

178. This kind of book is completely absent from the work of Vogel, *Introduction;* a brief and somewhat imprecise notice is devoted to this book in the nomenclature of Fiala and Irtenkauf, *Liturgische Nomenklatur,* 128; in Thiel's article, the notice is even shorter and, this time, downright erroneous, *Liturgische Bücher,* 2389. See also Huglo, *Livres de chant,* 110–111.

179. Gy, "Collectaire"; this text was reprinted in *Liturgie dans l'histoire,* 91–126.

180. We eagerly await the publication of Huglo's catalogue of the manuscript processionals preserved in the public libraries of France; this will no doubt initiate, or rather renew interest in research on this book.

181. H. Leclercq, "Processional," *Dictionnaire d'Archéologie chrétienne et de liturgie (DACL),* ed. F. Cabrol (Paris) vol. 14, pt. 2, col. 1896.

182. Hesbert, *AMS,* CXX–CXXI.

we must be content with arguments drawn from the examination of Carolingian chant books. In certain antiphonals of the ninth and tenth centuries, one encounters groups of procession antiphons forming a part of the books. Conversely, the absence of these antiphons from two of the most important pre-Carolingian antiphonals (the manuscripts of Monza and Rheinau)[183] suggests that these pieces were incorporated into the antiphonal after having existed separately. In the medieval library catalogues, the term *processionale* (one also finds *processionarium, processionarius*) does not appear before the second half, and even the end, of the Middle Ages. Mentions of chant *libelli* perhaps refer in fact to processionals under the form of separate booklets, but nothing allows us to affirm this: *Item alii libelli, quae [sic] in choro habentur* ["Similarly, other booklets which are kept in choir"] (catalogue of the Abbey of Schaffhausen, about 1083–1096).[184] On the contrary, an entry in the library catalogue of the Priory of St. Martin of La Canourgue en Gévaudan, dating from the twelfth century, attests the existence of processional booklets: *Caterniones [sic] de antiphonas processionales* ["quires of eight folios of processional antiphons"].[185]

In the tenth and eleventh centuries, the processionals were frequently included in composite books which were perhaps the result of a grouping of *libelli;* in these books, the processionals were gathered together with tropers and sequentiaries.[186] Several of these manuscripts have been described by Gy: Paris, B. N., lat. 1121 (its principal part dating between 994 and 1033), comprising troper, separate sequences, offertories, procession antiphons, gospel antiphons for the time after Pentecost, sequentiary; Rome, Bibl. Casa., cod. 1741, and Bibl. Nazionale, cod. 1343, two processional-tropers from the eleventh century. In these manuscripts, the different parts are clearly distinct from one another, without fusion of the pieces.

From the twelfth and especially thirteenth centuries on, the processional acquired a place among the many liturgical books that a church was expected to possess. The processional appeared first

---

183. Monza, Tesoro San Giovanni, cod. CIX (Monza, c.800); Zürich, Zentralbibl., cod. Rh. 30 (Abbey of Nivelles or Chur, eighth or ninth century); see Vogel, *Introduction,* 359.

184. Becker, *Catalogi,* 157.

185. Delisle, *Cabinet des manuscrits,* 2:no. 35, p. 506.

186. See J. Chailley, "Les anciens tropaires et séquentiaires de l'Ecole de Saint-Martial de Limoges," *Etudes grégoriennes* 2 (1957) 163–188; Huglo, *Livres de chant,* 126.

under the form of booklets,[187] as the reference in the catalogue of St. Martin of La Canourgue cited above attests, or perhaps it was already made up into a more substantial book. As time went on, the processional increased in size and was no longer limited only to procession antiphons. Several churches in France have preserved numerous processionals from the period between the thirteenth and fifteenth centuries. Among the new religious orders, some did not include processionals in the official list of liturgical books which was established rather early in their history. This was the case of Cîteaux, which, however, owned more than twenty processionals at the time of the compilation of the catalogue of John of Cirey in 1489.[188]

In the thirteenth century, one observes two developments: on the one hand, the processional was frequently included in official lists, notably in the Dominicans' established by Humbert de Romans, master of the order between 1254 and 1256;[189] on the other hand, the processional gained a new configuration as a descriptive book since the rubrics pertaining to the processions increasingly took precedence over the antiphons. The combination of the ritual and processional then appears as a logical step because the procession chants held an important place in the enactment of rites, such as funerals. By the end of the Middle Ages, although still retaining its specific character, the processional looked more like a ritual, more or less complete, depending of the rites it contained. In the fifteenth and sixteenth centuries, the processional became a book of utmost necessity in the churches, whether monastic or diocesan, to such a point that its contents were considerably augmented. Originally containing only procession chants with their rubrics, the processional now also included other antiphons, versicles, responsories, and complete rituals (for funerals, the washing of feet on Holy Thursday, the Adoration of the

187. As Gy noted in "Collectaire," 468, the reference drawn from the list of books commissioned, according to Leo of Ostia, by Didier, abbot of Monte Cassino (1058–1085), does not allow us to decide with certainty whether we are dealing with a processional in the proper sense or with a collection containing the orations said by the priest: *Id ipsum fecit, et de alio libello in quo sunt orationes processionales . . .* ["He composed this, and from another *libellus* containing the processional prayers . . ."], (*Chronicon Casinense* 3.18, PL 173, col. 736 A).

188. See Gy, *Collectaire*, 468.

189. In the prototype of the Dominican liturgy, kept in the convent of the Dominicans of Santa Sabina (Rome, Santa Sabina, XIV, I, 1), one finds the following references, *Processionarium* (fol. 1r) and *libellus processionalis* (fol. 58v).

Cross on Good Friday, various rites of ablution, and so on); some-times, the processional was even appended to a book of the Hours.[190]

190. See, for instance, the series of processionals used by the Dominican nuns of Poissy, recently studied by M. Huglo, "Les processionnaux de Poissy," *Rituels*, 339–346.

VII. The Ceremonials[191]

The ceremonials are in some ways the end result of the typological evolution of the ordinaries at a time (mainly the fifteenth and sixteenth centuries) the books used in worship had entered a further phase in their history. Compared to the ordinary, the ceremonial was at once more precise in its instructions concerning the performance of the rites and devoid of any reference to liturgical texts (chants, prayers, readings). To be helpful, it had to be used in conjunction with an ordinary, or even with the liturgical books properly so called. This typological difference appears clearly only from the fifteenth century on, at the time the "true" ceremonials appeared. Before that time, the books had features akin to the ordinary, the customary, even the pontifical and ceremonial. The lack of definite boundaries between these different kinds were due to the conditions which caused the emergence of a new book genuinely destined *for* the liturgy, the ceremonial. As Martimort has reminded his readers, "the need for a ceremonial properly so called would be felt especially at the time of the Tridentine reform,"[192] particularly in the pontifical court and some episcopal curias.

The strong resolve to regulate as precisely as possible the liturgy of the Roman Curia arose in the second half of the twelfth century and even more in the thirteenth. The liturgical usages of the Curia already constituted the principal elements of the papal ceremonial. The main purpose of these texts was to describe in detail the opulence which the rites demanded, from the material and human viewpoints, and to give all necessary particulars concerning the roles of the officiants. For this, the ordinary and pontifical were no longer adequate, and from the thirteenth and fourteenth centuries on, small ceremonials were

191. Concerning this book, see Martimort, *Ordines*, 89–100.
192. Ibid., 90.

composed which relate to particular rites; one of those was compiled for the papacy during its stay in Avignon.[193] In the fifteenth century, the existence of the papal and episcopal ceremonials is confirmed thanks to the elaborate work of persons in high places at the pontifical court. At the request of Innocent VIII (1484–1492), Agostino Patrizi Piccolomini and John Burckhard compiled a ceremonial presented to the Pope in 1488, printed for the first time in 1516, and often reprinted afterward.[194]

Along the same lines as the ceremonial, and also in the fifteenth century, diaries for use by the papal masters of ceremonies appeared; in these are noted, day by day, the actual performance of the ceremonies, the receptions, the corteges, the journeys, with a wealth of particulars relating to protocol and accounts the incidents that might have occurred.

The ceremonials for the episcopal Mass appeared in the second half of the fifteenth century, in the wake of those destined for the papal court, and reached their full development in the sixteenth in works commissioned by cardinals.[195] Before they came into being, the custom, as early as the thirteenth century, was to simply add particular rites to pontificals in the strict sense.

With the development of the ceremonial, the end of the Middle Ages and the Renaissance were characterized by an increased specialization of the books that describe the liturgy; the balance which existed in the ordinary between detailed rubrics and sacred texts was lost. For historians of the papacy as well as for specialists of rites at the junction of the Middle Ages and Modern Times, the ceremonials are an important source for their research.[196] For medievalists, they

193. See ibid., 96–104, and the study of Schimmelpfennig, *Zeremonienbücher.*

194. See the important studies of M. Dykmans, *Le cérémonial papal de la fin du Moyen Age à la Renaissance,* 4 vols., Bibliothèque de l'Institut historique belge de Rome 24–27 (Brussels, 1977–1985), and *L'oeuvre de Patrizi Piccolomini ou le cérémonial papal de la première Renaissance,* 2 vols., Studi e Testi 293–294 (Vatican City, 1980–1982).

195. See Martimort, *Ordines,* 107–109.

196. For the sixteenth century, the ceremonials can be the principal source for the interpretation of images representing papal ceremonies; see for example, N. K. Rasmussen's fine study of an engraving by Etienne Dupérac, dating from 1578, depicting the celebration of a Mass in the Sistine Chapel in the presence of Pope Gregory XIII (1572–1585), "*Maiestas Pontificia:* A Liturgical Reading of Etienne Dupérac's Engraving of the *Capella Sixtina* from 1578," *Analecta Romana,* Instituti Danici 12 (1983) 109–148.

are a far cry from their ancestors of the Middle Ages (*ordines romani,* pontificals, customaries, ordinaries) and enable them to evaluate the ways in which liturgical traditions were transmitted beyond the Middle Ages, sometimes down to Vatican II, thanks to their codification through print.

Conclusion

By way of epilogue to this history of the liturgical books in the Middle Ages in the West, I would simply recall three points, already met with in this book, for which the study of the sources of the liturgy proved of particular interest and whose important contribution to the history of the Middle Ages it highlighted.

These three points are: the use the royal and imperial powers made of the liturgical books in order to validate and strengthen political reforms; the central role played by these books in the history of the papacy, in particular in the thirteenth century after the Fourth Lateran Council; and finally, the impact of these books on the development of private devotion among clerics and lay people, which was on the periphery of the official liturgy.

Historians have often observed that in the kings' and emperors' search for political stability within their territories, liturgical books had played a fundamental role. First, the Carolingians, with the Gregorian Sacramentary, then the Ottonians, with the Romano-Germanic Pontifical, attempted, with different degrees of success, the liturgical unification of the empire. Each time, the liturgical books were part of an array of administrative "instruments" (juridical, political, economic) whose purpose was to impose new regulations. Already in the middle of the eighth century, Pepin the Short (741–768) had perceived the determining role of the books of worship in the success of a liturgical reform within the Frankish kingdom. First Pepin's and then Charlemagne's politics were aimed at liturgical unification based on the Roman model, supported by books in use in Rome, the sacramentary in particular. In the Carolingian sovereigns' eyes, the authoritative voice in matters of worship could only come from Rome, the see of the Western Church. The Christian empire willed by Charlemagne was to be founded on the Roman liturgy; as a consequence, the Gallican liturgical traditions in force throughout Gaul were supplanted. In the ecclesiological concept of liturgy during antiquity and the High

Middle Ages, the sacramentary occupies the summit of the hierarchy of the different books used in worship. This explains Pepin and Charlemagne's choice: the liturgy of the empire could be organized only around the sacramentary, the true core of Christian worship.

In the second half of the tenth century, the Ottonians imitated their predecessors by granting a preeminent role to liturgical books in the building of the empire; to this end, they favored the making of a new book, the pontifical, whose success was great in the second half of the Middle Ages. In contrast to the Carolingians, the Ottonians did not direct their liturgists to use an already existing book; they urged them to make a new book, and the fact that it was a compilation appears as its most innovative feature. It was destined for the bishop because of his role in the *Reichskirchensystem* ["imperial ecclesiastical system"] of the empire. Like theology and law, the (episcopal) liturgy was codified in a compilation, an undertaking willed by the political power.

The contribution of the history of the liturgy and its books to the knowledge of the papacy is well known, principally for the second half of the Middle Ages, beginning with Innocent III (1198–1216), a time when the notion of *Curia romana* makes its appearance. Let it suffice to recall the fundamental part the popes and the Curia played from the thirteenth century on in the process of enforcing the assimilation, and even the ecclesiological identification, of the *Ecclesia romana* with the *Curia romana*. In this process, the liturgy and its books hold a place of honor with, first of all, the composition of an ordinary (between 1213 and 1216), then of a missal, a pontifical, and a breviary. In order to impose upon the West a liturgy in conformity with that of the papal chapel, new books had to be made and diffused. For the sake of comparison, it would be interesting to study the liturgy of the royal chapels established in the course of the thirteenth century, especially that of the Sainte-Chapelle in Paris, in order to discern its own identity and measure its eventual influence elsewhere than at court,[1] alongside that exercised by the liturgy of the Curia.

---

1. Already spoken of by R. Branner, "The Sainte-Chapelle and the *Capella Regis* in the Thirteenth Century," *Gesta*, 10/1 (1971) 19–22; and C. Billot, "Les Saintes-Chapelles (XIIIᵉ–XVIᵉ siècle): Approches comparées de fondations dynastiqes," *Revue d'Histoire de l'Eglise de France* 73 (1987) 229–248, "Le message spirituel et politique de la Sainte-Chapelle de Paris," *Revue Mabillon* 63, n.s. 2 (1991) 119–141. On the liturgy of the Carolingian chapels, see J. Fleckenstein, *Die Hofkapelle der deutschen Könige*, vol. 1: *Die karolingische Hofkapelle*, Schriften der Monumenta Germaniae Historica 16/1 (Stuttgart, 1959).

In the thirteenth century, therefore, the papal chapel became the highest tribunal in matters of ecclesiology, dethroning the Lateran basilica, which up to then had represented the ancient tradition of the Roman liturgy. Prior to this development, the Lateran canons, who willingly welcomed the pope for celebrations, had not been inured to external influences. Thus, in the twelfth century, the canonical *ordo* of Lucca, regulating almost everything in the canons' lives, had played an important part in the writing of the Lateran canonical *ordo*. In the latter, the place of papal ceremonies, along with those prescribed in the canonical usages of Lucca, were kept intact.[2] But the transfer of liturgical and ecclesiological power from the Lateran to the papal chapel, which occurred in the thirteenth century, would nullify any external influence on the organization and definition of the Roman liturgy, from then on identified with the Curia.

Beginning with the Carolingian period, there developed forms of liturgical expression too often neglected by historians of worship because they were considered marginal when compared with the liturgy of the Eucharist and the sacraments. In large part, they concern private devotion and personal piety. For the High Middle Ages, textual attestations and the manuscripts that have been preserved reveal the devotional activities of the clergy and the educated laity (emperors and empresses, kings and queens, princes and princesses, and so on). To satisfy their personal piety, individuals needed appropriate books, such as the booklets of the Carolingian period (the *libelli precum*[3] ["prayer books"]) allowing them to celebrate privately the Hours or to devote themselves to exercises of devotion.

In the second half of the Middle Ages, especially from the twelfth century on, the rise of new religious orders, the Mendicants in particular, as well as the growing desire of the lay people to pray by themselves outside their participation in the liturgy of the Church, had as a consequence the flowering and spreading of forms of private piety up to then practiced by clergy, royalty, and nobility. This is attested by the many books of Hours from the fourteenth and fifteenth centuries, most widely disseminated among lay people, especially the

2. See P.-M. Gy, "Interactions entre liturgies: Influence des chanoines de Lucques sur la liturgie du Latran," *Revue des Sciences religieuses* 58 (1984), Mélanges A. Chavasse, 537–552; this text is reprinted in P.-M. Gy, *La liturgie dans l'histoire* (Paris, 1990) 127–139.

3. P. Salmon, "Livrets de prières à l'époque carolingienne," *Revue bénédictine* 86 (1976) 218–234.

bourgeoisie of the cities.[4] Several scholars have fully demonstrated the role of these forms of expression of devotion in the evolution of reading practices, especially among the laity, and the place of the book in Western culture.[5]

The Church, essentially the regular clergy, did not remain inactive in this movement and participated in the creation of new books of piety. Alongside the numerous abridged psalters and pocket breviaries for the use of monastics and mendicants—Franciscans and Dominicans—one sees the development in monasteries, particularly among nuns, of *libelli precum* that are adapted to the new monastic spirituality which, marked by the spirit of the times, tended to emphasize personal devotion and develop a visionary mysticism.[6]

It is also at that time that one observes the liturgical books of both antiquity and the High Middle Ages, called "first generation books," undergoing changes leading to "second generation books," the principal of which are the missal, breviary, and pontifical, all characterized by an increase in the local particularities which will be the rule in the life of the Church down to the Council of Trent.

But this is the subject of another book.

4. R. Wieck, *Time Sanctified: The Book of Hours in Medieval Art and Life* (London, 1988).

5. See P. Saenger, "Books of Hours and the Reading Habits of the Later Middle Ages," *Scrittura e civiltà* 9 (1985) 239–269, and "Manières de lire médiévales," *Histoire de l'édition française: Le livre conquérant: Du Moyen Age au milieu du XVIIe siècle*, 2nd ed. (Paris, 1989) 147–161.

6. As in the case of Hildegard of Bingen (1098–1179); some of these *libelli precum* contain an iconographic cycle meant to foster the exercise of prayer and devotion; see J. Hamburger, "A *Liber Precum* in Sélestat and the Development of the Illustrated Prayer Book in Germany," *The Art Bulletin* 73 (1991) 209–236.

Selected Bibliography

History and Typology of Liturgical Books
Heinzer, F. "Liturgische Bücher." *Lexikon des gesamten Buchwesens*. Vol. 4,
p. 580. Stuttgart, 1995.
Johnson, M. *Bibliographia Liturgica: Bibliographie der nachschlagewerke für
Liturgiewissenschaft*. Biblioteca "Ephemerides Liturgicae," Subsidia 63.
Rome, 1992.
Kranemann, B. "Liturgische Bücher als schriftliche Zeugnisse der
Liturgiegeschichte: Entstehung–Typologie–Funktion." *Imagination des
Unsichtbaren: 1200 Jahre Bildende Kunst im Bistum Münster*, 147–166. Ed.
R. Brandl. Ausstellung des Westfalischen Landesmuseums fur Kunst
und Kulturgeschichte, Landschaftsverband Westfalen-Lippe, Münster,
13. Juni bis 31. Oktober 1993. Münster, 1993.
Lowden, J. "Luxury and Liturgy: The Functions of Books." *Church and People
in Byzantium*. Ed. R. Morris, 263–280. Society for the Promotion of
Byzantine Studies, Twentieth Spring Symposium of Byzantine Studies,
Manchester, 1986. Birmingham, 1990.
Neuheuser, H.-P. *Internationale Bibliographie "Liturgische Bücher": Eine Auswahl
kunsthistorischer und liturgiewissenschaftlicher Literatur zu liturgischen
Handschriften und Drucken*. Munich, 1991.
_____. "Typologie und Terminologie liturgischer Bücher." *Bibliothek: Forschung
und Praxis* 16 (1992) 45–65. (Important, especially for the problems posed
by the search for a practical nomenclature for bibliographers.)
Palazzo, E. "Libri liturgici." *Enciclopedia italiana dell'arte*. Rome, in press.

The Cataloging of Liturgical Manuscripts
Balboni, D. "La catalogazione dei libri liturgici." *Ephemerides Liturgicae* 31
(1961) 223–236.
Baroffio, B. "Fontes italicae liturgiae: Osservazioni metodologiche." *Rivista di
storia della Chiesa in Italia* 23 (1969) 120–134.
Göller, G. "Methode des Katalogiesierens liturgischer Handschriften." *Mitteilungen der Arbeitsgemeinschaft für rheinische Musikgeschichte* 27 (1966)
90–91.

Palazzo, E. "Le catalogue des ordinaires des bibliothèques de France, une nouvelle entreprise de catalogage des manuscrits liturgiques." *Die Erschliessung der Quellen des mittelalterlichen liturgischen Gesangs* 39. Wolfenbütteler Symposion, 1996. In press.

Historiography of the Research on Liturgical Books

Johnson, C., and A. Ward. "The Hispanic Liturgy and Dom Marius Férotin." *Ephemerides Liturgicae* 110 (1996) 252–256.

Klöckener, M. "Bio-bibliographisches Repertorium der Liturgiewissenschaft." *Archiv für Liturgiewissenschaft* 35–36 (1993–1994) 285–357.

Sacramentaries

Davril, A., ed. *The Winchcombe Sacramentary (Orléans, Bibliothèque municipale, 127 [105])*. Henry Bradshaw Society 109. London, 1995.

Metzger, M. *Les sacramentaires*. Typologie des sources du Moyen Age occidental, fasc. 70. Turnhout, 1994.

Moeller, E., I. M. Clément, and B. Coppierters't Wallant, eds., *Corpus Orationum*. 8 vols. CCSL 160–160H. Turnhout, 1992–

Palazzo, E. *Les sacramentaires de Fulda: Etude sur l'iconographie et la liturgie à l'époque ottonienne*. LQF 77. Münster, 1994.

Books of Chant

Bernard, P. "Bilan historiographique de la question des rapports entre les chants 'Vieux-Romain' et 'Grégorien.'" *Ecclesia Orans* 11 (1994) 323–353.

____. "Les chants propres de la messe dans les répertoires 'Grégorien' et romain ancien, essai d'édition pratique des variantes textuelles." *Ephemerides Liturgicae* 110 (1996) 210–251.

Exultet: Rotoli liturgici del medioevo meridionale. Dir. G. Cavallo. Coord. G. Orofinoand O. Pecere. Rome, 1994.

Hiley, D. *Western Plainchant: A Handbook*. Oxford, 1993.

Hughes, A. *Late Medieval Liturgical Offices: Resources for Electronic Research: Sources and Chants*. 2 vols. and 5 computer disks. Toronto, 1994–1996.

Kelly, Th. *The Beneventan Chant*. Oxford, 1989.

Books of Mass Readings

Bernard, P. "La question du nombre des lectures à la messe dans le rit romain jusqu'au VIIe siècle: Quelques réflexions à propos d'un ouvrage récent." *Bibliothèque de l'Ecole des Chartes* 151 (1993) 185–192.

Chavasse, A. *Les lectionnaires romains de la messe au VIIe et au VIIIe siècle: Sources et dérivés*. 2 vols. Spicilegii friburgensis Subsidia 22. Fribourg, 1993.

Books of the Office

Etaix, R. *Homéliaires patristiques latins: Recueils d'études de manuscrits médiévaux.* Collection des Etudes Augustiniennes, Série Moyen Age et Temps
modernes 29. Paris, 1994.

____. "Le lectionnaire de l'office de Cruas." *Revue du vivarais* 98 (1994) 15–22.

Liturgia delle ore: Tempo e rito. Atti della 22 settimana di studio dell'Associazione
Professori di Liturgia, Susa (Torino), 29 agosto–3 settembre 1993. Bibliot-
eca "Ephemerides Liturgicae," Subsidia 75. Rome, 1994. In particular, F.
Dell'Oro, "Recenti edizioni critiche di fonti liturgiche," 197–303.

Ottosen, K. *The Responsories and Versicles of the Latin Office of the Dead.* Århus,
1993.

Books of Sacraments and Rights

Cygler, F. "Règles, coutumiers et statuts (V^e–XIIIe siècles): Brèves considéra-
tions historico-typologiques." *La vie quotidienne des moines et chanoines
réguliers au Moyen Age et Temps modernes,* 31–49. Wroclaw, 1994.

Klöckener, M. "Das Pontifikale: Ein Liturgiebuch im Spiegel seiner Benennun-
gen und der Vorreden seiner Herausgeber, zugleich Würdigung und
Weiterführung einer Studie von Marc Dykmans." *Archiv für Liturgiewissenschaft* 28 (1986) 396–415.

Palazzo, E. "Authenticité, codification et mémoire dans la liturgie médiévale,
l'exemple du 'prototype' de l'ordre dominicain." *Liturgie, musique et culture au XIIe siècle: Le prototype de la liturgie dominicaine.* Actes du colloque
international de Rome, 1995. In press.

____. "Le cataloque des ordinaires des bibliothèques de France, une nouvelle
entreprise de catalogage des manuscrits liturgiques." *Die Erschliessung
der Quellen des mittelalterlichen liturgischen Gesangs* 39. Wolfenbütteler
Symposion, 1996. In press.

Reynaud, F. "Un cérémonial de la fin du XVIe siècle à l'usage de la cathédrale
de Tolède." *Revue Mabillon* 67, n.s. 6 (1995) 225–241.

Index of Persons

Durand, U., 8
Durandus, William, 209, 210

Ebner, A., 12, 13
Egbert of York, 50
Eginon (bishop of Verona), 154
Elze, R., 14
Emma, 59
Eudes of Sully, 193, 228

Florus of Lyon, 141
Frere, W. H., 13
Fructuosus of Braga, St., 116

Gamber, K., 13
Gautier (bishop of Orléans), 31
Gelasius I, St., 41, 44, 50, 60
Gellent, Nicolas, 228
Gennadius of Marseilles, 29, 84
Germain, M., 7, 34
Gherbald (bishop of Liège), 31
Godescalc, 102–103
Grégoire, R., 15
Gregory I (the Great), St., 21, 28, 30,
    45, 50, 52, 60, 70, 73, 86–87, 93,
    139, 148
Gregory II, St., 45, 52, 95
Gregory VII, St., 118, 207
Gregory XIII, 234
Gy, P.-M., 16

Hadrian I, 30, 50, 52
Haito (bishop of Basel), 31
Haymo of Faversham, 118
Helisachar, 53, 99, 140
Henry II, 104, 212
Hervé (bishop of Beauvais), 212
Hesbert, R.-J., 14
Hilary, St., 47, 126
Hildegar (bishop of Meaux), 31
Hildegard of Bingen, St., 240
Hildoard (bishop of Cambrai), 48, 51
Hincmar (bishop of Rhiems), 197

Hittorp, M., 176
Honorius I, 51
Huglo, M., 14, 72
Hugh (abbot of Cluny), St., 219
Hugh (abbot of Farfa), 217
Humbert of Romans, 231

Ingeborg, 134
Innocent III, 169, 208, 210, 225, 227,
    238
Innocent VII, 234
Isidore (bishop of Seville), St., 63,
    88, 116

Jerome, St., 61, 88, 101, 130, 132, 152
John III, 40–41, 42
John of Cirey, 231
John the Deacon, 70, 139
Jungmann, J. A., 5

Klauser, Th., 13
Kunigunde, 104

Landulf (bishop of Benevento), 210
Leidrad, 141
Leo I (the Great), St., 39, 40
Leo III, St., 53
Leo of Ostia, 231
Leroquais, V., 11, 12, 53, 209–210
Louis the Pious, 53, 99, 140

Mabillon, J., 7–9, 34, 176, 177, 181
Maiolus (abbot of Cluny), St., 219
Maingaud (abbot of Corbie), 216
Mamert, St., 47
Martène, E., 7–9, 34, 85, 176, 181
Martimort, A.-G., 15
Martin (bishop of Tours), St., 47
Maximianus (bishop of Ravenna),
    29, 44
Ménard, H., 9, 34, 50
Muratori, L. A., 9, 50
Musaeus of Marseilles, 29, 84

Index of Places

Index of Liturgical Pieces

Index of Manuscripts

Verona, Biblioteca capitolare
    cod. 85: 35, 39–40, 42
    cod. 90: 75
    cod. 92: 183
Vienna, Österreichische National-
    bibliothek
    cod. 1861: 103

Wolfenbüttel, Herzog-August
    Bibliothek
    cod. 4160 (Weiss. 76): 85

Würzburg, Universitätsbibliothek
    cod. M.p.th.f. 62: 94, 98, 99

Zurich, Zentralbibliothek
    cod. Rh. 30: 230
    cod. Rh. 83: 148